What people are

Church Goi

Church Going Gone is the work of a man of great goodness, considerable stubbornness, and and not a little cunning. How can a person of liberal, humane, and imaginative instincts survive in the modern Church of England? Brian Mountford has not only survived, but for thirty years had the living of St Mary's, the University Church in Oxford, the site of events of enormous consequence such as the trial of the Oxford Martyrs in 1555, and the centre of a busy and intellectually challenging modern parish. In the course of his life as a priest Mountford aroused enormous admiration not only for his liberal stance but also for his personal qualities of kindness and open-mindedness, and for the imaginative (and occasionally provocative) way in which he welcomed speakers from many different traditions to his church. All his qualities are vividly present in this book, as well as a lively gift for scene-setting and character-drawing. I enjoyed it enormously.
Philip Pullman

Brian Mountford has written a witty and captivating memoir. He brilliantly evokes the utterly different world of the Church of England in the late sixties and, through the story of his own ministry, offers a fascinating — and sobering — perspective on the sea changes that the Church has undergone over the past fifty years.
Jane Shaw, Principal of Harris Manchester College, University of Oxford

This charming and deeply insightful book is a real pleasure to read, and has the power to make its readers rethink their most basic beliefs.
John Simpson, English foreign correspondent and world affairs editor of BBC News

Brian Mountford senses our deep hunger to have answers to the big questions; part of his deeply liberal, protesting faith is to encourage us all to keep on asking.

Sarah Lloyd, MD of BBC's QI

Church Going Gone

A biography of religion, doubt, and faith

Church Going Gone

A biography of religion, doubt, and faith

Brian Mountford

CHRISTIAN ALTERNATIVE
BOOKS

Winchester, UK
Washington, USA

JOHN HUNT PUBLISHING

First published by Christian Alternative Books, 2021
Christian Alternative Books is an imprint of John Hunt Publishing Ltd.,
No. 3 East St., Alresford, Hampshire SO24 9EE, UK
office@jhpbooks.com
www.johnhuntpublishing.com
www.christian-alternative.com

For distributor details and how to order please visit the 'Ordering' section on our website.

Text copyright: Brian Mountford 2020

ISBN: 978 1 78904 812 4
978 1 78904 813 1 (ebook)
Library of Congress Control Number: 2020951004

Design: Stuart Davies

UK: Printed and bound by CPI Group (UK) Ltd, Croydon, CR0 4YY
Printed in North America by CPI GPS partners

We operate a distinctive and ethical publishing philosophy in
all areas of our business, from our global network of authors to
production and worldwide distribution.

Contents

A serious house on serious earth it is,
In whose blent air all our compulsions meet,
Are recognised, and robed as destinies.
And that much never can be obsolete,
Since someone will forever be surprising
A hunger in himself to be more serious...
'Church Going' (1954) Philip Larkin

To put it another way, religious decline in Britain is generational;
people tend to be less religious than their parents, and on average
their children are even less religious than they are.
British Social Attitudes (BSA) survey for 2018

Becassocked in the Westminster Village

London 1969, Campden Hill Square

We're in the book-lined study of Ronald Goodchild, Bishop of Kensington. Outside, the thin, grey light of a November morning.

On the edge of his chair sits a **tall slender curate**. The **Bishop** stands behind his desk. In a padded leather armchair, with a dossier of papers spread over his knees, sits the ex-army officer **William Davidson, Vicar of St Stephen's, Rochester Row**. This is the ecclesiastical equivalent of a court martial.

Bishop

So, let us get this straight. The Vicar accuses you of irregular attendance at morning worship and of committing fornication in the clergy house. But he says he has no evidence. What have you to say?

Curate (angered)

Of course he has no evidence. Does he listen at the keyhole of my room?

Bishop

I think we've heard enough. You are going to have to find another job.

Back to Westcott House, Cambridge, March 1968

Were we in Hollywood, the above is how the script might have opened.

In the last year of my theological college training, I had to find a job. I wanted to work in London, but it was usual for students to return to the Diocese that had sponsored them, in my case Chelmsford, and although Chelmsford stretched into

1

East London as far as Stratford, I wanted to be in the centre. Top of my wish-list was Chelsea Old Church, so I wrote to the Bishop of Kensington to ask if there was a vacancy. His response was to offer me a curacy in Sunbury on Thames. When I visited for a weekend my heart sank: this was a part of London in a no-man's-land of reservoirs and faceless avenues. Having been raised in the outskirts, I wanted to escape suburbia to be in the city. The college Principal, Peter Walker, was astonished by what he considered my brazenness in rejecting the bishop's offer. He seemed to have an image of bishops as feudal lords, whom to question would be a kind of professional suicide, but having had little experience of church hierarchy, I had no qualms. When I told the bishop Sunbury wasn't for me, he suggested St Stephen's, Rochester Row, just off Vincent Square, in the part of London edged by Victoria Street, Westminster, and Millbank. St Stephen's was well known in church circles as a 'training parish' and a launch pad for clergy preferment, particularly its vicars, probably because of its proximity to the seat of Church government at Church House in Westminster. The two previous vicars had both become bishops.

When George Reindorp had been Vicar in the 1950s, he had six curates and expected each of them to visit six people a day, which meant 216 people in the parish received a personal home visit each week, so it wasn't surprising the church was well attended. He had attracted a clutch of aristocratic ladies, including at one time Princess Margaret, and a large number of students and nurses from the nearby St Thomas' and Westminster Hospitals. Were I to accept the job I would be part of a team of three curates, three nuns – Sisters of the Deaconess Community of St Andrew – and the Vicar, William Davidson. Reindorp had been an empire builder and not only had he built a new church for the Millbank Estate, St John's in Causton Street, he'd also built a clergy house in his back garden, with four study bedrooms for bachelors, two flats for married priests

2

and a very small apartment for a housekeeper. Being unmarried I would have one of the study bedrooms overlooking a tower block in Hide Place, not much of an improvement on student accommodation.

I was interviewed separately by the Vicar, each of the staff, and by the churchwardens, one of whom, Colonel Jim Haywood, was a bluff, likeable man who had been a prison governor. 'There's only one thing I want to ask you, my boy,' he said. 'D'you believe in the virgin birth?' This was a long time before David Jenkins as Bishop of Durham had made this question a public issue. I said my faith didn't stand or fall by it and that, while biologically I found it a ridiculous idea, I didn't want to ruin the poetry of Christmas by trying to demythologise it. Under the influence of Rudolf Bultmann, the notion of demythologising the gospel text was fashionable in the 1960s. Bultmann wanted to separate the gospel message, the 'good news', from the mythical world picture of pre-scientific thought to make it more acceptable to a modern public, but it was astonishing how difficult religious people found it to let go of myth, fearing, I suspect, that to do so was to say their faith wasn't true and let the side down. After evensong I was put on show in front of a larger group from the parish and Colonel Haywood, who was clearly the power in the land, announced to the gathered company, 'Good chap; believes in the virgin birth, y'know.' Thus I was appointed.

I have never been one of those clergy who thinks ordination changes their spiritual DNA, that the grace of laying on of hands resets their spiritual software, placing them in a category apart. I held a very low view of it. To me it was a means to an end, an institutional necessity if you wanted to do this particular job. The ceremony turned out to be a rather dry affair. Perhaps St Paul's Cathedral is inevitably a dry place, hemmed in by traffic and the dust and grime of the City, and too vast for intimacy. My one regret in retrospect was not to have taken an 'ordination name' as one is entitled to do. No longer a dull Brian, no longer the hapless, laughably blockish fellow lampooned (albeit ten years later) in the Monty Python film *The Life of Brian*, but Thomas, maybe, after the great Aquinas or Augustine. Gus Mountford, that would be it. One of our Oriel undergraduates took the confirmation name of Athanasius, meaning immortal, after the fourth-century Bishop of Alexandria. If you're going to change your name you might as well go the whole hog.

I parked my car in St Paul's Churchyard, having driven up from St Katharine's, Stepney, a religious house in London's Dockland, where the ordination retreat had taken place. As is still the case, immediately prior to ordination Anglican ordinands are separated from their families and expected to spend 48 hours like monks and nuns saying the offices, perhaps making their confession, and devoting themselves to prayer and meditation. On the Saturday afternoon, while we were supposed to be contemplating the spiritual enormity of what was about to happen to us, I sneaked off to White Hart Lane to watch Tottenham play West Ham. I needed something more down to earth than the laboured spiritual addresses from the priest leading the retreat. If you want to be challenged by the doctrine of the incarnation, where better to do so than the football terraces? This was raw religion: thirty thousand people made in the image of God shouting for their team, most of them the salt of the earth, but a good few intent on tribal warfare. Here the fallen nature of humanity and humanity's potential for good vied with each other in a contemporary outworking of Paradise Lost.

Tottenham were defeated 0-2 in a very dreary game, a reminder that glory comes only now and then, like a special treat, and isn't commonplace either in football or religion. If it were, they would both lose their lustre. Perhaps this was the best preparation for ordination, to feel the humiliation of loss on a shabby North London afternoon, a reminder that the glitz of St Paul's Cathedral is only a fraction of a theological story that also contains dullness, obscurity, and disappointment.

After the service I walked out of the cathedral wearing my cassock and a new starched-linen dog collar chafing at my neck and repeatedly popping loose from its front stud and flipping up over my Adam's apple. This was to be my everyday garb in the parish so I thought I'd better get used to it. We twenty-five factory-fresh clergyman were greeted by our families on that vast escalation, that Jacob's Ladder of steps, linking the great West door of St Paul's to Ludgate Hill. My mother wore an undersized smile under a homely hat from C&A and looked on shyly but, so far as I could tell, proud, no doubt reflecting that I had rejected her working-class Congregationalism for this puffed-up Anglicanism. My father was relaxed and jovial, my Uncle Alf, tall and masonic in bowler hat and pinstripe trousers, looked like the official in the TV advertisement who cajoles you to get your tax return in on time. Many of them carried in their hand a copy of the ordination service booklet containing the words of the service and the names of those ordained and also the following explanation, which I have edited slightly.

Some terminology you need to know.

There are three orders, or ranks, in the Church of England: deacon, priest, and bishop.

When you are ordained you hold the office of deacon for the first year, during which time you are not permitted to celebrate the Eucharist, give absolution (i.e. declare people's sins forgiven), or pronounce a blessing. After twelve months of this non-sacramental apprenticeship, you are ordained priest at another ordination service. Yes, in effect you are ordained twice, but to different orders. Those very few people who become bishops are ordained a third time – to the order of bishop – and thereby gain the authority to confirm people and to ordain deacons and priests. Theologically, the diaconate is the essence of ministry because to be a deacon means to be a servant. Jesus said that the Son of Man came not to be served but to serve and that whoever would be great among you must be the servant of all. When you are ordained a priest, or a bishop, you never relinquish the order of deacon, although some

5

do tend to forget it.

Quite separate from the three orders are the job titles:

Curate – which means to have the cure (or care) of souls and these days is used for an assistant clergyperson in a parish. They can be deacons or priests.

Vicar – must be a priest and is in charge of a parish.

Rector – must be a priest and is in charge of a parish.

Chaplain – a priest who looks after a chapel in a hospital, school or university.

Canon – a senior priest in a cathedral. Also, a term for priests who have been given the honorary title in recognition of their work.

Dean – the priest who is head of a cathedral.

Archdeacon – a priest with an administrative role assisting a bishop.

Suffragan Bishop – an assistant bishop in a diocese.

Diocesan Bishop – the chief bishop of a diocese, what Mrs Thatcher called 'Big Bishops' because they had seats in the House of Lords and could oppose her politically.

To celebrate we went with a few friends for lunch at *The Prospect of Whitby*, a pub overlooking the Thames on Limehouse Reach. According to most online accounts, the pub was once known as the *Devil's Tavern*, but was renamed in the 1800s *The Prospect of Whitby* because a ship of that name was frequently moored outside, but I had always understood the name derived from the trade of shipping coals from Whitby. The returning ships carried barrels of urine from the East End pubs to Whitby, where it was used in the tanning and dyeing industry. London sailors desperate for work had the prospect of being hired here for that unsavoury return journey. After a couple of pints, I needed to contribute to the tanning industry myself and the man standing next to me in the stalls of the *pissoir*, seeing me fumble with my cassock, addressed me as 'Father', and asked if I needed assistance. Within hours of receiving my sacred commission in St Paul's I learned that the 'cloth' invited ridicule as well as respect, although in this case benign ridicule. On the positive side, clerical garb at least made one's role unambiguous. And it assured people who saw you in it that you would probably be reasonably agreeable towards them, which encouraged people, variously sad, lonely, or just plain scoundrels, to sidle up and unburden their souls. This was particularly true in pubs where I discovered many drinking men welcomed the idea that the Church wasn't always locked away in a private ghetto of religiosity, but could be there in the midst of everyday society, just like Jesus getting bad-mouthed for mixing with publicans and sinners. If the priest can drink with us, we are somehow redeemed, and not such bad guys after all.

In my Westminster local, there were occasions when I had so many pints lined up on the bar, bought by well-wishers, that it was impossible to drink them all. These libations offered on the altar of residual folk religion were often conscience salvers from people who thought they might appease God by buying his representative a drink. It was salutary that I was unable to consume them all, because it showed salvation was not as easy as that and couldn't be bought for half a crown.

*

Built by the early Victorians in 1847, St Stephen's had only half a spire, the top having been shaken so badly by a World War II bomb that it had to be removed. I was embarrassed by the imperfection of my first church, as if it were a failure on my part; I wanted it to be admired. The interior was better. The vicar before Bill Davidson, Tony Tremlett, had had the neo-gothic arches painted and the oak pews limed, giving them a green-white patina. I hadn't reckoned on having to go to church so much. The discipline was much stricter than theological college had been, partly to meet the requirements of the nuns, who were under vows of obedience to their order. As junior curate I was expected to unlock the church at 6.50am for Matins at 7.00am. It was one of those inverted privileges like the junior fellow of a Cambridge college having to fetch more claret when the decanter was emptied at dessert. I didn't realise at first that we curates were observed as we rushed round Vincent Square, cloaks flying in the wind, by coach loads of nurses on their way to the morning shift at St Thomas' Hospital, who amused themselves in speculation about the marital status and private predilections of each of us. But they too were victims of outmoded sartorial requirements, trussed up in the starchy uniforms unchanged since Florence Nightingale and the Crimean War. We then remained at prayer for half an hour before hearing mass at 8.00am. This meditation period was a puzzle to me. I wasn't clear why we were doing it and I didn't have enough holy thoughts to fill the space. Listening for the voice of God proved a vain exercise. Perhaps I was to allow the Spirit, as St John put it, to blow over me 'where it listeth', even while my mind wandered back to the nurses or what I needed from the shops. I was told it was acceptable to read during this period and the books I read were Paul Tillich's *The Courage to Be* and Teilhard de Chardin's *The Phenomenon of Man* and *The Divine Milieu*, much in vogue at that time. How much more helpful it would have been to read *New Society*, the social commentary I picked up each week from the Rochester Row newsagent. Besides, wasn't it a new society that Jesus called for in the gospels? In the evening we returned at six for Evening Prayer.

Each day we were joined for evensong by the retired Bishop of London, Henry Montgomery-Campbell, who lived in a Church Commissioners' house at No. 3 Vincent Square. Henry had a long, distinguished face, square jaw and smoked Senior Service cigarettes in a silver cigarette holder, resembling a pair of miniature tongs, which he gripped between his thumb and forefinger. In his eighties, he had a friend of similar maturity by the name of Mrs Kuhl, whom he always referred to as 'that dear lady'. Mrs Kuhl was a wealthy widow who lived on the East side of the Square and owned a hearse-like Daimler with a peak-capped chauffeur who drove her and the

Bishop to church. If he saw a curate on the way, delighted to be able to dispense largesse at Mrs Kuhl's expense, he would stop the car and beckon with his bony finger, insisting you had a lift. But Mrs Kuhl's house was on a one-way system, which meant the car was travelling in the opposite direction from the church and had to detour via the Horseferry Road, often getting caught in traffic and making the occupants late to the annoyance of the vicar.

Very frequently after Evensong Bishop Henry invited me round for a glass of sherry and to attempt to complete *The Times* crossword with him, a feat we never achieved. But between the anagrams and cryptic clues he regaled me in his deep, cultured voice with a repertoire of much-repeated stories. 'When they made me Bishop of London,' he would say, 'some people suggested it was a "caretaker" appointment.' I pointed out a caretaker can sweep very clean, and *sweep very clean* was emphasised very slowly with a wonderful sparkle. When he was enthroned as Bishop of London he arrived at the door of St Paul's and, as tradition dictates, knocked on the door with his staff. They were an inordinately long time opening it, so he turned to his Chaplain and asked, 'Do you think we've come to the wrong place?' When at last the doors opened and he saw the Dean and Canons coming towards him he remarked, 'The See gives up her dead!' – an allusion to the biblical Book of Revelation where 'the sea gives up her dead'. As Bishop of London he was entitled to be buried in St Paul's, so after he had had an appendectomy, he asked the doctors for his appendix in a bottle, which he sent to the Dean of St Paul's with the message, 'This is the first instalment, the rest will follow later.'

There was a London Clergyman by the name of Jack Vyse, whose surname was pronounced somewhere between 'Vize' and 'Vice'. Henry quipped in his sermon at Jack's institution, 'Now that we have licensed Vyse, there is no knowing what might happen in the parish.' But he was particularly fond of his Athenaeum stories: 'Last time I was at my club I was asked by a member of the House of Lords if I knew a suitable wit to ask to a dinner party. I replied that there were two half-wits in the corner, and if he were to invite them both it was bound to be a good evening.' His favourite, however, was a neat play on words: 'Last time I was at my club they were discussing the amalgamation of the "Bath Club" and the "Conservative Club" and trying to think of a name for the combined society. I suggested the *Lava-Tory*.'

*

In the parish there was little sense of community. The public streets of Vauxhall Bridge Road, Victoria Street, Millbank and Horseferry Road were busy with workers and shoppers by day and empty at night. Vincent Square was vast and eerily quiet, except when boys from Westminster School were playing football there, its liveliness not increased by the King's College theological hostel on the north side or the Gordon Hospital on the west. Just set back from Victoria Street, the Roman Catholic Westminster Cathedral was disdainfully included in our Anglican parish and was surrounded by stylish redbrick apartments, many occupied only on weekdays by MPs and senior professionals. Not far away from these elite dwellings, further up the street, were the vast tenements of the Peabody buildings, built for 'the artisan and labouring poor of London' by the philanthropist, George Peabody, 'to ameliorate the condition of the poor and needy of this great metropolis and to promote their comfort and happiness.' One of my duties was to give house Communion to the sick, which took me regularly into these Peabody Buildings. St Stephen's was high church, more Liberal-Catholic than Anglo-Catholic. Our worship wasn't ritualistic: no incense – for that you went to Father Gerard Irvine at St Matthew's, Westminster – yet the clergy were addressed as 'Father', an appellation technically reserved for priests. There was a debate amongst the churchwardens and staff whether, as a deacon, I should be known as 'Father' and the consensus was that I should, probably influenced by Colonel Haywood. The manner of taking the reserved sacrament from the church into the streets, however, was positively Roman. Robed in cassock, cotta and stole, my colleague, Tom Maidment, also wearing a biretta, the three curates carried the sacrament in solemn procession down the street. It was thought sacrilegious to put the silver pyx containing our Lord's body in your pocket, so this we held before us under a velvet veil. The people of Rochester Row might have thought it was Christmas and they'd been visited by the three wise men, but no one ever mocked, although, as we passed by many looked away, as people do from a funeral, in a mixture of what I took to be embarrassment and respect, or perhaps simply from a desire not to be involved. But occasionally there in the street someone would cross themselves or genuflect.

How did I feel about wearing this gear? Part of me was beguiled by the clerical weakness for dressing up and showing off; another part thought that I had betrayed my radical roots. The Cambridge modernist theologians I admired – Alec Vidler, Harry Williams, and John Robinson – feared the clerical collar was a barrier between church and society so they wore a black shirt with white necktie and earned themselves the moniker, 'the white tie brigade'. Not very radical? It is easy to forget how conservative Britain was in the sixties and how difficult to break free. If I had walked down Rochester Row in jacket and tie with the sacrament in my pocket wouldn't something have been lost?

Included amongst the home communicants was a ninety-year-old woman born in 1878, whom I visited once a fortnight in her simple room, off the stone landing of a Peabody tenement. Her father had been a milkman and she could remember his keeping cows within sight of Westminster Abbey. Walking down the vertical gorge of glass-and-concrete government buildings in Victoria Street now, it was hard to imagine such a pastoral scene existing in living memory, despite the inferred rural past in a name like Abbey Orchard Street. As I reflect on this in my eighth decade, it illustrates how far living memory stretches back, and 125 years seems not a very long time. In 2018 St Hilda's College, Oxford, celebrated its 125th anniversary to the sound of trumpets, but a fortnight before we had held a memorial service for a former fellow, Nita Watts, who was 98 years old – one lifetime spanning most of the college's history. And I'd been Chaplain for almost a quarter of that time – a period which from my viewpoint had flown by. We can think time moves at a glacial pace, but there are always people who live to a hundred, more and more of them these days, who look back to their childhood as if it were yesterday. Put twenty of those lives end to end and you go back to Jesus of Nazareth. Nearly everything recognisable in our own age goes back no more than two of those lives and, such has been the progress of the last century, most people would feel uncomfortable with life as it was before 1900, no motor cars, no anti-biotics, no central heating, gaslight, no votes for women, no air-conditioning. Measuring human history by a single life helps to get time in proportion, but it does of course support the idea of linear history, one damn thing after another. The Bible has another view of time, despite the fact it has no notion of the 13.4 billion years since the Big Bang or the 4.5-billion-year life of our planet. Eternity is a sense that time can be transcended by values, by God. As Psalm 90.4 puts it, 'One day in your presence is like a thousand.' God is outside time and importantly might be thought of in terms of being itself, a constant in an ephemeral world. The notion of *being* or *existence* isn't one that needs to be qualified by beginning or end, even though our experience of it personally has limits. The same Psalm says:

> The days of our life are seventy years,
> or perhaps eighty, if we are strong;
> even then their span is only toil and trouble;
> they are soon gone, and we fly away.

Curiously, we rarely think of our beginning as a limit: we slip into life with a gradually increasing consciousness and rarely feel any resentment that we didn't exist before.

Over the years that followed I have taken the sacrament to numerous housebound people. At Christ Church, Lancaster Gate, I visited a delightful old lady, Miss Cardo, who insisted on a glass of *Nuits St George* beforehand to 'fortify me for the fray', as she theatrically put it. She also insisted, quite wrongly, that my father was a member of parliament, the Labour MP Ian Mikardo, of whose left-wing politics she approved. But when eventually she was taken to hospital, incontinent and seriously ill, the doctors told me they had found her underwear padded with the *Daily Telegraph*, a well-known Tory paper.

These communion visits were short in duration (one might have to make as many as eight in a morning) but they were a way of keeping people in touch with the church community. They were to receive the same bread and wine shared by the rest of the parish at the Eucharist on Sunday. For many it was the highlight of their week and I found it moving that it meant so much. Some prepared for a day beforehand, setting out a little home-made altar and making sure their shopper or carer bought the right biscuits to go with a quick cup of tea. Afterwards they refused help with washing up because washing up prolonged the meaning and purpose of it all, filling a much longer space in an empty life waiting for the last trumpet to call. In some homes one entered a bygone world: rooms musty with age, primitive kitchens, antimacassars, neo-gothic treasures on the sideboard. I could be whisked away in the time machine in a moment, as if hypnotised. It wasn't that you were entering a museum, you were living in someone else's memory, which was both fascinating and, to a very young man, stultifying. Sometimes I stepped back into the urban morning and was overcome by a freedom like being in love.

Every Thursday I had to visit a ward at the Gordon Hospital

in Vincent Square, built on the proceeds of Gordon's Gin. This was in the days when wards were arranged with twenty beds in dormitory fashion, before the more humane division of wards into bays of four. I appeared at the business end in black cassock, like an angel of death, calling on every patient. It was known as 'blanket visiting', the equivalent of 'blind calling', and the prospect always filled me with dread, but perhaps not so much as it did the patients. I knew very well that many of them would feel harassed by my spiritual attentions, seeing a black cassock moving inexorably towards them, and that, being seriously ill, they may well have difficulty in finding a way to tell me to clear off. But the politeness of the British *in extremis* was admirable; they were scarcely ever rude or dismissive and frequently helped me into conversation that was mutually enjoyable. Maybe it is pretentious to call those visits 'spiritual', as if the clergyman has some sort of secret ingredient of religious comfort to offer. In fact, most conversations were mundane, about children and grandchildren, the War (old people then had inevitably lived through two world wars), and life in rosier times. If there was a spiritual component it would be the patient who raised it – a question of doubt or faith or hope or the future, and now and then to articulate thoughts about death they found difficult to discuss with their family. Invariably I would leave the Gordon with an elated sense of having done something worthwhile, but by the next Thursday would be full of apprehension again.

One day I was called into the Gordon to baptise a dying baby. I found her parents, no older than me, mother in a hospital gown, father for some reason in a black woollen overcoat, gazing distraught into the incubator at the tiny purple creature who had swapped the umbilicus for a mesh of plastic tubes. It was not a moment for soothing words: I had been called to do a job, as practical as anything the medical staff were able to do, but nevertheless I trembled at the enormity of the situation and my own inexperience. The nurse, however, who was younger than all of us, was matter of fact and gave me a long, sterilised spoon on which she placed a drop of water. I was to insert the spoon through a circular window in the incubator (like a seed propagator) and touch the child's head with it. That drop of water symbolised the waters of the River Jordan where Jesus was baptised and the Red Sea, which parted for Moses and the Israelites when they escaped Egypt for the Promised Land. But as I baptised the baby 'Mary Jane' I thought particularly of the healing waters of the Pool of Bethesda, which became agitated when touched by the angel of the Lord. In the end it was easily done, as was the subsequent listening to the story of how Mary Jane had taken a turn for the worse that afternoon and although they weren't churchgoers the mother had been brought up Catholic and when the nurse asked if they wanted a priest they had said yes and she phoned for me.

I have no idea whether Mary lived or died, but it was only days later that I was called to the Gordon again to meet a lady who was too frightened to go alone to view her husband's body in the hospital morgue. Although she didn't know it, this was a case of the blind leading the blind as I had never seen a dead body before and was probably more apprehensive than she was, but I assured her it was a natural thing to do and would be in a way reassuring. I wanted to say this would be a dignified and satisfactory experience, rather than the scene from a horror movie she had in mind. In such situations, I discovered, it's much more important to talk than to be tongue-tied for fear of being crass – a case of jaw, jaw, jaw.

She was a motherly woman whose husband had always called her 'me old duck' and as we walked the few yards down the Vauxhall Bridge Road to the mortuary entrance she chatted away as if I were the one who needed to be put at ease. When we entered the morgue, she simply said, 'O there he is, dear old Bill.' His body lay on a trolley with the sheet folded down to reveal a craggy face, hair neatly combed, and skin having the waxy, porcelain pallor of the dead. She told me he had spent his life in the building trade. I imagined he was one of that rare breed of good-hearted tradesmen who went out of his way to help his clients and who was proud of doing a good job. Now he had died of heart failure in hospital. It felt completely comfortable in the presence of this mortal frame to be talking about the life that had until so recently inhabited it. At the end she kissed his forehead and wistfully stroked his hair, like a mother sending her child off to school. Then we left that shivery, refrigerated, clean-smelling chamber to re-enter the world of traffic, widowhood, and, for me, youthful prospects. It was a sunny day and when I turned into Vincent Square I was aware of the abundance of cherry blossom and that the air had that cold clarity of spring, detectable even in central London, reminding me how much I was alive.

*

The clergy house was scarcely an ideal bachelor pad. Opposite my bedsit on the first floor the Vicar had his study, the location of which seemed to me greedy and intrusive when he had a spacious vicarage on the other side of the garden. It reminded me of being at home; you always wondered whether, in imitation of your mum and dad, he might open your door at an inappropriate moment or tell you to turn the music down. Downstairs was a dining room, furnished like a boardroom with a massive, contemporary mahogany table and limited edition prints on the walls, where the curates ate their meals and the whole staff took lunch on a Monday after the staff meeting. These repasts were prepared by the housekeeper, Mrs Simpson, who occupied a small apartment opposite the dining room, whence, through her ever-open door she observed all comings and goings. Nothing circumvented the gaze of Mrs Simpson, who had about her a touch of Mrs Danvers from Daphne du

Maurier's *Rebecca*, menacing, and devoted to previous curates whose stock had risen even more in her eyes by their no longer being there. The climax of her day was the serving of dinner at 7.00pm. She was a marvellous cook and her signature dessert, I remember with relish to this day, was the very apotheosis of 'Queen of Puddings'. But I was not her favourite. She had once looked after Fr Malcolm Johnson at St Mary's, Portsea, who had set the bar high for what it was, in her eyes, to be a pleasing young man and sensitive priest. When I showed too little enthusiasm for a little yellow sleeveless pullover she had knitted me, not only because it was the colour of Malvolio's stockings, but because it sat a little too pertly over my bottom, I could sense her attempt to like me gurgling down the plughole of the kitchen sink. Her seething sense of being undervalued was exacerbated by my repeated lateness for dinner with the excuse that I had been drinking sherry with Bishop Henry.

Every Monday the whole clergy staff met at nine and ended with lunch in the dining room at twelve-thirty. In addition to the Vicar, the curates and the nuns, we were joined by two other clergymen, the Chaplain of the Westminster Hospital and The Revd Lord Sandford, an hereditary peer and former naval officer, who was working in politics in the House of Lords and became a junior minister in the Department of Education at the fag end of the Heath government. One of the questions to come up early in my time was what we were to do about the falling numbers at Sunday Evensong. I suggested that instead of a sermon we should have a presentation on moral issues of the day followed by a panel discussion, an idea taken up enthusiastically by the vicar, although dubbed by the cynics as 'show biz evensong'. We started with Crime and Punishment, particularly the moral purpose of imprisonment and whether it could be reformative as well as punitive. South African Apartheid had been brought back to popular attention by the question of whether the black England cricketer Basil D'Oliveira would be included in the team to play there that winter and the Ethics of Heart Transplant Surgery, recently pioneered by Dr Christiaan Barnard, attracted a group of St Thomas' nurses from their nearby hostel in Ashley Gardens.

As the junior curate, I was far from being the show biz supremo. I needed to know my place and was often deputed to play the organ at Evensong in our daughter church, St John's Causton Street, which had been built in the 1950s by George Reindorp to serve the Millbank estate in the brief post-war surge of church attendance and missionary zeal. His intentions were no doubt worthy, but the result was a class divide in the parish between the colonels, professors, bishops, MPs, barristers and titled ladies of St Stephen's and the artisan tenement dwellers of St John's. This meant we had a structure alien to New Testament teaching. We paid lip service to Jesus' radical idea that the last shall be first and the first shall be last, but our own social organisation ran counter to it. The dilemma was subtly symbolised in the number of people who found it perfectly charming that the St Stephen's caretaker always addressed the Dowager Lady Falmouth as 'Mrs Falmouth'. He probably did it on purpose, in protest against the *frisson* of class discrimination beneath the surface of our society.

On one occasion (it must have been an anniversary of the building) the 'Raindrop', as Bishop George Reindorp was popularly known, came back to preach at St John's. He was greeted like royalty, an approach which George, ever the prince bishop, did nothing to allay. When he had been to speak at my theological college, the more left wing amongst us had been appalled by his silver buckled shoes and purple socks. Members of both congregations packed the church and the three curates sat at the back in cassocks and cloaks because there was no room or liturgical role for us up front. George had them rolling in the aisles with a joke-a-minute sermon. In the middle of his address, looking at me, he raised the roof with a quip about being able to see a bored curate sitting at the back reading the *Racing Times*. The thrust of his humour was magnificently unsubtle but not so much as afterwards at the bun fight downstairs in the hall when he introduced to me a shy but handsome nurse as 'the girl you're going to marry', before passing imperiously on leaving the two of us embarrassed but united in our astonishment at the crass episcopal pomposity. I think that was the last time she attended.

A parish is a very public stage on which to seek a partner. The clergyman has a conspicuous role, up at the front and dressed in robes intended to set him apart; with that goes an implicit ambiguity about the appropriateness of conjoining of any kind. In some ways religion is intrinsically alien to sexual relationship, particularly amongst its cultic representatives. Nevertheless, I was aware of a host of well-wishing, matronly women willing me on and watching my every move, hopeful of being gratified by romance. At just twenty-three years old, my love life clearly held an Austenian fascination for some parishioners otherwise bored with the predictability of church going and looking for a little spice in their lives. Lord Sandford had two daughters, both very beautiful, and one about my age, but I was no Mr Darcy, and I certainly lacked his fortune, so I could only admire them from afar. At Buckingham Gate School, where I taught one day a week, there was a slim, dark-haired and stylish teacher, Astrid, who always wore black. To me she was chic and worldly wise, but she was an atheist and clearly pitied me for what I stood for. In any case, she fancied an older, craggier, married teacher and I got the message that attention from me would not be welcome.

Each Wednesday I renewed my campaign to teach Religious Education at this secondary school, within a stone's throw of Buckingham Palace. Although the assignment was part of my parish duties, I was engaged by the local authority and had a contract quite separate from the Church of England. My full-time ecclesiastical stipend at that time was £504 a year and my one-fifth salary as a teacher was £268 a year. But there was a catch. The Church of England demanded I pay the whole of my teaching salary to the Diocese to be offset against my stipend, with the result that I cost the Church a mere £236 a year. At less than a pound a day, I regarded this as exploitation. Okay, I hadn't become a clergyman for the money, but I felt a level of injustice in this arrangement. First, I hadn't asked to be a teacher, but had had teaching thrust upon me; and, secondly, a day in the classroom of a school like that was very demanding, and was additional to my church duties which, as I said, began at 6.50am and included further commitments in the evening. Yet I regarded myself as one 'under authority' – the authority of the Church and my vicar – in a way that few would accept in today's climate of employee's rights and tribunals.

When it came to sexual preference, I was enthusiastically heterosexual. But this didn't prevent me from being propositioned by men. Young clergymen hold a potential lure of this kind and I was naïve about the preponderance of homosexuality amongst the clergy, simply not recognising it. That so many were unmarried seemed to me more a matter of vocation than nature and I always found the camp humour of certain bachelor clergy enticing – they seemed natural entertainers and to endear themselves easily to parishioners, and I wondered why I found this trait impossible to cultivate myself.

My wooers were older men. At the age of nineteen I had been prepared for confirmation by the Rector of Chingford, where I was assistant organist. He was both godly and clumsy, and had once made the ungainly suggestion that we hold our next class in Epping Forest. He had a brother, whom I had met at parties in the Chingford Rectory, much more sophisticated, unmarried, a lawyer in London with a flat in Bryanston Square. His brother was also a musician, a pianist, who had two grand pianos in this flat, so it seemed natural he should invite me over to play duets and I was pleased to accept because Westminster wasn't exactly the hub of London social life and he was like a father figure with access to a fascinating world beyond my experience. He took me to dinner in the Army and Navy Club, introduced me to the clarets of the Medoc and the naïve paintings of the Cornish artist Bryan Pearce who was just then coming to notice. Then one day, on the sofa after dinner, he put an arm around me and a hand on my knee and tried to embrace me. I could feel his heart pumping and his blood racing, which induced in me not so much disgust as surprise that an old man would experience the same nervous passion for me as I felt when I first tried to kiss a girl. When he recognised my lack of response he quickly drew back and I told him it was women that turned me on, not men. I didn't want him to be humiliated. I couldn't imagine I'd ever given him signals I might be in the least interested in him in a sexual way, except, perhaps by naïvely accepting his invitations at all.

It happened, you've guessed, one of the St Thomas' nurses had already triggered in me that same chemical reaction that had set his blood running, and caused me to find in that London spring what Gerard Manley Hopkins had called 'the dearest freshness deep down things.' Annette Rowe was nineteen, the daughter of a Cornish farmer, wore her hair up beneath a starched linen cap and was immaculate in purple and white pin-striped dress, black stockings and a 'Nightingale' belt. Nurses too were under authority and the regime at St Thomas' was as rigorous as the armed forces, where thoroughness of personal presentation was regarded by the ward sister as a barometer of the thoroughness of nursing care. She had been present at the heart-transplant show-biz evensong and afterwards I had managed to rein in my shyness enough to ask her out. Off duty she was different, brown hair tumbling to her shoulders and, I remember, a blue and white horizontally striped mini-dress – a true 'bird' of the swinging sixties. So, we 'walked out' together, as the parish ladies put it. But there was an underlying relationship management problem: our trysts had to be arranged around the anti-social hours of nursing shifts, and we had to meet in the clergy house because the St Thomas' Hospital hostel in Ashley Gardens, where Annette lived, was completely out of bounds to men. Even fathers were suspect and were expected to wait in the lobby. Night shift presented us an obvious difficulty: she would work by night and sleep by day, and there was little opportunity to meet. But the afternoon/evening shift created what was to become a *cause célèbre*. Nurses came off duty at half past nine, which meant Annette would arrive at the clergy house, having made the journey across Westminster Bridge, at about ten o'clock, when we would run the gauntlet past Mrs Simpson's door to go to my room. It was clearly the lateness of the hour that so scandalised the beloved housekeeper. In a religious house an evening's social intercourse might appropriately end at ten o'clock, but to begin then was dubious in the extreme. Weren't these poor nurses, who rotated their sleep pattern, at some personal cost, to provide twenty-four-hour care for the sick and the dying, entitled to a social life? I was reminded of the visiting hour restrictions at Newnham College in the 1950s, when men had to leave the college by 6.00pm. One young woman caught with a man in her room after hours, when hauled before the Principal, protested there was nothing a young woman might do with a male visitor after six o'clock that she couldn't do before. After a pause, the Principal replied, 'Ah, but she could do it again.'

I have no idea what scenes of depravity played out in the redoubtable Mrs Simpson's imagination, but, unbeknown to me, she was sharing them with the Vicar, Barbara the Parish Secretary, and presumably anyone who had time to join her for a cup of tea.

Three quarters of the way through a curate's diaconal year the vicar, or supervising priest, is asked to give the bishop an assessment of the deacon's suitability for priesthood. Bill Davidson decided *not* to recommend me.

The Revd Bill Davidson had been in the army and played cricket for Oxford University and Sussex. He strode round Vincent Square in his cloak and highly polished black shoes with a purposeful waddle. He told the Bishop of Kensington, Ronald Goodchild, that given another year he 'could make a man of me'. It was never clear to me, or I suspect to the Bishop, what that really meant. My response to this bombshell was one of bewildered numbness rather than anger. Instead of protesting furiously and defending my rights, as curates would do today, I found myself passively absorbing the shock, and introspectively asking myself whether he was right and what I had done wrong. This has been the way I have always dealt with disappointments, personal, professional and financial, internalising them deep inside because to speak of them has been too humiliating or painful. There was certainly deep humiliation in this rejection because, without being arrogant, I had always been told I was cut out for the job – my final report from college had said, 'This man will make a remarkable priest.'

What went wrong? What aggravated my vicar so much? When I arrived at St Stephen's, I had no idea he was already deeply unpopular with a significant number of the parishioners, but I soon discovered the parish was divided between those for and those against him. The most active opponents tended to be the more influential parishioners, intellectuals like Honoria and Francis Wormald, an art historian who was Professor of Palaeography at London University. They were open with me about their criticisms of Bill Davidson. He was known as 'Silly Billy', and constantly compared unfavourably with his two predecessors, the aforementioned George Reindorp and his successor, Tony Tremlett, then Bishop of Dover, an ex-Cambridge Chaplain, charmer, aesthete, and darling of the upper classes, especially titled ladies and rosy-cheeked young men. My loyalty was certainly tested at almost every dinner party and pastoral visit, and occasionally found wanting.

Despite the parish's misgivings, I liked Bill and thought he liked me. Apart from the fact that I was bringing youthful ideas and innovations to his parish, we had in common a love of cricket. We both played for the London Diocese team of which he was the captain. In a match against the 'Licensed Victuallers', who had in their side that day the Australian fast bowler Neil Hawke, the Vicar was determined to show his mettle and managed to score 30 runs against the distinguished guest. This obviously gave great pleasure and when he was out, he returned to the dressing room like a man who had scored a hundred at Lord's, raising his bat to acknowledge the crowds. When our turn came to field, I was posted to the long on boundary. Neil Hawke came in to bat and hit the ball ferociously. Eventually he hoisted a drive in my direction, which seemed to be in the air for an age before thudding into my chest where I managed to clutch hold of it before throwing it triumphantly into the air. The following Sunday in church Bill announced how proud he was to have a 'curate who can hold his catches', an accolade I assumed meant that perhaps I was a man after all.

King's College, London, still had a theological hostel in Vincent Square under the Principalship of Sydney Evans, later Dean of Salisbury, and it was the annual custom for the students, all of whom were training for the ministry, to attend St Stephen's for a morning Eucharist. On the Sunday appointed, I happened to be on the list to preach. At the staff meeting Bill raised the question whether I ought to be replaced by someone more senior, but after due deliberation the senior curate, John Fuller, said he couldn't see a reason why I shouldn't do it. To me it was a great honour and like so many clergy charged with preaching to an academic institution I tried too hard and tried to be too clever. I took my theme from D.H. Lawrence's essay 'Climbing down Pisgah', the mountain from which Moses saw the Promised Land which he was never to enter. Lawrence, as the writer of *Sons and Lovers* and the *Rainbow*, was one of my literary heroes, but this essay is five pages of stingy pessimism in which he describes the vision of 'oneness' from the top of the mountain – the Spirit or God – as a 'gigantic cold monster', and, for the purposes of the essay, the Promised Land turns out to be Pittsburgh, and the 'chosen few' millions of people smelling of kerosene. Of course, that wasn't the emphasis I took, and I hadn't read the essay properly. I simply thought it looked smart to pin my real theme – the promise of the future – on Lawrence. I was thinking, rather, of Martin Luther King's great speech: 'Let freedom ring from the heightening Alleghenies of Pennsylvania. Let freedom ring from the snow-capped Rockies of Colorado. Let freedom ring from the curvaceous slopes of California.' I didn't build on Lawrence's pessimism, but on the image of climbing up the mountain in order to see the possibilities that lay ahead. I felt a passion for this because I was a young, new clergyman who had climbed the mountain of ordination only to see before me a land that Bill Davidson intended to prevent me from entering.

He told me, as a parable for my situation – and perhaps an explanation of his own action – that when he had been a curate, he had been invited to play in the annual cricket match between the 'Gentlemen and the Players'. This was a highly prestigious fixture, involving the best of the amateur and professional cricketers in England, which functioned as an unofficial trial match for selection to the national Test side. When he asked his vicar for time off, he was refused, and he had regretted that lost opportunity ever since. I think the moral of his story was that you must expect to give things up for your vocation, which might in many ways be true – there are many sacrifices along the way, not least financial ones – but it has never seemed of any merit to me to engage masochistically in suffering for its own sake.

There were, however, more concrete reasons for his refusal to recommend me, which, naturally from my side of the story, I try to play down. The most material was a disciplinary one. We were not obliged to attend the morning worship on our day off. Mine was on Friday but the vicar took Monday, and very soon I fell into the habit of being absent that morning too because I knew he wouldn't be there to check on me. It was a deceitful thing to do and I ought simply to have said I found burning the candle at both ends too exhausting to cope with. The pattern of being in church so early every day, and for such a long time, was physically and mentally exhausting and I was still expected to be out at night helping to run a youth club, attending meetings and visiting parishioners who would often want to talk until late.

Then there was the fact of my grey suede boots, worn under my cassock and definitely against army regulations. Oh, and the fact that on a cold morning, during meditation, I liked to stand over the heating grill outside the Lady Chapel and let the warm air rise up under the skirts of my cassock and huge black clerical cloak, instead of kneeling, lifeless, in the pew, and, even worse, to read the *Church Times* while standing there. That was a mistake in more ways than one. The great John Robinson, Bishop of Woolwich and writer of *Honest to God*, once quipped that he had neither the faith, the hope, nor the charity to read it. It would have been much more defensible to be reading *The Times* or the *New Statesman* because current affairs and social ethics are the stuff that prayers ought to be made of. You need raw material for prayer and a wider perspective than your own introspective concerns.

But the problem, at root, I am certain, was my relationship with Nurse Rowe, to whom by this time I was engaged to be married. There was still a strongly censorious and proprietorial attitude towards sex in the Church, an uncomfortable contrast with the secular culture of 'Swinging London'. For example, if you wanted to get married in your first year of ordination, permission from the bishop was required on the grounds that the demands of holy matrimony and the demands of this quasi-marriage to the Church were incompatible. These days you'd tell interfering superiors to mind their own business and have the law on your side. And speaking of law, I can see in retrospect that various senior clergy took a prurient interest in my relationship which would today amount to sexual harassment.

Why should the vicar have shown the least interest in my private life, anyway? Was he jealous? Did he receive complaints? At least from anyone other than Mrs Simpson, who resigned as housekeeper, much to my relief and his annoyance? Was the presence of star-crossed lovers in the sterile clergy house a neon-lit metaphor for the clash between religion and the secular culture? One vital clue was gleaned from Barbara, the highly indiscreet parish secretary, who I didn't realise until too late was a double agent. Bill had been away on a clergy training course leaving his wife Sylvia and their children in the Vicarage. On a couple of occasions Sylvia had had difficulty starting the car and had asked me to help her, which I was able to do successfully. It seems that on his return Sylvia extolled the virtues of the young curate rather too enthusiastically and for one mad moment, according to Barbara, it crossed his mind that she had been unfaithful. In his imagination, the curate's sexual precocity had reached paranoid proportions, where, like some sort of Rasputin, he stalked about seeking women whom he may devour. He had once told me, when trying to explain why I shouldn't be ordained priest that 'the most dangerous thing known to man is between his legs.'

'What? More dangerous than the crocodile, Bill? More dangerous than gravity or *Bacillus anthracis*?' But I had learned deference the hard way from my mother. I wondered what experience at school, or in the army, or as a priest had led him to this conclusion and hoped he'd not extend his argument to biblical allusion and deduce the obvious from Jesus' words that 'if thy right hand offend thee, cut it off, and cast it from thee: for it is profitable for thee that one of thy members should perish, and not that thy whole body should be cast into hell.' Did he want to make a man of me? Or did he hope to take my manhood away?

The person ultimately responsible for my professional welfare was the Bishop of Kensington who suggested we meet to discuss my future. By this time, I was so disillusioned I was in two minds whether I wanted a future in the Church at all. I had had ambivalent feelings prior to ordination symbolised by my sense of foreboding while on holiday in France, at Saint-Benoît-sur-Loire, when I counted the days until I would have to abandon my casual shirt for a clerical collar. The experience of holy orders so far did little to resolve my dilemma. The Bishop seemed as bemused as me about why I was not to be made a priest, but it quickly became clear that in what he perceived as a disagreement between a senior and a junior clergyman he must take the side of the senior. There was no attempt at any point, by any of those involved, to give a written account of the reasons for their decisions. The Bishop was so compromised he tried to persuade me to choose to become a 'permanent deacon', which he said was an honourable tradition within the Church. Why didn't I get a secular job and continue to serve in that capacity?

The delightfully oxymoronic 'Westminster Rural Deanery' contained some famous churches, not least among them St Margaret's, Westminster, and St Martin's-in-the-Fields. At the clergy chapter meetings I had got to know the Vicar of St Martin's, Austen Williams, whom I had admired since I was a boy from his appearances on television. When I explained my situation to him, he told me he needed a warden for his new youth centre in St Martin's Place and immediately offered me the job. This was a wonderfully exciting opportunity. I was being invited to join the staff of one of the great churches by a

Rector whom I considered a fine preacher and a great man, to initiate an innovative and challenging job which carried with it a large flat overlooking Trafalgar Square where Annette and I could live when we got married. I knew the Bishop would be delighted and impressed by the alacrity with which I had met his criteria and solved a tricky problem. When I told him, however, he looked perplexed and strangely irritated; he pondered a long time and then said, 'Austen cannot do that. I cannot have one incumbent poach a curate from another incumbent in the same deanery. It cannot be done.' And there and then he picked up the telephone and rang Austen Williams and, in my presence, berated him for his proposal. Bill Davidson was right: someone needed to make a man of me. I should have handed back my letters patent, ripped off my dog collar, and walked out of the Bishop's study and out of the Church of England there and then, never to return. But I didn't. Feebly I agreed with the Bishop that I would once again look for a job that this time would not cause him any embarrassment.

Meanwhile Buckingham Gate School had been absorbed into the monstrous behemoth, Pimlico Comprehensive, where on a Thursday I took the ninth and tenth streams of thirteen, fourteen, and fifteen-year-olds for divinity. First you had to locate your classroom, which was like hunting for your car in a multi-storey car park having failed to make a note of which floor and row it was in. When the room was found, the next challenge was crowd control and calming down, which might take up to half the lesson. It was a kind of group therapy. These were the strugglers, the disheartened, those in danger of going under. They wanted to talk about sex, drugs and rock 'n' roll, not St Pauls' missionary journeys. In other words, they wanted to discuss how to cope with relationships and society. Although one boy asked me each week in a zombie like voice, 'Please, Sir, what d'you think of Gandhi?' which at first I thought was an absurd ruse to divert me from my task, but later recognised as a symptom of his attention deficit hyperactivity disorder (ADHD).

Such were the emotional and behavioural problems of children in this vast school, it was decided to appoint a school counsellor and the head teacher wanted me to take on the task. Not only did this strike me as a particularly daunting assignment, which I doubted my ability to manage with any success, it would mean effectively giving up being a clergyman altogether. It was all very well for the bishop to talk of the permanent diaconate, but in practice I felt this would have meant finding my own accommodation and slowly being absorbed into the secular world. It would have meant that I had slipped into a job not by positive design but on the rebound from a fiasco of pastoral mismanagement.

By now the vicar's decision to postpone my ordination to the priesthood had become public knowledge in the parish and, I am happy to say, that with the exception of one of the churchwardens, John Crowe, no one seemed to agree with him. It was around the time when men had first landed on the moon. Bishop Henry, puffing on his *Senior Service* cigarette said very solemnly one evening, 'I don't like having to say this, but I advise you to get out of this parish,' and then added, 'we are thinking of establishing an archdeaconry of the Moon, and I am going to propose William Davidson as Archdeacon.' Others, unbeknown to me, had asked Bishop Tony Tremlett and Sydney Evans, the Dean of King's, to intervene on my behalf. Sydney Evans, being in the theological college world, knew that a former Vice-Principal of Wells Theological College had just become Vicar of Christ Church, Lancaster Gate, and was looking for a curate. Between them they put pressure on the Bishop of Kensington to think again. This time both Bill Davidson and I were summoned to the Bishop's grand house in Campden Hill Square. I decided to travel by underground from St James' Park to Notting Hill Gate. When I got down to the platform there was Bill carrying a large leather briefcase containing what I presumed must be the evidence for the prosecution. I had nothing. We sat next to each other in the train and had the kind of polite conversation I imagine one might have on the way to the scaffold. And so, we are back to the film script with which this chapter opened.

When we sat down in the study at Campden Hill Square the Bishop spoke of the seriousness of what we were about to discuss, but I cannot remember whether or not he began with prayer for the guidance of the Holy Spirit. The Vicar spoke first rehearsing the complaints familiar to me: irregular attendance at morning worship, reading the *Church Times* during meditation, wearing grey suede shoes under my cassock, not making sufficient pastoral visits in a week. One of the things he had accused me of in our many conversations was not 'playing by the Queensbury rules' – a reference to the rules of boxing and suggestive of honour amongst gentlemen – particularly in relation to my failure to turn up to church on his day off. As I say, he had a point, but now he decided to punch below the belt himself and accused me of 'fornication'. In ecclesiastical law fornication was a sackable offence – that is to have sexual relations with someone to whom you are not married. Fornication is certainly a delicious word to relish and roll around the tongue, and not very complimentary either, deriving as it does from the Latin 'fornix' meaning a brothel. He then added, as an aside, 'But of course I have no evidence.' He'd got the idea from tittle tattle with the parish secretary, with whom, clearly, he had had some very salacious conversations. For prosecuting counsel to admit they have no evidence blows a fatal hole in their case. I was irate. I found it offensive and impertinent that anyone should spend time speculating about the nature of my relationship with my fiancée, let alone consider it appropriate to raise as a matter for public discussion. Perhaps I was naïve given the Church's record for sexual repression and the residual Augustinian view that all sex, even within marriage, is tainted with sin. I simply replied, 'Of course he has no evidence. Does he listen at the keyhole of my room?'

Getting up from his chair, the Bishop said, 'I think we have heard enough' and asked Bill to leave so that he could speak to me alone. As soon as he had gone a great wall of emotional pressure that had been building up over the last few months ruptured like a fractured dam and I broke down into uncontrollable tears, which made me feel childish and vulnerable. Obviously, the Bishop had had no training in how to deal with this – no arm round the shoulder, no pause for recollection; he carried on speaking as though nothing unusual was happening. He said I clearly couldn't remain at St Stephen's any longer and I might as well clear my desk immediately, but that there was a vacancy on the far side of Hyde Park at Christ Church, Lancaster Gate, with a man called Reginald Askew, who had recently arrived in London from Wells Theological College with high hopes.

After I left St Stephens, I thought good riddance, but soon discovered there were many affections I had developed in that short period of fifteen months, not least for the nuns, the Sisters of the Deaconess Community of St Andrew in their blue habit, who during my fall from grace with Bill Davidson had always been supportive and open-minded. Sister Joan Irene was the senior in their small household, a wonderfully complete person, motherly and attractive and, it seemed to me, in tune with the world and contemporary life, not in any way cloistered or too heavenly minded to be of any earthly use. And Sister Lena, who eventually became Superior of the order, sweet and canny and the most obviously 'holy' of them. There was also a young novice, Juliet, who joined the parish after I had arrived. She had a good figure, was a bit laddish, like a youth club leader, but with a sexy spark. Although I wouldn't have used such Freudian language in those days, she had about her an air of having been hurt, messed with, abused, and, since I had a visceral antipathy towards monasticism which I regarded as unnatural and repressive, I wanted to keep her out of the nunnery and convert her to the King's Road culture. But probably it was exactly that peer group pressure to have a good time and exploit the popular culture that she was running away from. There was one overarching regret for the nuns: despite their sense of vocation they couldn't at that time be priests, and the depth of their jealous frustration was exposed by their repeated ironic jibes at my dog collar as the 'ring of confidence', a slogan taken from a Colgate toothpaste ad for white teeth. It seemed their only descent into bitterness.

And there was Raymond, the organist, newly graduated from the Royal Academy and the music we made together, and his beautiful fiancée, who repeatedly came to my room for afternoon tea and spiritual counsel without incurring the spite of Mrs Simpson or striking the bell of the vicar's fairground randiness strengthometer.

I missed the unlicensed diner in Warwick Way, where you could take your own wine and nearly always see the actor Wilfrid Brambell, who played Alfred Steptoe in *Steptoe and Son*, sitting in the corner, looking as dishevelled as he did in his role of rag and bone man. And at the other end of the feudal scale, being invited to dinner with the Dowager Viscountess Falmouth in her Chelsea flat to discuss Fr Mario Borrelli, whom I had met at a post-ordination training day – known by the clergy as 'potty training' – at St Katharine's, Stepney, and had mentioned in a sermon. Lady Falmouth had expressed her admiration for Borelli's work with the street urchins of Naples and wanted to hear more about it. I, of course, knew no more than already stated in my sermon, but we sat at either end of a long table and, since she was a touch deaf, had to holler at each other to be heard, whilst being waited upon by an aged maid, just like Julie Walters in the 'Two Soups' sketch from the *Victoria Wood* show, all bent over and shaking, and enquiring whether Sir would care for more soup.

On another such evening the Wormalds, who had taken me under their wing, asked me at dinner if I could recommend a film they might like and I suggested Luis Buñuel's classic,

Belle de Jour, mainly because I had a crush on its star, Catherine Deneuve. It's the story of a respectable young wife who takes up prostitution by day while her husband is at work. Hence *de jour* rather than *de nuit*. On the following Sunday they told me how much they had enjoyed it, but thought it wasn't the sort of film a clergyman ought to recommend to parishioners. Too racy by half. So, it is okay for me and for them to see it, but not for anyone else? One of the great curiosities of an incarnational religion in which God becomes human and embraces the world that he loves, is how much of that life, its nature and passion, is considered 'unsuitable' for its adherents to contemplate, particularly if you are one of its official representatives.

At our Christ Church flat in Bayswater we had no outside space at all and I missed the window boxes outside my first-floor room, in the shadow of Hide Tower where, at Annette's behest, I had grown nasturtiums that summer, their vibrant blood orange flowers providing a Proustian memory of falling in love.

The only time I returned to St Stephen's was for the funeral of dear old Bishop Henry Montgomery-Campbell, 1887–1970, with whom I had drunk all that sherry. I can't remember now whether it was conducted by Bishop George Reindorp or Lord Fisher, the previous Archbishop of Canterbury, whom Henry had referred to as a hard man: 'He boils his potatoes in the tears of widows,' he used to say. Henry had served in the First World War and won the Military Cross for bravery at Gallipoli. He had had a charmed life in the Church of England, born into a church family, moving from post to post and then bishopric to bishopric with what you might almost describe as divine right. It was before the age of political correctness and I recall this service happened in the same week as the funeral of Lillian Board, a British Olympic runner who had died of cancer aged 22. As I have said, Henry was known for his eccentric manner of smoking cigarettes, which he held in a miniature silver grip contraption. Afterwards George made a terrible joke that Henry would be in heaven saying to Lillian Board, 'Do have a cigarette?' which I am sure Henry would have found to be in bad taste. Archbishop Geoffrey Fisher meanwhile spent a deal of time chatting up my fiancée.

*

Twenty years later, Bill Davidson showed up one morning at the University Church, Oxford, with a new wife and apologised for what he had done. I felt no resentment because things had turned out well for me despite that experience and I had dined out on the tale many times.

What Rash Fellows These Christians Are

I am finding it frustratingly difficult to paint a mature portrait of myself as a young man. In his brilliant novel *The Only Story* Julian Barnes asks whether all the retellings of your personal story bring you closer to the truth of what happened or move you further away. Later in the novel one of his narrating characters ponders, 'which are truer, the happy memories, or the unhappy ones? He decided eventually that the question was unanswerable.' I worry whether I have remembered accurately; surely justice and truth depend upon it. But what does it matter? Do we not all embellish our story in the light of experience. That, surely, is the nature of life writing – somewhere between history and the novel – never dispassionate, often exaggerated, but at its best seeking creatively to say something worthwhile.

*

I was only twenty-four when I went to Christ Church, Lancaster Gate, barely out of college, and inexperienced in the ways of the world. My most vivid and persistent recollections of that period are of people and attitudes which were not only new to me, but fundamentally challenged the lower-middle class values I had taken for granted as a teenager. Nothing was as permanent as I had imagined, all was fluid: quite contrary to my parents' view of life that their social framework and values had somehow been fixed by the gods.

In front of the church in the centre of Lancaster Gate was a churchyard overlooking Kensington Gardens. It was dry and infertile, leeched of nutrients by the roots of plane and lime trees under whose canopy little would grow, but Harry Cantwell, our local greengrocer and self-appointed gardener, was undaunted. Harry was as sharp as the neat double whiskies he knocked back in the *Cleveland Arms*. In the war, he had run a scam selling His Majesty's Navy's sugar on the black market. He brought the same roguish touch to his church work and was reckless for our success. Every morning he went early to Covent Garden market to buy fruit and vegetables for his greengrocery store in Leinster Terrace and then one day in March he came home with trays of geraniums which he proceeded to plant in the borders of the church garden setting them ablaze with red. This instant garden was a joy for a day or two until a frost destroyed them. In a parish letter, the vicar said that people seeing this unseasonal juxtaposition of daffodils and geraniums would be bound to think 'what rash fellows these Christians are'. That phrase summed up everything I admired about Christ Church, Lancaster gate. One Christmas Harry bought a Christmas tree to rival the one in Trafalgar Square annually given by the people of Oslo, but it was so enormous none of us was able to erect it either inside the church or outside in the churchyard where it remained on its side throughout the Christmas period, a symbol of laudable over-ambition for the Kingdom of God.

*

I first visited the church on a Sunday night in December 1969. Annette and I were invited to attend Evensong to meet the congregation. Assuming the service began at 6.30pm, as it did at St Stephen's, Rochester Row, we made a bad start by arriving half an hour late and hoped to slip in unnoticed at the back, but I was wearing a large clerical collar leaving little doubt that I was the expected candidate and the sidesman on duty, the same Harry Cantwell, led us ostentatiously down the central aisle to a pew at the front of the church on the right-hand side, so that the eyes of all in the temple were upon us.

We had arrived in time for the anthem, which rose exquisitely in the heavenly acoustics from a mixed voice choir of young and beautiful people – beautiful, not in the hippy sense popular at the time, but youthful and vigorous and dynamic. This was followed by the sermon. The vicar, an enormous red-bearded figure, like Isaiah or one of the prophets, ascended the marble pulpit and leaning over its parapet began, 'Tonight atheist I am speaking to you.' Isolated in the front pew, like the squire in a *Punch* cartoon, I thought, 'but he hardly knows me. Surely he can't be speaking to me.' It was an arresting oratorical ploy. In the large congregation, believers, agnostics, and sceptics alike sat up to listen to see how he was going to present the claims of Christianity to the real or imagined atheist.

The pulsating atmosphere afterwards was a complete contrast to stuffy Rochester Row. There was a buzz, a critical mass, which made you want to be involved and get to know these people. Bayswater was to Westminster as a nightclub to a poorly attended political meeting. For a start there was no church hall, so every social gathering had to happen in someone's home or in a local hotel. On this occasion, being a public viewing of the new curate, we gathered in the Vicarage in Porchester Gardens. The whole of the downstairs, kitchen, living room and Vicar's study were crowded with people of all sorts and conditions: an Etonian churchwarden, the other the Principal of the Camberwell School of Art, a gaggle of old women led by the onomatopoeically named Edie Withers, who wanted a kiss and got it, along with her friend Mrs Branstone whose cleaning mops were kept in the cupboard off the choir vestry, and the greengrocer sidesman who had so flamboyantly shown us to our seats an hour earlier. But the majority were young, many in their first job after university, living in bedsits, effervescent, socially committed, predatorily heterosexual, of the 'flower-power' generation, talented and holy. Suddenly it was possible to be in love with the Church and recklessly ambitious for it.

I moved from my study-bedroom in the Westminster clergy house to a ground floor flat in Cleveland Square that same

December, managing to shift all my stuff – a desk, two chairs, books, pictures and vases – in two journeys in my clapped-out Humber Supersnipe, an enormous maroon limousine I had bought as a student for a holiday job driving Americans around London. There were four huge, high-ceilinged rooms in 26 Cleveland Square, two either side of the double front door that opened onto the street, and two at the back, with a poky kitchen off one of them. On the living room wall was a full-size billboard poster proclaiming 'Guinness is Good for you' left by the previous curate, and when I bought a seven-foot Broadwood grand piano for £25 from a lady in South Hampstead, it was lost in a corner at one end. There was no central heating and I had to make do with a two-bar electric fire. For this bohemian luxury I received a heating allowance of £60 a year, which, in accordance with diocesan rules, was taken away when I married, presumably on the grounds that a man married a wife not only for better or for worse but for additional warmth.

During my first two months there I continued to live in a single room – the 'Guinness' room – as the other bedrooms were still let to two young spinsters of the parish, Chrissie Radcliffe and Pippa Benson. Who could escape the irony that after all the kerfuffle about concupiscence and lust at St Stephen's I should now be expected to cohabit with two girls in a Bayswater bedsit; an irony magnified when my fiancée was prevented from staying overnight on the grounds that it was immoral. She was on a three-month nursing placement in Portsmouth's psychiatric hospital and when she came to visit needed accommodation. So the vicar arranged for her to lodge on these occasions with Diana Panting, an unmarried civil servant in her mid-thirties, the ambiguity of whose name did not escape us, especially when we discovered she in turn was visited most Friday nights by a mystery lover.

Looking back, it seems absurd either of us should have tolerated such denial of our privacy and control of our personal lives, but the Church was locked into the past and we did not demur, taking its authority for granted. Not only that, I felt angry at the double standards: it was one rule for me and another for the rest of the congregation of Christians, who presumably shared the same moral values. The vibrancy of the young congregation was partly fuelled by the making and breaking of relationships and they came to church not only for the worship and discussion groups and social outreach, but for its community. In the age of the pill, Christ Church celebrated liberation. Strange that a Church that has made so much fuss about priests being gay, should also get so worked up about someone being straight. The Bishop couldn't let the matter drop and insisted, as part of my post-Rochester Row therapy, I receive counselling as if I had a mental health disorder – sex addiction, I suppose. I was sent to David Martin, the Chaplain of King's College London. Fortunately, I knew David and his wife from my days in Westminster and he was able to treat these sessions as a joke.

*

Having moved me to Lancaster Gate, the Bishop of Kensington decided I must be ordained priest at the earliest possible opportunity and, since the Advent ordination was a matter of weeks away, I once again went to St Paul's Cathedral for the great service where the Bishop of London, Robert Stopford, assisted by other priests laid his hands on my head in the act of ordination. There was none of the life-changing symbolism this time round, no sense of leaving the world of the collar and tie for the dog-collar, no hint of a special relationship with God. This was a belated, matter of fact imparting of the right to celebrate the Holy Communion. It should have happened three months previously and had been delayed by the bizarre circumstances I have described.

The real change, however, was my new life in Bayswater. Reggie Askew had a high sense of drama and generously suggested I celebrate my first mass on Christmas Eve at the midnight service. In those days the priest still faced the altar with his back to the congregation and Reggie had decked the altar with ranks of candles like a birthday cake for God, which from a distance looked bright and Christmassy but at close quarters was like being in King Nebuchadnezzar's burning fiery furnace. As it had been for Shadrach, Meshack and Abednego, the situation was compounded by the number of garments I had to wear. They were bound in their mantles, their tunics, and their hats; I wore a white alb over my cassock and on top of that a heavy chasuble of lined cloth and gold embroidery with amice and apparel around my neck. The perspiration poured from my head and ran down my face.

That year Reggie had made a linocut for the parish Christmas card, *The Heavenly Host appearing over Queensway*. It had seemed a preposterous idea. For a start, the streetlights were far too bright for anyone to see the night sky, and why should the heavenly host appear above a street more noted for its brothels than its holiness? Queensway was, besides, the place where Reggie had been accosted by a prostitute who, when he had protested that he was the local vicar, had retorted, 'Then to you, Dearie, it's free,' and also the location of the French patisserie he gave up visiting the following Lent because he lusted after the girl behind the counter. 'Marriage is Lent,' he was to declare in a sermon, and although people looked at his wife, Kate, with both curiosity and sympathetic embarrassment, we knew what he meant: marriage requires self-control, not because love is so fragile, or his marriage vulnerable, but because the drive of the selfish gene is irrepressible and can make even a French patisserie a dangerous place to lurk. But in the heat of my first mass I suddenly recognised in a moment of inspiration that the 'Heavenly Host appearing over Queensway' was a metaphor for the belief that Bayswater could be miraculously transformed and that my vocation was to enable that process.

Queensway was not only a sort of down-market King's Road, it boasted London's first department store, Whiteley's, the founder of which had left an endowment of money to be distributed to the poor at Christmas. One of my jobs was to cycle round the Paddington area on short frosty afternoons delivering what had become known affectionately as the 'Whiteley's Pound'. It wasn't a great deal of money, even though by then it had become two pounds, but enough to buy the ingredients for a Christmas dinner for one and a bottle of sherry besides. I felt guilty for enjoying these errands of mercy and hoped they did not bring me more pleasure than the recipients. The experience was a like stepping back into Dickensian London, me playing a sentimental and reformed Scrooge bringing turkey and good cheer to all the Cratchits of Bayswater as I became the bountiful visitor to lonely people in circumstances as varied as a flat in that exclusive and delightful quarter of Little Venice, to a damp basement down by the railway line in Westbourne Park Villas, which then, if not now, were run-down houses in multi-occupancy, with casement windows no match for the cold. Scrabbling my way through one dark and stinking basement passage, I was aware of a scuttling movement around my feet and a furry brush around my trousers. My sense of guilt was intensified by the fact I knew I would return to a companionable Christmas and that the delivery of the Whiteley's Pound was an added pleasure to my enjoyment of the festive season. Would I stop on Christmas Day to remember the twilight loneliness of those people who had only Christmas past to reflect on and maybe not particularly happy memories of those either?

Like St Stephen's, Christ Church had had a larger-than-life previous vicar who, through his flair, oratory, and unorthodox leadership had shaped this extraordinary community. He spoke in a cultured, avuncular voice about Christian love with the same prodigal enthusiasm as the Beatles sang about secular love: 'All you need is love', 'love is all you need.'

He preached about Lolita and Picasso and the imagery of God – and hugged everybody. Young and old flocked to sit at his feet. In his early forties, Tony Bridge had been an artist and atheist, but then, deeply affected by his experiences in the Second World War, he became more and more convinced by the Christian story to the point where he felt compelled to be ordained. Because he spoke out of that background and experience, many found his message irresistible: it meant the priest and prophet had visited the same wilderness so many of them had struggled through, or were currently battling against with varying degrees of success and failure. People don't want to hear from a person for whom spiritual confidence is a matter of effortless ease; they don't want sugared certainties; they prefer faith that has been through the mill and faced up to the realities of life, or as the First Letter of Peter says, has been tried as gold is tried in the fire.

By the time I moved to Lancaster Gate, Tony had become Dean of Guildford, so I never worked for him, but we very soon met on his return visits and immediately hit it off. This rapport was entirely unrelated, I might add, to the fact he swore like a trooper. But I did admire the fact that his expletive inventiveness could extend to prayer as well as ordinary conversation. I remember that he had prayed for those 'poor bastards' suffering in the Vietnam War. The Dean of St Paul's, Alan Webster, once told me the reason Tony had been made a dean rather than a bishop was his propensity for 'four-letter' words. Yet he loved the beauty of the Book of Common Prayer. In that prosaic era when *Series III*, the precursor of the 1980's *Alternative Service Book*, was published he criticised it in the national press as being written in the 'language of seaside landladies', an unreconstructed comment he wouldn't have got away with today. But there was a refreshing honesty about the freedom of his extempore prayer. Throughout my theological college days, we had prayed for Vietnam until blue in the face and the prayers had become tired and ragged at the edges. To pray for those 'poor bastards' was not only a wake-up call for the congregation, but for God too, in the best Old Testament tradition, as the prophet Habakkuk puts it, 'O Lord, how long shall I cry for help, and you will not listen?'

Vietnam had prompted the slogan 'Make love not war', which had become the catchphrase of the hippy movement: it was a double protest – a battle cry for the free love that female contraception had recently made possible (and which so tormented the imagination of the Vicar of Rochester Row) as well as a cry against the empty cruelties of Vietnam, symbolised, by the famous photograph of the little girl running down the road in agony, burnt with napalm, an image that somehow manages to bring a visceral shock of revulsion into every school playground and every parent's heart and thus to give radical credence to the call for love. Power should not be found in the dropping of napalm, but in flowers and the beauty of nature. That was the idealistic dream of our generation and we were all taken up with flower-power to some degree. I made my own 'kipper' tie from an off-cut of material from a flowery dress my wife was making. Laura Ashley had hit the market with prettily innocent, floral dresses from Wales, that young women wore like woodland dryads. However, many were still too hard up to buy their clothes and the seamstress's art had not yet been lost. Most girls I knew could use a sewing machine and would expect to receive one amongst their wedding presents. For all that, I was confident Christianity was capable of propagating the length and breadth and height of love a hundred per cent better than Flower Power.

On his vicarage wall, Tony Bridge had painted in large white letters, 'I love you'. It was his Christian version of 'make love not war' and the effect had been prophetic. I wasn't so naïve, however, that I didn't recognise the culture of 'love' at Lancaster Gate was somewhat affected and self-indulgent. Everyone kissed everyone else, or at least the younger women were kissed a great deal, not least by Reggie whose bear-hug embrace was legendary. My fiancée, a nubile nineteen, was also the object of this kissing frenzy which men undertook with seeming impunity under the guise of Christian love. More kissed against than kissing, the women of Lancaster Gate never kissed each other, the sisterly embrace not yet the commonplace it is today. Such was the men's uninhibited confidence that they had the right to ogle the women, a young medical student from St Mary's Hospital, who sang bass in the choir, led me one evening to a mini-skirted, leggy soprano sitting on the floor at a coffee party and invited me to admire the perfection of her legs. She seemed unfazed by this, I suppose flattered – he said why else would she display her legs if they weren't to be looked at – but I was embarrassed and found his prurience gauche. Basically, I did not get along with the kissing culture. Not that I was a prude I hope, if anything the opposite, but I thought there was too much *eros* and not enough *agape*. Perhaps had I been unattached I would have felt differently, but I confess to being vulnerable. Potentially a jealous lover, I did not relish the idea of my fiancée being embraced by a host of young men however Christian they might be. So I didn't go in for kissing, hugging and squeezing. Bill Davidson would have been proud of me.

Mrs Bridge, Brenda, was just as posh as Tony and on one of their return visits to the parish, Reggie greeted her with an excessive, over-enthusiastic embrace that caused her to protest that she wanted to get out of his clutches. Afterwards she complained to me, 'When I want him to squeeze my f****** tits, I'll f****** well tell him.'

But Lancaster Gate flowed with *agape* nonetheless: an ugly word, those three Greek syllables, but a noble concept. It is the word used for love or charity in St Paul's hymn to love, so often read at weddings, in 1 Corinthians 13 and, in the early church, for a religious meal, akin to the Eucharist, sometimes called a 'love feast'. The student demonstrations of 1968 had been characterised by protests known as 'sit-ins', where students occupied buildings and lecture theatres to the considerable inconvenience of the authorities at the LSE and the Sorbonne. Inspired by that imagery we instituted 'eat-ins', occasions for hospitality in each other's homes, which were open to people from the parish without discrimination. They weren't exclusive or elitist, but as it were protested the hospitality that flows from the prodigal hand of God.

'Hospitality' was for us as important a theological word as 'salvation' or 'redemption', and it spoke loudly and effectively in the bed-sit London of shilling-in-the-slot gas fires and dingy staircases. Reggie often spoke of 'Franciscan' hospitality, which gave a theological ring to what we were about. I think he meant the Franciscans started as beggars and subsequently welcomed beggars into their houses and, although poor, were happy to share generously what they had. The same approach was evident in our mass migrations to the pub on Sunday nights. In any community or association of people some will be more attractive than others and their company preferable to that of the club bore or tongue-tied introvert. That is why in-groups develop, but in our community, friends didn't always sit together; everyone made an effort in the course of an evening to move round and to share their company and conversation. I came to regard this as a special example of true *agape*.

Tony Bridge had encouraged people to show their love to one another. Edie Withers and her delightful old friend Mrs Branstone who cleaned the church and left her disgustingly smelly mop in the choir vestry cupboard, told me each week that they loved me. It might have been dismissed as the foolish talk of old crones, but it was their attempt to find the love of God in lonely lives, and their genuineness was confirmed to me when Edie paid the ultimate tribute of calling me the 'Young Tony'.

*

Whilst at Lancaster Gate I played every wedding-day role except that of the bride. I was the groom at my own wedding, officiated at several, and played the organ when the organist was away. Then one day a young American in the congregation asked me if I would give her away. She was to be married in Christ Church but her family weren't well off and her parents couldn't afford the fare over the Atlantic. I rather fancied myself walking down the aisle with her on my arm, saying, 'I do' in reply to the vicar's, 'who giveth this woman to be married to this man?' and making a speech at the reception. Then she raised the question of how we were to get to the church. So I said that since I was standing in for her father I might as well be her chauffeur as well and collect her in my car, which at that time was a duck blue Hillman Imp with the engine at the back. On the happy day, I arrived at her flat in Queens Gardens, rang the bell, and she let me in via the answer phone. When I reached the third floor her door was open but she was still in her underwear, unable to get into her wedding dress. 'I'm sorry to do this to you,' she drawled, 'but can you ease this over my shoulders and do up the zip?' I pulled the zip up the length of her spine; in the cool air I couldn't help noticing the goose bumps on her shoulders. As we left, I said, that now I was her bridesmaid as well, she mustn't forget to hand me her posy when we get to the chancel steps.

Reggie and I both had a maverick streak. We would have called it 'imagination', others might have said we were embraced by that common clergy weakness, the desire for attention, attested by a fondness for dressing up, fancy titles, and walking in solemn procession. It's a trait shared by academics, who besides were once all clergymen, viz the Clerk of Oxenford in Chaucer's *Canterbury Tales*. When Oxford held a memorial service for its Chancellor, Lord Jenkins of Hillhead, in 2003, there was a discussion whether there should be a procession of all the Heads of Colleges through the streets from Balliol College to the University Church. The argument was settled when the Vice-Chancellor said in all seriousness, 'What do we do when we meet together as a University? We process.'

Part of the maverick streak was contrariness and in Lent, instead of fasting, we decided to have a weekly fry up for breakfast – bacon, egg, mushrooms, black pudding, and fried bread, eaten in the vicarage kitchen on Tuesdays following early matins. After one of these paradoxical Lenten breakfasts we sat in the Vicar's study, lined with books about ethics, including a much thumbed copy of *Five Types of Ethical Theory* by Reggie's hero, the Cambridge philosopher C D Broad, and agreed that the end of Lent, Good Friday, was the one day of the year when the Church was symbolically dead: all the pomp and ceremony, institutionalism, and even the sacraments were suspended as we contemplated the enormity of Christ's crucifixion. How were we to mark this? We decided that for the Three-Hour Meditation, which coincides with Christ's three hours on the cross from noon until 3pm, instead of wearing clerical collars and cassocks we should put on civvies. Reggie was much more conservative than he let on, and when it came to clothes a bit of a snob. I guessed exactly how he'd dress. Was he able to predict me in the same way? In the event we both turned up in dark suits, striped shirts with separate starched white collars, sporting old school ties. What rash fellows! The only difference being his was a Savile Row suit, mine was from Monty Burton's; he was an old Harrovian whereas I had been to an Essex County high school.

There was a conventional side to our Lent as well. In Passiontide the crucifixes, statues and pictures in church were veiled according to High-Church custom with purple satin cloth. As curate it fell to my lot to cover the reredos behind the high altar, which involved climbing a ladder and stepping onto a ledge, deep with the ecclesiastical dust of ages, above the statues, fifteen feet from the ground. Rather than feeling nearer heaven, I became frozen with vertiginous fear, especially at the moment of transferring from the ladder to the ledge, where I felt the ladder might easily slip away and the saint's head I was clinging onto easily separate from its body. But this wasn't half so bad as changing the light bulbs in the nave. The lights were suspended from the apex of the neo-gothic arches, which reached almost to the clerestory windows. To reach them I had to hoist a three-sectioned ladder onto the wall above the centre of the arch and then climb into mid-air until the lights were in reach. Thus, precariously hanging, I groped for the dud bulb, poked it into my trouser pocket, extracted the new bulb from the other pocket and twisted it into the socket. I tried not to look down because to do so was like falling from the sky without a parachute. In those pre-health-and-safety days I undertook these tasks unquestioningly and alone in that great building. It frightened me and afterwards I would have nightmares about climbing a spiral staircase with stairs that sloped into a great void with no banister, but I knew someone had to do the job and it might as well be me. In a way, although this might easily be a retrospective view, it felt like an initiation rite, the painful and dangerous task that a young man had to undergo in order to prove his worthiness for the priesthood. The nightmares continued for many years, long after Christ Church, Lancaster Gate, had been pulled down and replaced with flats. When I pass on the bus down the Bayswater Road and look up into Lancaster Gate, it seems odd that that space, which once to me was holy, and in this instance terrifying, should now be someone's bedroom on the third floor. Maybe one day someone sleeping there will have a dream of a young man climbing a ladder with light bulbs in his pocket. It seemed to me then, as now, that a willingness to get your hands dirty is an essential quality in a clergyman and ever since those days I have judged my assistant clergy by asking myself whether they would be willing to change the light bulbs.

Being in the centre of London it was not unusual for the church to be visited by distinguished or famous people. Deans and bishops often came to preach, actors such as Frank Windsor from the TV series Z Cars and Peter Jeffery, the Headmaster in the film If read at the carol service. On one occasion Iris Murdoch, Bernard Levin, and Monica Furlong publicly debated their views on Christianity. Afterwards Reggie and Kate hosted a literary supper party at the vicarage and kindly invited me. All hospitality centred around the scrubbed pine table in their kitchen with a pine dresser displaying their collection of pale blue and white *Asiatic Pheasant* china and a row of New Hall teapots. We sat on elm country chairs and drank the house red from Justin de Blank's shop in South Ken. All this evoked the Somerset rusticity of Wells, where Reggie had been vice-principal of the theological college. Reggie was in his element, and for most of the time 'ran' the conversation from the head of the table as Sir Michael Howard, when Regius Professor of History, would do at lunchtime in Oriel College. At one point he said, 'Since we have all recently published a book perhaps each of us might say something about their work.' It would have been about the time of Iris Murdoch's novel *The Black Prince* (drawing on the theme of Hamlet) – one of her very best books. Levin had written about politics, a housemaster from Eton had written about the philosopher J L Austin, and Reggie had written *The Tree of Noah*, an imaginative story about Noah set in Somerset, but one of those cross genre books it is almost impossible for a publisher to market, being neither fish nor fowl. It was too much like a novel to be a religious book and too much like a religious book to be a novel. In any case Iris Murdoch famously disliked talking about her novels and the conversation concentrated on the housemaster from Eton and Austin.

I had been reticent in the conversation at dinner and afterwards, over coffee, Iris made a bee line to talk to me. I could easily get tongue-tied when I met famous or clever people. As I child I had suffered for a few years from a stammer, which I tried to beat by finding a synonym for the word I couldn't get out, which could lead to misunderstanding. I once failed to get a job in BBC religious broadcasting because, for the sake of my stammer, I substituted *religious* broadcasting with *Christian* broadcasting because I was having difficulty with the 'r'. Immediately the interviewer jumped on me supposing me to be some sort of campaigning dogmatist and almost shouted that what they were interested in was RELIGIOUS broadcasting. Sometimes I did the same kind of thing with paragraphs and ideas, and say something quite opposite to what I knew to be the case to break the ice of a conversation, and then be annoyed with myself when my collocutor looked at me as if I were an idiot. Naïvely I asked Iris whether they had been talking at the table about Austin Farrer, the theologian and Warden of Keble, knowing full well it had been the philosopher John Austin. In this case, Iris was extremely gracious and said that although they were discussing John Austin, they could 'easily have been talking about the work of that wonderful priest, Austin Farrer'.

In subsequent years, when we were living in Oxford, I met Iris Murdoch quite often. I would sometimes find her standing in the University Church apparently absorbed in thought, perhaps contemplating the sovereignty of Good if not of God. On several occasions she came to speak at the University Church, the first time as a part of a series on religion and literature. She insisted she wouldn't give a lecture but would 'engage in conversation' and that this should not be in the church but in the Old Library. I advertised the meeting in the usual way and on the night there were queues outside the church – far too many to fit into the library which has a capacity of eighty people. Once the first eighty had been admitted I had no alternative but to bar the door and the person in whose face I had to shut it was Professor Denis Nineham, the former Warden of Keble, who had taught me briefly in Cambridge. He told me in certain terms that I ought to have had the sense to organise the event properly. On another occasion I invited Iris, but she suggested it might be better to ask her husband, John Bayley, who 'gives a very good talk on Barbara Pym'. I knew John from St Catherine's College where I was a member of the SCR and he immediately agreed to speak, but he too had a proviso, that we were to dine together beforehand in St Catherine's. Iris and John loved their food and wine and we were consequently twenty minutes late in arriving. To my dismay there was Denis Nineham sitting in the front row looking at his watch in a disgruntled way and not hesitating to advise me that it would have been better to have started later. John soon got into his stride, which was rather a faltering one because of his stutter and because he found Barbara Pym's depictions of high church foibles so hilariously amusing that repeatedly he was reduced to tears of laughter by jokes, which because of his stutter, he had not yet told.

In Iris's last months when Alzheimer's had taken its full and ghastly grip, we were invited by the Levi's to a dinner party with Iris and John. The Levi's always produced wonderful food in their kitchen/dining room which resembles a film set for a French cooking programme, with copper pans, earthenware vessels and hanging garden herbs. The wines Paul had been given to review for the *New York Times*. The children buzzed about and Iris smiled benignly. Although I felt intimidated by her, she had warmly encouraged me to write when I showed her my short stories which were eventually published as *Changing Faces*. Now I felt foolish for ever having feared foolishness. It seemed self-indulgent in the light of her intellectual disablement and I realised how important it is to be yourself and not struggle to be the image of the ego you want to project. After supper one of the children, the buzzing Georgiana Levi, brought a copy of three of Iris's novels to be signed by the author, who happened to be her godmother. Iris smiled but clearly had no idea what to do. Eventually John took out a pen and wrote a draft ascription on a separate piece of paper and told Iris to copy the words into the book. Like a child she began to do so; then faltered and John had to guide her hand to write not just his words but her own name.

*

I continued to teach for a short time at Pimlico Comprehensive, but since the purpose of my having a teaching job was to build relationships between the community and parish I was working in, it made little sense to return to Pimlico for a day every week. We had no church school in Bayswater, so Reggie and I agreed I should approach the local junior school. Between my flat in Cleveland Square and the Vicarage in Porchester Gardens lay the Hallfield Estate, a 1950's high-block, modernist development by Denys Lasdun that rose in jarring contrast to the elegance of Porchester Terrace and the local squares. Hallfield had its own junior school and I persuaded the headmaster to give me a job.

Because of the concentration of embassies around Kensington Palace, each employing domestic staff from their home countries, the school had children of twenty-eight different nationalities, many of whom struggled with English. In consequence we had a larger than usual number of what were then called 'backward' readers. My job was to give them intensive teaching in small groups. I had no training for this – indeed I had no teacher-training at all – but was qualified simply by having a degree, and relied on instinct and imagination, immodestly regarding myself as a natural. Taking a leaf out of my father's book I gave nicknames to the children, which amused them and, I think, suggested a kind of affection and sense of common humanity. The teaching methodology then was still pretty basic with 'flash cards' as one of the main tools. I held up a card showing, say, 'bus', 'pan', 'man', or 'shop', and they shouted out the word. This could easily become tedious and concentration was difficult, so I had to invent ways to liven it up. As a probationary teacher I was due to have my work evaluated by the school inspector. Having been forewarned by the headmaster I prepared my *pièce de résistance*, a periscope, which I constructed myself out of a cardboard box and bits of mirror glass. In the classroom I hid flash cards on the top of all the cupboards and bookshelves. The balding inspector was frosty and aloof, determined to assert his professional impartiality. The children were puzzled by the presence of this incongruous figure, a man with a middle age spread seated on a junior chair, trying not to be noticed. He would have looked more at home behind the cashier's desk in Barclays Bank. But they were fascinated by the periscope and wanted to read words as never before. I had been told it was good practice to involve any visiting adult in the activities of the class and not to treat them as an outsider, so I said, 'Children, we are very glad to have Mr Perkins with us this morning and I am going to ask him if he can find any of the hidden words using this periscope.' This seemed entirely natural to the children, if not to Mr Perkins who felt obliged to go round the classroom on his knees shouting out 'big', 'cow', and 'pie'. The kids applauded his efforts but were keen to get the periscope back for themselves, Kwaku, my star Ghanaian student, grabbing it from a grateful Mr Perkins. 'Me next, Sir. Oh, pleeese, me, Sir.'

For 'joined-up' reading we used the *Ladybird* Key Words Reading Scheme. These books were beautifully illustrated by J H Wingfield who had a penchant for lazy rivers, straw-purple meadows and country houses. His larger-than-life colours evoked an idealised Oxfordshire or Gloucestershire and provided me with a much yearned for antidote to the relentless pavements of the city. *Adventure at the Castle* looked so romantic: Cinderella with her pan of ashes from the stove and her antithesis, Prince Charming, at the Ball. During these lessons I was drawn into a reverie of rural escape and nostalgia. Having come from such diverse cultures, I wondered what the kids made of these idealised depictions of English country life. One story was set in a walled garden with a herbaceous border of hollyhocks and delphiniums and elegant ladies on a striped lawn. Despite the proximity of Kensington Gardens, I felt hungry for real nature, for hedgerows, wildness and wet. Every holiday we drove eight hours south-west to Cornwall and my wife's family farm; as soon as we reached Devon, we stopped for a break and, while the dog ran free in a field, I would kneel down and kiss the red earth. By terrible contrast, when we returned to London, the nearest bit of grass was in the Hallfield Estate and when I took the dog for a pee there, both he and I knew this was a travesty of nature.

*

If the Heavenly Host was to appear over Queensway in ways other than merely on a Christmas card, we had to work out how to make that happen. We decided to put on a play, 'The Trial of Job', written by Reggie. In the biblical story, Job, you will recall, is the victim of a game between God and Satan in which Satan taunts God with the claim that Job has only lived a blameless life because he's had it too easy. Job's faith is then tested by the death of his children, bankruptcy, pustular skin diseases, and so-called Comforters who tell him he must really have upset God to deserve suffering like this. It is about the problem of evil – why God allows suffering in the world – and the seeming inconsistency of divine blessing and punishment. It is one of the greatest literary pieces in the Bible and reaches sublime poetic heights when God speaks from a whirlwind about the wonder of his creation, challenging Job to respond.

In the play there were thousands of words to learn.

'I have written the part of Job for you,' said Reggie, seeking to flatter.

'And how about you? Who will you be?' I asked.

'I,' said the vicar, 'will play God.'

He had friends on the West End stage and one day visited a theatrical costumier, coming away with a bundle of costumes from a then recent film – Tony Richardson's *The Charge of the Light Brigade*. In his role as God he wore the uniform of Lord Raglan – scarlet jacket with gold brocade, spurs and black jodhpurs – sort of English aristocracy stroke Mussolini, equals God. He also directed the play and suggested I wear my old Burton suit, interpreting the part of Job as a businessman on Skid Row. All of which, you may be forgiven for thinking, was such an odd and unbalanced model for vicar/curate relations, diocesan HR should have been called in.

We put on the play in two venues: first in our own Christ Church, Lancaster Gate, and subsequently for two nights in the crypt of St Paul's Cathedral, where, in both places, God was able to read his script from the pulpit, without having to learn any lines, while I acted being plagued by boils and having breath that was 'noisome to my friends'. Then Lord Raglan spoke out of a whirlwind in his finest Harrovian tones to ask me, 'Where were you when I laid the foundation of the earth? Tell me, if you have understanding... Can you bind the chains of the Pleiades, or loose Orion's belt?' 'Can you draw out Leviathan with a fishhook, or press down its tongue with a cord? Will it make many supplications to you? Will it speak soft words to you?'

I was overwhelmed by the awesome majesty and power of God. It's not just the macho image of an angler with the great sea monster on the end of his line, but the infinitely creative power, the sheer inventive genius – 'Were you there when I laid the foundation of the earth? Who laid its cornerstone when the morning stars sang together and all the heavenly beings shouted for joy?' Hearing this poetry Job had no alternative but to repent. His life takes a new direction and he comes not to resent his trials but to look at life through God's eyes.

The play was eventually performed on television, with professional actors, and when the BBC came to pay the author, they said they could only give him 44 per cent of the fee because 56 per cent of the script had been lifted straight out of the Bible. We were familiar with jokes about the parsimony of the BBC's pre-chat show drinks, but this seemed too stingy by far, because he was a good writer – quirky, but good. Take this prayer for integrity in vocation, written when he was Principal of Salisbury Theological College, as an example:

> Give us a man of God,
> Father, to pray for us,
> Longed for, but insignificant,
> But excellent in mercy...
> Someone who loves the mystery of the faith,
> Whose conversation seems
> credibly to come from heaven
> a poor man, a hungry man
> Whose hospitality is endless.
> (Reginald Askew ACCM Prayer Card 1975)

The style is poetic and punctuated by surprise and paradox: a priest who is 'longed for but insignificant', as if insignificance is a virtue. In one way, of course, it is: it is the self-emptying and humility of Christ. Or a 'hungry man whose hospitality is endless': what deeper generosity than the hungry man who gives another hungry man his food? I am reminded of Christ who refuses to turn stones into bread in the wilderness, yet feeds the Five Thousand from fives loaves and two fishes.

'Preach the gospel everywhere if necessary using words,'

said St Francis of Assisi, or so tradition has it, when he sent his brothers into the surrounding towns and villages of thirteenth-century Umbria. It's another form of the adage, practise what you preach, or as Jesus put it in the Sermon on the Mount, 'by their fruits shall ye know them'. The vigour of this youthful faith in Bayswater was much more than self-indulgence; we knew that to be convincing Christian faith must be backed up by Christian action. For far too long in recent church life the agenda has been set by self-regarding structural concerns: should gay people or women be admitted as priests and bishops of the Church? Who should be allowed to get married in church? How can we keep the buildings going? Naturally, we have also puzzled over how to make Christianity relevant in a secular culture. The answer to that question doesn't change: by looking outwards to serve the community and embracing society as something we belong to, rather than something to be shunned with a 'my kingdom is not of this world' attitude. In short, God is enacted, and the Kingdom of God is a 'how' not a 'what'.

Apart from the tireless hospitality of Christ Church people, there was a group that decorated the flats and houses of those who couldn't afford to get it done professionally, some were involved in the Paddington Christian Housing Trust, others in youth work, and as a Church we were committed to a relief project in Tanzania, where president Julius Nyerere was much admired for his left-wing leadership, anti-apartheid campaigning, and stand for African unity. These social commitments were pressed on us by prophetic members of the congregation who basically refused to shut up about their personal commitments until the rest of us fell into line. Ian Hoare was one such: a bearded young man with a passion for kissing as well as for social justice, who presented himself as the social conscience of the parish. When he was to be married to Jacquie, Reggie read the banns and accidentally stumbled into saying, 'I published the banns of marriage between Ian, Hoare of this parish...' but no more was audible above the congregation's convulsive laughter and applause.

But top of the bill in our practical Christianity enterprise was what Reggie grandiosely dubbed 'The Belfast Air Lift'. He had a penchant for triumphalist embellishment; never, for example, content to call the carol service simply a carol service, it had to be the great carol service. On this occasion he had returned from his summer holiday thinking big. The family had been to Somerset in, 'Cardinal Wolseley', the car he'd bought with the Easter collection, which in those days a vicar received as part of his stipend. It was, of course a variable, and a genuine example of performance related pay: the kinder you were and the better you preached, the more you got. His sermon the next day began, 'I have a dream'. He built up successive paragraphs about having a dream for reconciliation between Catholics and Protestants in Northern Ireland, where the 'troubles' were boiling up again. He even began to echo the tremulous modulations of Martin Luther King. Oratorically, of course, it wasn't a patch on MLK. As I write now forty years since King's speech in Birmingham, Alabama, commentators are saying it was perhaps the greatest piece of oratory of all time. But Reggie's version was effective nevertheless. As a first step he proposed we provide an ecumenical holiday in London for Catholic and Protestant children from Belfast and asked the congregation to put their hands in their pockets there and then to finance it, which they generously did. Having revealed the dream, he asked me to implement it. Why else have a curate? We persuaded the Roman Catholic church in Edgware Road to come on board and together we invited twelve children from either side of the sectarian divide, along with supporting parents and clergy. Institutions and individuals were immediately enthused with the idea and wanted to give generous support. Our first coup was to persuade the RAF to fly the party, free of charge, into their Oxfordshire base at Brize Norton – hence the ludicrous soubriquet, 'Belfast Air Lift', deriving from the 'Berlin Air Lift' of June 1948, when the RAF kept up an eleven-month supply line to West Berlin in the face of a Russian blockade of road, rail and water routes into the city.

Annette and I had two ten-year-old Protestant boys staying in our flat and when the news came on the television with reports about killings in Northern Ireland, they sat fidgeting anxiously in their chairs, until it became clear the victims were Catholic, and then they cheered. Thus, sectarianism was already being seared into their young minds, laying down uncompromising prejudice for years to come.

My principal task was to fill the week with a programme of entertainment and social events. On the religious side we held combined worship in both C of E and RC churches, and a press conference in the Sanctuary outside Westminster Abbey, with Askew in his element. The officers of HMS Belfast showed us round their battleship on the Thames, the grooms and ostlers at Buckingham Palace introduced us to the Windsor Greys and Cleveland Bay horses in the Royal Mews, and the kids were photographed alongside the gilded Gold State Coach, landaus, carriages, and footmen's livery. They had tea in the Fishmongers' Hall by London Bridge, saw *Willie Wonka and the Chocolate Factory* at the cinema and *Ali Baba and the Forty Thieves* on ice at Olympia. When the stage maroons went off with loud bangs, the children cowered in their seats – too much like home. Each of these events was donated by the institution concerned. We thought we ought to include a visit to the circus. I scoured the papers and all I could find was something at the Round House in Chalk Farm entitled, *Le Grand Cirque Magique*. The Round House was known for being a shade avant-garde, so I phoned up to check the performance was suitable for children. 'Oh, yes,' they said, 'bring 'em along.' And kindly gave us tickets. I wore a prominent white clerical collar, as did the vicar. The Roman Catholic priest was in full clericals, and the nuns in their habits. When the performers came on to the stage, the whole ecumenical party slowly began to process the fact that they had no clothes on. This was a nude show. 'Do you think we ought to leave?' asked the vicar.

'Oh, no,' I said, 'the tickets were free. It would be churlish.'

Also, I did not want these rash Christians to look prudish. Christ Church was, besides, a liberal, progressive church. The nuns loved it, the kids loved it, and when the performers came out into the audience as part of their routine, I knew it would happen, one of the young female jugglers decided to sit on my knee. But, lest you get the wrong idea, this wasn't a louche or sexual show: the nudity (or semi-nudity) soon fused unobtrusively into the clowning, juggling, tight-rope walking, and music of genuine circus acts. It was another example of 1960s boundary pushing. In the wake of the Belfast Air Lift, several of our community pushed other boundaries by becoming involved with, and in two cases working for, the Corrymeela Community, the oldest peace and reconciliation organisation in Northern Ireland.

*

For me, the sense that all things were possible to the rash fellows of Christianity changed how I saw the Church with a capital C and filled me with a fresh enthusiasm for it. You could say, I was *converted*. Not *born again* – I can't get on with the charismatic evangelical theology that underpins that idea – but certainly finding a new dynamic in religion that outclassed the inherited religion of my upbringing. I began to reflect that I had progressed from school to university on theological auto-pilot, and stayed the course through theological college because, like Macbeth, I was 'in blood/stepped in so far that, should I wade no more/returning were as tedious as go o'er'. I had joined the Church of England in search of liberation only, in my first job, to run into the buffers of its conservatism, which, as I have said, very nearly resulted in my cancelling my membership card within the first year.

But Lancaster Gate *was* the liberation I had hoped for, not purely from its own merit, but from its serendipitous location in a wider historical revolution where society, sometimes reluctantly, was casting off the conservative culture of Second World War Britain like a snakeskin: Women's Lib, Gay Lib, the end to censorship in 1968, 'the new morality'. God was announced not to be a bearded old man in the sky but the 'ground of our being'; Peter Cook publicly mocked the patrician arrogance of prime minister Harold Macmillan in *Beyond the Fringe*. I think all ordinands could give a passable rendition of Alan Bennett's sermon in that same revue on the text, 'My brother Esau is an hairy man but I am a smooth man,' declaring that life is like a sardine tin: 'there's always a little bit in the corner you can't get out.' We sat around the vicarage TV to watch *Monty Python*, women in mini or maxiskirts, taking the pill, feeling free. We went to boozy parties, where there was always plenty of cannabis if you wanted it, and plenty of meaning-of-life discussion if you happened to want that as well. In the parish we had eat-ins and supper parties and grand parties in hotels, all modelling the heavenly banquet described in Jesus' parables of the Great Feast, the Wise and Foolish Virgins, and the Guest without a Wedding Garment. Heaven was to be a wedding feast, a Holy Communion, a great party, a welcome to strangers from off the street, an abandonment of class and a celebration of reckless commitment.

I don't remember whether I used the word *liberal* for it then, but that's what it was, and it became the foundation, the underlying philosophy, for all my subsequent ministry. It matured and adapted from that heady sixties cocktail into a radical, questioning, protesting faith.

Such liberalism is scarcely tolerated now in the Church of

England, goodness knows why, subsumed by a spirituality that is honourable and well meaning, but less generous, less universal, less connected to its social and intellectual history, and timid beyond belief, glancing anxiously from side to side lest the great Leviathan, secularism, should suddenly swallow it whole, never to be seen again. Maybe even then it was unusual and not so highly regarded amongst the black-suited priestly cast. Yet Tony Bridge became a cathedral dean and Reggie Askew a theological college principal, preferments they would not gain in today's managerial Church with its fears of 'reputational risk' and desire for impact reports. Risk is one of the virtues of liberalism and risk is what attracted me to the religion of these rash fellows.

Risk is also an aspect of revolution: rise up against the establishment and you risk being cut down. We have seen the Hong Kong democrats facing the water cannon and tear gas of Xi Jinping's communist soldiers, the assassination of Saudi Arabian dissident Jamal Khashoggi and the tense debate in the Liberal West over the toppling of statues and the 're-writing of history'.

During my three years at Christ Church I didn't always find it easy to do the basic things well. When it was my turn to preach, I often found myself stuck for what to say. I used to wander around Kensington Gardens trying to conjure up something interesting. Others came and gave virtuoso displays in the pulpit, but I had to find a way not to sound banal. Basically, I lacked experience of life and my theology wasn't sufficiently well informed to be able to unpack the great Christian ideas. Our red setter, Solomon, used to accompany me on these walks, frequently causing embarrassment by interfering with other park users. One June day, while investigating the sunbathers disporting themselves in deckchairs by the Round Pond, he became engrossed with the open bag of a young woman and began to pull out items of underwear and toss them triumphantly into the air. Her anger was not appeased by the fact that the penitent owner of the errant dog was wearing a clerical collar. No 'for you duckie, it's free' for me. Then I would go back to the flat and tap away at my 'Olympia' typewriter, unable to find the theological significance of that story, thus forging an address which was less interesting than real life. I knew it would be better to speak *ex tempore*, that the communication would be more alive, more heartfelt, more compelling, but I was afraid of drying up in the pulpit before all those people. My breakthrough came at the end of a very busy week when we had been away on a parish conference in Sussex and I hadn't had time to prepare anything. I had been reading Solzhenitsyn's *One Day in the Life of Ivan Denisovich* about the adversities and struggle for survival in Stalin's Siberian labour camps – what became known as the 'Gulag Archipelago'. I had been moved by the hardship men had to suffer and struck by the values induced by the experience of life on the edge, provoking amongst others those religious questions of what finally matters. For example, the prisoners soon learnt to value every mouthful of their meagre daily bowl of porridge, savouring it, taking their time over it and not leaving a single oat on the plate, but licking it clean with relish. They had to think positive and therefore turned a pauper's dish into a feast, which gave us a different take on the Heavenly Banquet. I spoke freely about this and from the heart, unscripted, and suddenly the congregation were on the edge of their pews.

Chaplain and Fellow

Every Thursday Alan Yates served at the 6.30pm Mass, and afterwards we went for a pint. He was a lonely guy, single, who loved going off to Yugoslavia (Croatia) twice a year with a group of mysterious friends to tan his body a burnt umber hue. To 'serve' at the Eucharist meant dressing up in black cassock and white cotta, setting out the communion vessels – chalice, paten, veil and burse, containing the folded corporal, so called because it is the linen square of cloth onto which any crumbs of the Body of Christ might fall – and at the offertory to pass these objects to the priest before pouring the water of the 'lavabo' over the priest's hands in the act of symbolic cleansing. For many men, this was a half-way house to priesthood, providing them with a public religious persona and giving access to the sacristy, an inner sanctum for the sacerdotal class. In the musty Lady Chapel, where we were usually joined for mass by two or three old ladies, I could hear the reassuring noises of the world outside, which induced in me a sensation somewhere between transcendence and entombment, one of the paradoxical seductions of priesthood when you remember Christ's words, 'My kingdom is not of this world.'

Beyond this arcane ecclesiastical bubble, Alan took my general interests to heart, not in any sort of toadying way, but out of genuine friendship, and he had spotted an ad in the *Church Times* for the post of Chaplain at Sidney Sussex College, Cambridge, which he thought I ought to apply for. Without his indefatigable churchiness, I would never have known the opportunity existed. I applied and was appointed. Reggie Askew and I had discussed whether I ought to wear a dog collar for the interview. I was all for collar and tie as an indication of what I regarded as my radical modernity, but he was emphatic clerical garb was the only viable option, his point being that one ought not to be ambiguous about, or embarrassed by, the profession you represented. It was a chaplain they had asked for, not an agent of theological angst. Only one other of the five short-listed candidates was dressed as a clergyman, and I was trussed up like a catalogue illustration of what you might expect to see were you to enter Harrod's and ask for a Church of England curate.

*

By far the most significant event in my time at Sidney was the debate about whether the college should admit women. It had been an all-male bastion for three hundred and seventy-nine years, but there was a growing view that, in the interests of social justice and academic progress, change was necessary and probably inevitable. Three colleges – King's, Churchill, and Clare – had already successfully gone mixed and, as a small and less well-known college, hidden away in the shopping part of town, it was important for Sidney not to be left behind. But opinion was divided. In college there were three levels of government: The Master and Fellows, which included all Fellows, the Governing Body, comprising Fellows holding current posts, and the Council, an executive elected from the Governing Body to execute its day to day business. In order to change the statutes to admit women, a two-thirds majority would be required in the Master and Fellows, which included the retired Fellows. Inevitably the prospect of change was threatening to the traditionalists who adduced any argument available to them to frustrate this new-fangled idea, one of which was that the accommodation of young men and women in close proximity would encourage fornication thus breaching the college's duty to uphold Christian principles, and an appeal was made to me as Chaplain to support the view that it would be immoral. I believed their argument was spurious and contrived, but the full panoply of a Cambridge Fellowship is a daunting audience to address and my heart thumped as I suggested there had been a shift in moral theology, as well as in society, towards a more open attitude to sex and that we would not wish to diminish the place of sexuality in human relationship by equating it with sin, as in the old expression 'living in sin'. This intervention apparently carried weight and won me many friends among the younger, progressive fellows anxious for change, and, to their great credit, the older men whom I had opposed seemed totally unresentful.

When it came to the moment of decision, it was the tradition for us to cast our votes in reverse order of election, so that the most recent fellows would not be influenced by the vote of their more senior colleagues. It meant I voted third. The result was overwhelmingly in favour, but there was a final drama when a popular and very senior member, Professor Edred Corner, stood up and with a flourish threw three things onto the table. 'Here, Master, are my keys,' he proclaimed, 'here are my Statutes, and here is my letter of resignation. You will never see me in this college again.' It was mildly shocking that he had planned this exit in such detail and had written, as it were, a suicide note for us all to read. True to his word, he never entered the college again despite many entreaties from his contemporaries who missed his jovial company at dinner on Friday night and the strange vegetables and fungi that, as a botanist, he regularly brought for the chef to include in the menu.

One afternoon when I had just returned from playing in a second eleven football match, muddy and bruised from the encounter, I received a phone call from Professor Derek Beales to tell me the Master had died from a heart attack in London and would I come into college as quickly as possible. That morning he had chaired an important meeting, had lunch, and later been found slumped in a toilet at the Athenaeum. It was a Friday, the night when in term the Fellows dine together in conspicuously gastronomic and vinous style, and one of the first questions was whether the dinner ought to be cancelled as a sign of respect. The Master's wife, Rae Linnett, said that was not what Jack would have wanted and we were to go ahead, which I was very glad to hear. 'He can't be dead,' she repeatedly said, 'he can't be.' Clearly not just a rhetorical response, she added emphatically, 'I shan't believe it until I've seen his body.' The senior dons: the Vice Master, the Bursar, Roger Andrew, the medical Fellow, Christopher Parish, and the Senior Tutor looked at me, the young Chaplain, for some sort of pastoral strategy. Little did they know that, although I had been ordained for five years, I had never conducted a funeral. It wasn't that people didn't die in Bayswater, but in both my London parishes, if there was a funeral to be taken, and there weren't many, the vicar would naturally officiate. Thinking on my feet, I said that as soon as Jack was brought back to Cambridge, I would go with Rae to see him in the mortuary – at least I'd had practice at that in the Gordon Hospital – and we would fix a date for the funeral as soon as Rae was ready.

Two days later we went to a funeral parlour in Cambridge. When the attendant pulled back the sheet the Master's great head was revealed, like a wax model, not unlike the death mask of Oliver Cromwell in the college library Muniment Room. Rae looked long and tenderly at her husband with her head at a quizzical angle; then she pronounced, 'He is dead,' and came right up to the bier and leant over him. 'Hasn't he got lovely bushy eyebrows,' she said, brushing them with her fingers, 'Just like Dennis Healey's.' Would I like to stroke them? For me this intimacy was extremely odd. The corpse before me was the awesome figure who had appointed me to the chaplaincy and who, until a few weeks previously, had been the Vice Chancellor of the University. Now we were twiddling with his eyebrows. What a puzzling contrast between public and private life, even in death.

Unsurprisingly, Rae was very emotional in bereavement; she had suddenly lost her life partner who still had five years of an illustrious career before him and she was pretty highly strung in normal circumstances. When Archibald Cox, the Watergate prosecutor of President Nixon, was a Visiting Fellow of the college, she secretly taped a private and candid talk he gave to the *Fellows' Wives* and couldn't understand why he objected when she offered to play it to anyone who cared to listen. Tapes of Richard Nixon's Whitehouse conversations had been crucial in the investigation of the Watergate scandal. She loved America and all things American. She also had adored having a succession of famous visitors to the Lodge during the vice-cancellariate, from the Queen of Denmark, to Alistair Cook, much loved for his weekly *Letter from America* on BBC radio. Now she wanted people to come and pay their respects to Jack. Perhaps they could be invited, she suggested, to the undertaker's funeral parlour and see him as we were seeing him now. At theological college I had been encouraged to be open about death and not to sweep it under the carpet, and in the light of that largely untested theory, at least by me, I rashly suggested we might take the Master's body back to the Lodge where it could 'lie in state' in an open coffin until the funeral so that those who wished could pay their respects. 'I'd love to have him home with me just for a few more days,' she said. And although completely counter-cultural and un-English that is what happened. One night before dinner the Fellows solemnly processed into the Old Library to pay their respects at the open coffin, some out of duty, others genuinely pleased to linger awhile and consider the man who had led the college into a new era. No one ever accused me of being a lunatic priest, even if some thought it.

Yes, you did hear me say *Fellows' Wives*. In those un-woke days of 1975, we were all men and our club was the college, so it seemed only fair for the Master's wife to run a club for wives, meeting once a term in the grand surroundings of the Lodge, when they could enjoy the college's hospitality. I was complicit in this, as were my radical young colleagues who had just voted to admit women as Fellows and students. In social revolution the penny drops slowly.

Obviously, my principal role as Chaplain was to conduct the worship in chapel, a building refashioned by T H Lyon in the early twentieth century as a monument to the Anglo-Catholic movement. There was an irony in this move up the candle since Sidney, along with Emmanuel College, was one of only two post-reformation colleges in 'old' Cambridge. Outside its walls, the nineteenth-century Baptist tub-thumper from Waterbeach, Charles Hadden Spurgeon, subsequently the Minister of the Metropolitan Tabernacle in Southwark, had raised his hands to heaven, and publicly praised God for its protestant foundation. The chapel's present furnishing would have been an abomination to him: the black and white marble altar decked with six ebonised Italian candlesticks, and between them Pittoni's altar-piece of the Holy Family, with the superscription, *Gustando Vivimus Deo* – 'by tasting we live in God', words taken from the seventh-century Latin hymn for Easter Vespers, 'The Lamb's high banquet we await'.

The hymn refers both to tasting the Eucharistic bread and to the Exodus, reminding us that God provided the Hebrews with manna in the wilderness, which became part of their national narrative. Jesus is also that bread and when we share the bread and wine of communion, we make him present among us.

The vestment chest contained a fine collection of 'fiddle back' chasubles, a delicious feast for liturgical gourmets, that would have delighted Barbara Pym or John Betjeman. When the Archbishop of Canterbury, Michael Ramsey, came to preach on Ascension Sunday 1974, he told me that, as a boy in Cambridge, he had watched with delight the rebuilding of Sidney Chapel. His father had been President of Magdalene College and a

Congregationalist. So, the archbishop had made the same inter-denominational journey as me. On that day he took for his text a verse from Psalm 139, 'I am fearfully and wonderfully made'. The congregation roared with laughter at the mere announcement of the text because as a physical human being he was a bit Heath Robinson. Like Rowan Williams, he needed a haircut and, of course, he spoke in a sing-song voice with a bit of a stutter. But Sidney's High-Church revival went off not with a bang but a whimper because, in the aftermath of the Great War, some of those who had conceived it lost their faith, most notably the Dean, B T D Smith.

The chapel possessed one other notable but invisible feature, the head of Oliver Cromwell, who had studied at the college as a Fellow Commoner from 1616–1617, buried in an unmarked place beneath the small antechapel. When Cromwell died, he had the status of a king and therefore his body was embalmed and preserved prior to burial in Westminster Abbey. At the Restoration Charles II had Cromwell's (intact) body disinterred and hung, drawn and quartered at Tyburn before commanding his head be displayed on a pole above Westminster Hall, where it remained for thirty years until blown down in a storm. It is said to have been picked up by a passing actor and sold on to private owners eventually ending up on the Wilkinson family mantelpiece for two hundred years until 1960 when Horace Wilkinson died and left it to his son, also a Horace, who offered it to Sidney Sussex College. Naturally, there was concern it might be a fake, but Dr Otto Smail, the distinguished medieval historian and college Archivist, was persuaded of its authenticity and accepted it for the college. While the episode made a good after dinner story, the antechapel never became a place of pilgrimage or tourist attraction.

When I arrived in 1973 the worship was middle-of-the-road Anglican: we used the 'modern' communion service, known prosaically as 'Series 3', and Book of Common Prayer Evensong, just like Christ Church, Lancaster Gate. Every day in term I said Matins and Evening Prayer in the Lady Chapel according to the Prayer Book, supported by undergraduates who signed up on a rota to keep me company. On the morning of the vote on the admission of women, several Fellows also turned up to Matins to seek the guidance of the Holy Spirit or perhaps to pray for the conversion of their opponents.

I was happy working within this traditional framework but anxious to engage more interest from the undergraduates. I found ways of spicing up the plain diet of worship, first by introducing girls from the Perse School to sing in the previously all male choir and, cornily in the opinion of some senior members, decided to celebrate in 1975 the fiftieth anniversary of the re-dedication of the chapel. The organ scholar at that time, James Wood, was a very able young composer studying with Nadia Boulanger and I asked him to compose an anthem for the occasion. If I could find him some avant-garde words 'other than the traditional biblical stuff', he said he would do it. After much head scratching, I found an E E Cummings poem with the opening line, 'I am a little church, no great cathedral', which described the chapel and its recent history rather well. We wanted a famous preacher and after being turned down by a few well-known bishops (they existed in those days) I was tipped off that an actor, Andrew Cruikshank, was a Christian and enjoyed speaking to students. He had played the role of Dr Cameron, the patriarchal Scottish doctor in the famous, long-running TV series, *Dr Finlay's Casebook*. As far as the undergraduates were concerned this was a coup and they turned up in great numbers drawn by the lure of fame. The Fellows were ambivalent about my choice and the professor of Modern History told me at least five times that Cruikshank scarcely had the intellectual clout to speak in a Cambridge college, especially on a major occasion. It was curious how this esoteric anniversary, susceptible as it was to ridicule, and a mere trifle in the context of a four-hundred-

year history, had morphed into a 'major occasion', reflecting, I
believe, our deep need for markers as we tell our story.

Evangelicals

In the 1970s, religion in the University tended to polarise
either side of a conservative/liberal fault line, in college terms
represented by a stand-off between CICCU (the Cambridge
Inter-collegiate Christian Union) and Chapel. The same division
persists today, but is significantly more nuanced as a result of
widespread secularisation, where 70% of 18–24-year-olds say
they have 'no religion', and the high proportion of students
from other cultures and countries where Christianity is not
historically the dominant religion. Each college had two CICCU
reps, usually self-assured public-school types with nascent
leadership skills. In Sidney, one of these, Giles, who had
been at Marlborough, forbade his followers to attend chapel
because they were not yet 'secure in the Faith' and presumably,
therefore, wouldn't be able to resist the liberal theological
ideas of the chaplain, who was known for 'unsound teaching'
– a biblical phrase coined for *ideas we don't agree with*. In an
attempt to build bridges, I used to attend college Bible studies
and have memories of sitting around in student rooms in the
twilight of winter days while an earnest undergraduate led us
through some verses from the New Testament. First, someone
was nominated to read the passage, then we would be asked
in turn to say what we thought it meant, and finally the leader
would give a definitive account of what it *really* meant. It was
hopeless trying to introduce any discussion of how one might
read the text more broadly in the light of biblical criticism
or its historical setting because, when all said and done, the
rules stated this was the infallible word of God and therefore
must be susceptible to an infallible interpretation, which the
undergraduate leader invariably was prepared to provide.

Every three years CICCU held a centrally organised mission

to the University, led by an international evangelical speaker, who would present the traditional claims of evangelical Christianity. Invariably this would include the infallibility of scripture, the idea that Christ's death was a penalty paid to God for human sin, the divinity of Christ, and marriage as the only moral *locus* for sex. One of the missions in my time was entitled, 'Who's Jesus?' and the question was blazoned everywhere across Cambridge. Besides, this concern had obsessed the Church ever since Jesus asked his disciples, at Caesarea Philippi, 'Who do people say that I am?' However much bishops had insisted that Jesus of Nazareth was the Messiah or the Christ, the question wouldn't go away. It was central at the Council of Nicaea in 325 CE, where one side said he was God and the Arians on the other said he was not. In the 1970s, Andrew Lloyd Webber and Tim Rice's rock opera, *Jesus Christ Superstar*, depicted Jesus more as a revolutionary popstar than God, and in 1977 Don Cupitt, the Dean of Emmanuel College, came up to me at our street party for the Queen's Silver Jubilee in Humberstone Road, to confess gingerly that he had contributed to a book which would 'ruffle a few feathers', *The Myth of God Incarnate*. So, by this time people were feeling brave enough to question again one of Christianity's most compelling and dramatic ideas, that God is visible in the self-giving, inclusive life of Jesus. No wonder the mission should ask all over again, 'Who's Jesus?'

But the aural pun which this title created didn't pass me by. I was beginning to fear that the answer being given to this biggest of theological questions was narrow and exclusive. In the jargon of the promoters, Jesus was to be accepted as your personal saviour, a kind of special friend, the bond of which relationship could only be discerned through faith, and who one must accept had paid the penalty for your sin to a legalistic God who seemed to demand his pound of flesh, yet was also to be known as 'loving father'. Troubled by this tribal and retributive theology, I decided to preach a sermon entitled,

'Whose Jesus?' and advertised it around the place. I knew I was being provocative and perhaps a little gauche, but I was young and, to justify myself, my response was motivated by conviction. I believed passionately that the picture of a punitive God was wrong and equally that, to coin a phrase of T S Eliot, we had the right to 'work out our own salvation with diligence', not rejecting the cumulative reflection and theology of the Church, but using our own experience and intelligence. Had I thought of it then, I would have said faith isn't a binary choice between one thing and another, but usually an ambivalent position in which faith and doubt tend to play off against one another in a kind of counterpoint, like a Bach fugue. But it was my conviction which was my strength, even though I didn't recognise its power at the time; it was this that earned me the respect of more conservative colleagues because they saw my message was not lukewarm or watered down, like the Laodiceans.

Catholics

But theological tribalism is a spaghetti-junction of contraflowing loyalties and to accuse others of it is frequently to become tribal oneself. Two of my predecessors as Chaplain of Sidney, George Tibbatts and George Braund, were campaigning Anglo-Catholics and members of the *Oratory of the Good Shepherd*, a Cambridge-based religious order committed to celibacy and Catholic discipline. Canon Tibbatts, as he was always known, came in to dinner on a Wednesday and soon took a liking to me. Like several clergy of his generation, including the Revd Wilbert Awdry who wrote the famous *Thomas the Tank Engine* stories for children, he was a railway enthusiast of such accomplishment that, in a Second World War emergency, he had taken charge of a steam locomotive and driven the train from Cambridge to Liverpool Street. He was also a trustee of the Cleaver Trust, a fund to support Anglo-Catholic ordinands. He thought the trust needed younger blood and persuaded the chairman, Chancellor

Garth Moore, to appoint me. I had friends from Corpus Christi College, where Garth had been law tutor, and knew from them the tradition there that it was unwise to accept an invitation to tea if Garth invited you, and by 2016 it was established that he had not merely been the kind of amusing eccentric who according to folk tradition liked to conduct tutorials from his bath, but, while Vicar of St Mary Abchurch in the City of London, had allegedly abused an underage boy, to whom the Church of England subsequently paid compensation for his suffering. The only thing I remember about his letter to me was its opening line: 'My dear Mountford, (I think I know you well enough to address you by your surname).' I had agonised how to reply and ought to have followed my instincts, 'My dear Moore,' but caved in to politeness and began instead, 'Dear Chancellor.' Despite my diplomatic restraint, once I attended the meetings, in the *piano nobile* of Lutyens' neo-Georgian Faith House in Tufton Street, Westminster, I immediately sensed a *froideur* between Garth and myself, an instinctive chemical unease, and an intuitive mistrust of my churchmanship on his part. The problem was, I wasn't one of nature's Anglo-Catholics and must have seemed like an undercover agent in their ranks. George took it for granted that I was a Catholic, because of my time at St Stephens, Rochester Row, but he didn't know I had been reared a non-conformist; that I had never been an altar boy, or swung the thurible, choking the congregation with incense, or consumed under-age pink gins with lonely bachelor clergymen in the rectory drawing room. It made a difference. To learn to be a high churchman in adulthood is a bit like learning to ski, never having done so as a child.

When it came to dishing out the funds of the Cleaver Trust, I began to despise the one-of-us mentality, the approval of only certain kosher referees, the exaltation of what Garth called 'Catholic theology', the snide comments of Cheslyn Jones, Principal of Pusey House, every time I spoke. It became clear this tribe was closed to me, self-protective and one-dimensional. Eventually, I had had enough and made a speech to the assembled gang that I considered theology in principle an open-ended and intellectually disinterested discipline that ought not to be shaped to fit the needs of any particular party or interest group, and resigned. There was no anger, no riposte, no gleeful rubbing of hands, but they were sure glad to see the back of me.

*

Whilst the worship in chapel was conventional, couched principally in the rhythmic prose of Thomas Cranmer's evening prayer and Myles Coverdale's poetic translation of the psalms, I always wanted to make the variable input interesting, which, funnily enough, even the sermons of visiting dignitaries didn't always achieve. So, I decided to hold a series of events on other religions. This caused a massive hoo-ha from the Christian Union, who considered it somehow blasphemous to pollute the true religion with any mention of other gods. For them, the text from St John's Gospel where Jesus says, 'I am the way, the truth, and the life; no one comes to the Father except by me,' was conclusive and incontrovertible – they would have to boycott the whole term's programme. The dispute was resolved by holding choral evensong, without a sermon, and after the blessing, I would remove my clerical robes, those who objected could leave, and then we would hear from the other faith representative in, as it were, a neutral space. This was cutting edge, and long before inter-faith projects were in vogue, or college communities were sufficiently diverse to raise the need for a 'faith' room where a Muslim student might pray and even have the facility to wash in preparation for prayer.

The series seemed to some a mixed success, and to others a mixed failure. Don Cupitt had warned me it was impossible to find a swami who wasn't an Englishman. Swami Yogananda turned out to be an oddball Aryan from South London dressed up as a Yogi and, not wearing a watch because it was too worldy, repeatedly asking me if I had a *timepiece*. Presentations which are vague in my memory were given by Jewish and Muslim speakers, but the highlight as far as the young men were concerned was the session on Tai Chi, involving some description of its philosophy and an extensive demonstration of balletic movements enacted by one of our neighbours, Bronwyn Hipkin, athletic, pretty, graceful and clothed in a body-hugging leotard. It was the most voluptuous event I have ever witnessed in a church and even my critics were reduced to awestruck silence – 'gobsmacked' is probably the word.

I had no regrets about this term's unusual programme because it pushed the boundaries holding back the Church in an increasingly secular society, and only by breaking through those boundaries did I think we could keep our integrity in an intellectual society like Cambridge. To get out of the cage was a matter of theological integrity for me. I identified with the words of W H Auden in *In Memory of W. B. Yeats*:

'In the prison of his days

Teach the free man how to praise.'

With the same passion for freedom in religion, I protested against the fact Roman Catholics and Anglicans could not share communion with one another. The crazy thing was by now their respective liturgies had become hard to tell apart, because the Church of England's *modern* liturgy had reverted to the historic order of the mass, undone by Cranmer at the Reformation. I hit it off with the University Catholic Chaplain, Fr Richard Incledon, himself a radical, and we decided to con-celebrate the mass together in Sidney Chapel, which we did on several occasions without the heavens opening, or either of us being struck down by lightning. When Jesus said, 'Do this in remembrance of me,' he didn't add, but only those of you who have been authorised, trained, and certificated by one of the many churches that will rise up and claim to be the true heirs of my kingdom. When Jesus said, 'Suffer the little children and let them come unto me,' he could have meant: if a child should break bread in memory of me, that will have more value than the meanness of any bigoted exclusivist.

The students didn't find our con-celebrations problematic and when I worked at the University Church in Oxford a decade later I probably gave communion to as many Catholics as confirmed members of the C of E, since most visitors from continental Europe thought we were Catholic, couldn't tell the difference, and in any case weren't theologically bothered. Most people never understood what all the fuss was about. But Richard Incledon was succeeded by Fr Maurice Couve de Murville, a conservative, who later became Bishop of Birmingham, a Roman Catholic diocese which included Oxford, and under him con-celebration between Anglican and Catholic was unthinkable.

Pastoral

Apart from the requirement to conduct chapel services and to live within a mile of the college, there was no job description and I don't recall ever having had a written contract. Nor did I have a line manager – if such a role had been invented by 1973. I was technically my own boss, the *ordinary* of the chapel, which meant that, ecclesiastically, I had sole authority over it in the same way as a bishop did over churches, and, like nearly all colleges in Oxbridge, the chapel was a *peculiar*, technically outside the diocese and therefore beyond the bishop's jurisdiction. As a matter of goodwill, the chaplain might seek the bishop's licence to officiate, which I did, and remember entering on a cold day, into an empty Ely Cathedral and, in a side chapel near one of the mighty Victorian heating stoves, receiving a licence from the Bishop of Huntingdon. Job description or not, it was clearly part of my role to be pastoral – what now is termed 'welfare'. If you attend a Welfare Committee meeting in Oxford today, you can expect about twenty people round the table deliberating on the well-being of undergraduates, who, for their part, see themselves as in particular need and often under-cared-for. In St Hilda's College in 2019, a student-organised survey of welfare provision reported the extraordinary statistic that 62% of them had, or had had, mental health disorders and they attributed this principally to the stress created by intensely busy terms, competition, high expectations from dons (and surely parents too), and frequent examinations. Those pressures were similar in Cambridge in the 1970s, but the culture of the time said you just had to get on with it. We had 'moral tutors', dons who cared for pupils whom they didn't teach, the Chaplain, and in a quite unofficial counselling role the Librarian, a substantial former opera singer, Jean Reddy, who hailed from Blackburn, the town which also nurtured the great contralto, and former telephonist, Kathleen Ferrier. Jean was immensely jolly, inquisitive, and anti-establishment. The students loved her for that and told her everything.

At central 'Deans and Chaplains' meetings we would sometimes discuss pastoral situations and dilemmas, with a view to obtaining mutual help and advice, but people could easily become competitive as they tried to outdo one another with tales of the enormity of what they had had to cope with and their students had had to endure. It reminded me of the Monty Python 'Four Yorkshiremen' sketch, where the participants compared the privations of their youth: 'you were *lucky* to live in a house, we had to live in one room/a corridor/ hole in the ground, etc.' And while I felt a prim disapproval of wallowing in others' misery as a means of giving your own ego a boost, there was little doubt that how you coped with a major crisis in college could make or break a reputation. The long-faced Edward Norman, Dean of Peterhouse, once described these meetings in an article for a national newspaper as 'cocoa time in a theological college', even though they were attended, in addition to us junior clergy, by such luminaries as Bishop John Robinson, Professor Charlie Moule and Professor Geoffrey Lampe.

From my point of view there had been several landmark pastoral situations at Sidney, the death of the Master being the first. The second concerned a very creative English student called Tom, suffering from a form of schizophrenia which had convinced him he was the 'Third Son of God'. Who the second was, he couldn't explain, but it didn't seem to be important. His condition became rapidly worse and his behaviour very disruptive and notorious in college. Since, in the minds of some tutors, I was the agent for the first Son of God, they assumed I'd be able to help him out and one night, when his symptoms were particularly acute, I drove him, writhing and foaming at the mouth, to Addenbrooke's Hospital where I assumed he would be admitted as an in-patient or be 'sectioned' under the Mental Health Act to Fulbourn Psychiatric Hospital. No such logic. His condition did not justify or necessitate any treatment. So, Annette and I took him back to our college flat in Sussex House. I had had no sense of any physical danger to ourselves, even though he continued to thrash about in the bed in our spare room, to foam at the mouth, and to yell out a rhythmic cry, like a football chant, 'Fuck-ing, Fuck-ing, Fuck-ing', so that all the neighbours could hear and wonder what the Chaplain was up to. News of this loud night of profanity spread quickly in college and around the neighbourhood and it was this that turned Tom's case into a *cause célèbre*. Within days, however, Tom had left the college, unable to continue with his studies.

Then there was Dave from Bristol, also reading English, who before the beginning of each term would stroll down to the Bristol docks and buy a plentiful supply of Marijuana to sell on to his fellow students by way of supplementing his grant. The

Senior Tutor had noticed a funny smell outside Dave's room, but thought no more about it, until one day news broke that Dave had been arrested. He was sentenced to three years by a notoriously severe local judge and at the next Governing Body meeting the question was raised whether Dave should ever be readmitted to the college. While having little sympathy for the guy, whom I found aloof and weak-willed, I thought the college had a duty towards those it had selected as undergraduates, not to abandon them necessarily for either their academic or moral failings. Dave would serve a minimum of eighteen months in a British jail, and having borne his punishment, on the principle of double jeopardy, I thought no one should be tried or punished twice for the same crime; his slate should be wiped clean. Others regarded double jeopardy as a principle of law restricted to the law courts, and that it ought not to provide an argument to prevent a prestigious educational institution from protecting its reputation and making a public declaration that it would under no circumstances condone drug crime. I argued that strong, creative ethics required honesty and risk-taking: we could sit back smugly and declare there was no place for wickedness in this college, or we could recognise the positive value of forgiveness, reconciliation, and second chances. Dave returned to finish his degree a chastened, but a lonelier man, since by the time he got back his contemporaries had left and he experienced the great vacuum created by the triennial departure from 'Cambridge' of each set of undergraduates – the dispersal of successive networks of relationship, which enable people to speak affectionately of 'my Cambridge'.

Through the deliberations of the Governing Body I first saw clearly the contrast between corporate and individual morality, the key phrase being, 'the good of the college'. For the good of the college you might find yourself taking a moral position that as an individual you would feel uncomfortable with. Although Dave was given back his place, concern for corporate reputational risk very nearly persuaded the Fellows to throw compassion out of the window. Or there's the perennial moral maze of money. Many of the large donations have their dodgy side, but the good of the college persuades us to take a broad view: however tainted, the money could be put to good use by our stainless institution. It seems to me 'dodgy money' is a careless moral concept: most money has a suspect side just as most donors are imperfect beings and those who pull down the statues of great benefactors are sinners too. The good of the college turns out to be a notion with little substance.

*

One of the most principled and ecumenical undergraduate supporters of Chapel was Ed, a gentle, humane medic and devoted member of the Christian Union. In his third year he put medicine on hold to take advantage of the Cambridge 'tripos' system, which allows for a degree to be made up of different 'parts', to read for a Part I in English. That summer, not long before the beginning of term, he went on an evangelical mission hop-picking in Kent, and one afternoon, riding on a tractor-drawn trailer, the tractor took a corner too sharply, the trailer turned over and Ed was trapped beneath. He lived for a day before dying of his injuries. His last words were, 'over to you, Lord.' Shock waves reverberated around college, utter disbelief at the loss of such a young and engaging life. Many of us attended the funeral in Kent and, to our surprise and, I believe, general consternation, found ourselves in an atmosphere of bright clothes and joyous smiles. It was to be a day of resurrection: not tragedy, but triumph. His family, too, were ardent evangelical Christians who believed Ed's death had somehow been willed by Jesus so he might immediately enjoy the bliss given to those in union with Christ. It seemed crazy. Could his parents really be so pleased? What were we to say:

Yes, isn't it wonderful Ed has jumped the queue for eternity? My very elementary knowledge of the psychology of bereavement suggested not only that this euphoria wouldn't last, but that it ought not to. Even in Christian triumph you had to feel the pain, and I arrogantly feared the family's sugar-coated certainties had led them to imagine the future as a sort of utopian dreamland, whereas I thought the rewards of Christianity were to be found more in terms of discovering that faith could bring strength in adversity, not as a panacea, but a way of coping and coming to terms with a life that was not always fair or easy. In that surreal, sunny, smiley day I wanted to shout out Dylan Thomas' line, 'Rage, rage at the dying of the light.'

A different kind of poetry helped build a friendship with Phil Davis, a brilliant but difficult young man who came from High Pavement Grammar School in Nottingham to read English, black-haired, acerbic, and racing in the literary slipstream of D H Lawrence and Stanley Middleton, his novelist/English teacher at school. Phil's essays were frequently more than twenty pages long, rather than the six pages required, and he expected his supervisor to read them with the attention required of a major review in the *London Review of Books*. On one occasion he sacked a supervisor assigned to him from another college for not being clever enough to teach him. By sacked, I mean he had the audacity to refuse to be taught by this person any longer. Tim Langley, the English Fellow, who had been on my interviewing panel and become a great friend, told me about this with a mixture of amusement and exasperation and I decided to take Phil for a pint. Initially wary, I wondered if we had anything to say to each other, but the key was I took Phil seriously. That was all he wanted. In return he rewarded me by attending chapel despite being Jewish. By the time he was a graduate student, he and I ran a creative writing class in my rooms for students who wanted to write poetry. Despite the fact I had embraced the early twentieth-century's rebellion in poetry against romantic escapism in favour of social realism – T S Eliot's 'smell of steak in passageways' and his anti-hero, J Alfred Prufrock, measuring 'out his life in coffee spoons' – Phil thought I needed further education and said I ought to get a copy of *High Windows*, just published by Philip Larkin, which I bought, together with the then ten-year-old *The Whitsun Weddings*, where, in *Mr Bleaney*, Larkin portrays the loneliness of life in a bleak bedsit in a Midlands town, reflecting his own experience, and asks what life adds up to. 'I don't know,' is the reply. Larkin takes the ordinary and looks it in the eye, out-stares it like a man that can tame wild beasts. In an early book, Andrew Motion says Larkin 'clearly has no faith in inherited and reliable absolutes', but, unlike many critics, he doesn't accept that Larkin is gloomy but that his poems have an 'unmistakably affirmative aspect.' Phil was convinced we must write about what matters deeply to us and not think of poetry as something decorative or in any way prettified. I had written about two stone lions standing guard at the gates of the manor in Fen Ditton, which Phil clearly regarded as in the latter category and thought not a proper subject for poetry. As soon as I detected his anxious frown, I realised he was right: this was insipid, more heritage guidebook than life changing. No holds were to be barred.

Despite our vigorous efforts, Annette was unable to get pregnant, and she became more and more agitated about it. We both did. We had considered ourselves the classic fertile couple. Then at 7.00am one morning her sister, Sally, rang to announce she was 'in the family way', an expression so banal and soap-operatic I fumed at its triviality and my envy was all the more aggravated. But Sally was older and so, perhaps, entitled to reach motherhood first: it was no consolation. We were about to tread not the Family Way, but the brave new road of *in vitro* fertilisation. I wrote a poem entitled '304 CY 2 (Histology)', which I'd found written at the top of a form given to me in Addenbrooke's Hospital. It began:

They asked for a specimen of love
    To test it,
Wanted it delivered by hand
    Within two hours –
Evidence of ancient craftsmanship
    In a plastic bottle.

Since this was obviously difficult for me, I'd been uncomfortable about allowing the poem to be discussed in the group, but Phil was insistent, and my reluctance was vindicated when one young female undergraduate said she found it offensive and disgusting. As a poet I was dispirited, as a man humiliated. Just as I had been by the young male doctor in the hospital who referred laughingly to the room where specimens of semen were produced as the 'Masturbatorium', a joke no doubt to him and his colleagues, but to me a cruel reminder that the consummatory moment in the creation of any possible future child of mine might have to be achieved in the presence of a two-dimensional centre-fold tart fondling her nipples, or with her fingers up her crutch.

Class

Not a college for toffs, Sidney kept a balance of proletariat and bourgeoisie, a few Etonians, the occasional Radleian or Rugbeian, but plenty of grammar school boys, and within the Fellowship a good proportion of young fellows, including the five of my own intake in 1973, who were generally relaxed and leftward leaning when it came to social attitudes. But tradition runs deep and old habits die hard. Never having regarded myself as a social radical, I was surprised when my objection to the term 'college servants' in the prayers at the Commemoration of Benefactors service, on the grounds it was elitist, met with opposition. I wanted to replace it with 'college staff', but Professor Derek Beales maintained there was nothing discriminatory in the term *servant* since they quite clearly served the college. But then that could have been said about all of us, Fellows included, we all served the college. In the service there was a hierarchical list of those being memorialised: the Master, Fellows, Scholars, graduates, undergraduates and college servants, not to mention the extremely exclusive list of specific people to be given a religious puff merely on the grounds of their having given a load of money. It was telling, too, that these men, so neutrally and nobly described as 'servants' were called by their surname: the college butler, Dennis Pettit, for example, was addressed to his face as Pettit, albeit with a tone of affection, whereas he would address us as, 'Sir'. It was all a bit Downton Abbey, yet one hot day without thinking I went into lunch in my shirtsleeves, and afterwards a group of older fellows opined what a good idea it was; how odd no one had ever thought of it before, and that in future they might well try it themselves.

Somewhere between servant and fellow was a layer of personage designated 'Mister'. Such a one was Mr Mathan, the Chief Clerk, always properly, if never well-dressed, in his sixties, a Dickensian figure who functioned in an office piled high with files and papers and all the accoutrements of pre-digital administration. Mr Mathan could act 'umble, but his ironical servility was all-knowing. On the day the first women undergraduates arrived, I entered his office and beheld in front of the counter a black-haired young woman in a flowery frock. When she had left, I asked Mr Mathan who she was. 'That, Sir, is Bethel,' he replied unflinchingly, using her surname to deflate my enchantment. Her name was Miranda.

Then there was Mr Bentley, the groundsman at the college playing field up the Huntingdon Road, halfway to Girton. A countryman and gardener, he was the salt of the earth, and kept those bleak meadows on the edge of the fens like Elysian Fields, and with the compost of plentiful grass cuttings grew prize-winning vegetables. Any conversation with him might easily be hijacked by the single-minded Mrs Bentley. Mrs Bentley had been nanny to Ben de la Mare, grandson of the poet Walter de la Mare and at that time Chaplain of Trinity. 'How's my Ben doing? He hasn't been to see me since Christmas,' she'd interject, and I'd try to think of a bit of news different from last time to fill the vacuum of proxy-maternal longing in that isolated pavilion.

*

At North Oxford dinner parties, and on other occasions too (although mainly at North Oxford dinner parties), I've often been asked to sum up the role of a college chaplain, usually by interlocutors who imagine it doesn't add up to much and think that, since the three Oxford terms are each a mere eight weeks long, it's money for old rope. Once the obvious ecclesiastical role of officiating at services has been taken out of the equation, it can be difficult to know how to describe the rest. The tales of Tom, Dave, Phil, Ed, Mr Mathan and Mr Bentley might do the trick.

Towards the end of my career and in retirement, I have developed a portfolio of work which includes hosting international conferences and giving seminars on leadership. In a seminar for the executives of the German engineering company Thyssenkrupp I tried to draw on my understanding of the role of chaplain to help them think through a problem they themselves had identified within their own group of companies. In the business world, the survival of a company depends on the crude economics of the bottom line. Executives know that, but the more sensitive ask themselves how they can add to the quality of life in the workplace; how they might help employees find reward in the daily grind and see work as more than a means to an end – paying the bills and enjoying a drink at the weekend. It is a question of how to nurture commitment to the organisation in such a way as to help it to flourish and transcend itself. In other words, how to develop interests other than the balance sheet or how to make it through to Friday.

I asked whether there is a case for employing what I called a 'community animator'. Not a welfare officer, because that makes people think there's something wrong with them, and sometimes encourages them to look for a problem. Not a human resources person, because HR is linked with discipline, arranging your holidays and explaining the number of days sick you have clocked up, but a minister without portfolio, a free-ranging networker who crosses over boundaries between board level and shop floor, without any disciplinary or evaluation role. One London law firm, for example, has a grand piano and arranges piano recitals in the middle of the day and even pays for lessons for employees who would like to learn how to play. There is evidence that such attempts to add value to life in the workplace can improve well-being and productivity.

In university life there's a bottom line too, sometimes known as the '2:1 culture', where the sole criterion for assessing the effectiveness of a higher education institution is the number of first class and 2:1 degrees it can produce. Anything less is considered failure and one of the consequences is a collective neurosis amongst students, fed by the belief that the stress of exams is unbearable and the expectations placed upon them by their tutors tantamount to abuse. It used to be that a University education set out not only to provide degrees, but to nurture the whole person and, within a community of people studying different subjects, prepare students for leadership and a commitment to the common good, which hopefully would give them the mettle to fight nationalism, prejudice, exclusion, bigotry, demagoguery, and fundamentalisms of all kinds. I always thought it part of my job to be such a free-ranging generalist in a society of specialists, promoting music, the arts, ethics, serious discussion, political commitment and connections to the world beyond academia. In footballing jargon, I had a midfield role as playmaker.

Leaving Sidney

During my six years at Sidney I had often wandered around Midsummer Common and Jesus Green with my dog, the mad red setter, Solomon, pondering what job I might do next. This was never from a sense of discontent, but I knew this paradise ought not to last and, at some stage, I must become a parish priest if I wanted to re-join the main stream of the Church of England. Almost from the moment of my arrival in Cambridge I had begun to receive invitations to consider other jobs. I had only been at Sidney a year when Reggie Askew left Christ Church, Lancaster Gate, to become Principal of Salisbury Theological College. Since I had been a curate there, a group of parishioners wanted me to return as vicar, a proposal I found both flattering and seductive, because I had loved that place and those people, but my new Cambridge job offered wider horizons.

Eighteen months after that Tony Bridge, the Dean of Guildford, asked me to become Canon Precentor of the cathedral there. Much as I admired him, when we got down to details it seemed far less exciting than working in a Cambridge college and I said no.

Michael Roberts, who had been Chaplain of Clare College, asked if I was interested in 'the most beautiful parish in England'. Prior to ordination he had been on placement in Dartmouth in Devon, and now the private, land-owning patron, had asked him if he knew of a young man who might become vicar, obviously thinking of Michael himself. It seemed off the map even if it did boast the Royal Naval College. The patron said he wanted a young man because there are so many hills in Dartmouth, which seemed as good a criterion as any for appointing an incumbent. The attractions were obvious: very great natural beauty, a wonderful town centre church, and, on a small promontory at the mouth of the river, an ancient church dedicated to St Peter, a fisherman. Before refusing the offer, I consulted my old college Principal, Bishop Peter Walker, then resident in Tom Quad at Christ Church, who said I needed more of a challenge – like Milton Keynes – which seemed a bit rich coming from a man who had been a public schoolmaster, a Cambridge Don, a theological college principal and now lived amongst the ivory towers of Oxford talking to W H Auden about poetry. What did he know about challenging parochial life?

A year later Tony Bridge offered me another canonry at Guildford and again I refused him.

Mark Santer, the then Principal of Westcott House, told me I had a soft job and tried to persuade me to take a parish, but chaplaincy was my skill, as I discovered again in 2018 when I spent a year as Acting Chaplain of Corpus Christi College, Oxford. Although I could no longer play football with the lads, and had no inclination to stand at the bar of the JCR buying drinks for anyone who cared to talk to me, and although the great majority of college members didn't attend chapel, I knew I hadn't lost my touch. Each week I was expected to email every member of college with information about chapel services and events, and I turned this into an illustrated blog, one week writing about my response to my four-year-old granddaughter's timeless query, 'Who made God?', and the next about the ethics of the TV reality show, *Love Island*, after the Daily Mail had asked me to contribute to a feature it was running on the programme. When *Love Island* comes on air, the JCR fills up: the mysteries of sexuality, body-image, relationship, and rejection being an everlasting cause of disquietude for students. Even the non-attending dons joined in the discussion.

Mark was not inclined to give up. The Dean of St Paul's had asked if he knew anyone who might become Vicar of Southgate, in North London, and Mark suggested me. When I met Alan Webster in the deanery of St Paul's, he gave me the big sell: to be Vicar of Southgate was 'an important job', and the church had the largest electoral roll in the episcopal area, over 750 people, and there would be two curates, an excellent choir, magnificent parish halls. He had talked me into it and I was immediately despatched to meet Bill Westwood, the Area Bishop of Edmonton. Driving out of the City through the Victorian hinterland of Kings Cross towards Finchley away from the Capital's energetic centre, I began to have second thoughts. When I reached the North Circular Road, instead of feeling freedom and excitement, a sickening spasm of doubt took hold and I felt trapped by the verbal commitment I had just made to the Dean.

God's Own Examination

I only wish men would pay more attention to acting (i.e. to practising what they preach) and less to dogmatising.
Brook Fosse Westcott

I think it is time to fill in some gaps. Rather than going right back to my entrance upon life's stage, let us flash back to 1966 when I began my formal training for the ministry in a Church of England seminary.

Those who advised me about which theological college to apply to said it was a choice between Ripon College, Cuddesdon, six miles outside Oxford, and Westcott House, in the centre of Cambridge. At the end of the summer of 1965 I drove from North London, through Aylesbury, into the Oxfordshire countryside to be interviewed at Cuddesdon. I was lodged overnight in the dour guest room just above the chapel, a crucifix above the bed, and a Bible on the bedside table. Even this proximate location didn't enable me to get to the chapel in time for 7.30am matins. I had overslept and my suitability for the college was immediately thrown into question.

The college had been erected in the late nineteenth century, adjacent to the Bishop of Oxford's palace, as a place of retreat and reflection for Oxford men who wished to prepare for holy orders. Its setting in beautiful and remote countryside was intended to isolate the young men from the fascinations of the flesh in Oxford city, deterred by the long cycle ride into town and a particularly gruelling, uphill journey home. There was a gothic, introspective air within, which the *Spy* cartoons of Victorian divines in the corridor outside the common room did nothing to dispel.

One of the current ordinands had been assigned to look after me, but apparently his duties didn't stretch to waking me up

93

in time for chapel. At tea he introduced me to other students who earnestly informed me this was a place where they were 'measuring you for your gaiters' – gauchely self-regarding I thought, even though I knew the majority of Church of England Bishops at that time had been students at either Cuddesdon or Westcott House. Indeed, the Principal, Robert Runcie, was very soon to become Bishop of St Alban's. Before evensong I was to meet him for interview in the elegant Cuddesdon Vicarage where he lived with his family. After fifteen minutes talking on a sofa in his study, he suggested we stroll around the orchard in the extensive garden. Tall, cassocked, and ever so slightly effeminate, he quizzed me on my faith and interests and, as we walked, plucked at the apples on the tree, gazing up to heaven like a monk illustrated in a medieval book of hours.

Not holy enough. Those weren't his exact words, but when Runcie wrote to me afterwards, he considered I would find it difficult to live in that isolated place with its ascetic, quasi-monastic discipline and that therefore Cuddesdon was not for me. He implied he often felt that way himself about the place and, having been Vice-Principal of Westcott House, he believed that would suit me much better. How my ego was pricked by this negative, yet realistic, assessment of my character and spirituality, and how the earnestness of my youth sprang up to goad me into the self-flagellation of writing back to say I recognised in myself the need to develop a more robust spiritual discipline and that I would like to come to Cuddesdon nevertheless. He insisted I go to Westcott and he was right.

*

On the evening of my first day at Westcott I was so nervous I could scarcely eat my dinner, anxious whether I would be liked and which of these strangers might become my friends. At just twenty-one years old, I hadn't yet learned that the people you meet first in a new situation are unlikely to be the ones you eventually bond with. On arrival earlier in the day I had been shown to my room, a drab cube of space on the first floor of the 1880s red brick court, facing dimly through a heavily leaded window onto the garden. After dinner I was reluctant to return to it too early. Fortunately, I was invited for drinks by Simon Acland, a wealthy, High-Church charmer, whose charisma immediately attracted me, and thought myself particularly favoured. When I made my *entrée*, I wasn't the only new boy to have been invited. There was a babble of noise and the clink of glasses as equal numbers of first- and second-year men juggled with their apprehensions. An extravagant buyer of books, Simon had just received a package from the *Folio Society*, which contained a beautifully bound copy of Coleridge's poems which I so admired and enthused over he leant it to me and, I fear, I still have it today.

In 1966 Westcott House retained the vestiges of a finishing school for young clergymen. It wasn't quite *de rigueur* to wear your old school tie for Sunday lunch, but many did, and the social structure of the college was still delineated by a tribal and esoteric nomenclature, not dissimilar from the kind of boarding school satirised in *Private Eye* as 'St Cakes'. The college itself was always referred to as 'the House', the weekly open-meeting of staff and students as 'the Moot', the senior student, 'the Sheriff', his two deputies, 'the Bailiff of Beer' and 'the Bailiff of the Flat Iron', the student who kept a record of the year's events as 'the Archivist', and the student gardener, somewhat prosaically, as 'the Gardener'. The rest of us were 'henchmen'. The student who played the piano in chapel was 'the Minstrel' and those who looked after the chapel and the sacristy were 'Temple Keepers'. A key part of our pastoral training involved visiting patients at two of Cambridge's hospitals: those who arranged the rotas were known as 'the Chaplain General of Addenbrooke's' and 'the Bishop of Chesterton'. There was an entirely optional opportunity to preach at local churches both in Cambridge and in the surrounding villages, the organiser of which was known as 'Episcopus Vagans', meaning wandering bishop, usually one whose consecration had been irregular. Elections were held termly for each of these posts, except for the Temple Keepers and the Hospital Chaplains, whose appointment was reserved to the Principal.

If you had read theology as a first degree, as I had, the curriculum wasn't demanding. In two years I sat the five papers of the General Ordination Examination not covered by my degree, including, ethics, liturgy, and pastoral theology. To satisfy the examiners in GOE, generally known as 'God's own examination', was the basic academic qualification for ordination, which everyone had to pass; what, in these days of degree inflation, would be a B.Theol or a B.Min. It was expected in addition that students would participate in the daily round of worship: Holy Communion, meditation, matins, mid-day prayers, and evensong. Of these, matins and evensong were considered 'as of obligation', a curious phrase intended to imply something obligatory yet at the same time loose-ended enough to fit in a liberal society.

Having only moved from Congregationalism to Anglicanism two years previously, this liturgical rigour was new to me and I battled with it both culturally and intellectually. I thought, for example, that the Eucharist was devalued by daily repetition: in my home church it had only been celebrated once a month and therefore been a special occasion, and we had savoured it. Now it was a quotidian event, in danger of becoming habitual and mechanical. In my view the same could be said of prayer. I wanted to apply the principle of moderation in all things, but we had a very heavy diet of it – like oarsmen eating steak for breakfast to build up their muscles for the race, so prayer was considered the protein of spiritual might. An older student, who had worked in the civil service, started taking a copy of

The Times with him to read during meditation, which agitated the Principal no end. Where might it end? *The Sun*? In a liberal society there could be no censorship. When challenged, the student said he found it difficult to pray without having the national and international news in front of him, an argument with which the great Protestant theologian Karl Barth concurred when he said that you should preach 'with the Bible in one hand and the newspaper in the other'.

Some days I just couldn't face chapel and skived off, as did others, but to do so tended to result in an 'as-of-obligation' pep talk from the Principal, or, in extreme cases, being sentenced to a term as Assistant Temple Keeper with its associated duty of ringing the bell that called the college to worship at 7.25 every morning. Inscribed upon the bell, in Greek, were the words, *pistos ho kalon* – 'faithful is he who calls', a quotation from the First Letter to the Thessalonians referring to Jesus Christ. With my pyjamas under my cassock, in the middle of the winter term, it was a quotation that could on most days apply to me. On my days of failure, the French song we learnt in childhood would have been more appropriate:

> *Frère Jacques, frère Jacques,*
> *Dormez-vous? Dormez-vous?*
> *Sonnez les matines! Ding, dang, dong.*

The Temple Keeper's duties also included serving at the Eucharist. Since this was not one of the mainstream services, it could also be an occasion when priests visiting the House might preside. One morning a very conservative, old-fashioned West Indian priest, on sabbatical leave from his parish in Barbados, officiated in a particularly eccentric manner. When he reached the Peace, he turned to the Temple Keeper and said, *Pax tecum* – peace be with you. The bleary-eyed Temple Keeper recognising the change of language, summoned the first Latin that came into his head and replied, 'Et tu, Brute.'

Apart from being Temple Keeper, I also served in the offices of Bailiff of the Flat Iron, Archivist, and Deputy Minstrel, the post of minstrel always being occupied by my friend and best man Gerald Broadbent, an accomplished pianist who had studied at the Royal Academy of Music. Each summer the House showed its appreciation of the college staff by taking them on a very boozy boat trip from Jesus Green to Ely (and back) through the calm and tranquil water of the Fenland River. Prior to this event there was, of course, the customary evensong. As it happened, I was on duty as Minstrel on one of those occasions. At the last minute I changed the number on the hymn board from the one that had been chosen by the Chaplain and when the minister announced it, struck up with 'Eternal father strong to save/ Whose arm doth bind the restless wave'. Each time we reached the climactic chorus, 'Oh hear us as we cry to thee/For those in peril on the sea', contemplating the still waters of the Cam and the ludicrous contrast with the 'mighty tumult deep' the Principal, Peter Walker, shook his head from side to side and wept copiously into his handkerchief.

Compared with Cuddesdon, this was a liberal place, but we were nonetheless governed by the monastic paradigm, despite the irony that the Church of England had been born out of Henry VIII's suppression of the monasteries and the confiscation of all their wealth. Much was made of 'being in community', to the extent that married men had to leave their wives and families for a term each year and live in college with the rest of us, observing the daily round of services and meals together. While this experience bore no obvious relation to the working conditions we were being trained for, I found a value in belonging for a short period to a community of people trying to share a common discipline. I came to regard shared meals as an extension of the sacrament of the Eucharist, not in a pious way but much more broadly as a part of everyday life, as the Quakers do, who have no formal communion service as part of their worship. The rationale behind what was initially an intuitive theological instinct was a view that the eucharistic symbolism only really has substance if it is underpinned by some experience of hospitality beyond the domestic unit, beyond the immediate circle of friends, and also of making do on occasions with very simple food, which we did every Friday and during Lent in solidarity with those who don't have enough to eat.

I have only recently understood the fundamental importance of hospitality in the ancient human experience. The Hebrew Bible speaks of being open, friendly and fair to 'the stranger within your gates' (Exodus 20.10). And the Greeks spoke of *xenia*, or hospitality to the stranger, from which we get our word xenophobia meaning the fear of strangers. Xenia only appears twice in the New Testament once in Acts and once in Philemon where it is translated as 'lodging'. And that is the point: in the ancient world, when people began to embark on long and perilous journeys to expand their nations and prospects, before there was money, hotels, or public transport, they had to rely on hospitality, and help with transport, from the richer people in the places they passed through. This is a feature of the Hebrew Bible and of the *Odyssey*, for example, where the theme of *xenia* is explored both in the hospitality given to Odysseus on his journey home, and in the abuse of hospitality by 'the suitors' of Odysseus' wife, Penelope, back in his home village on Ithaca, where a group of young nobles exploit the hospitality of Odysseus' estate, killing hundreds of his animals for their feasting and drinking his cellars dry.

*

On Friday night there was an event regarded as totally sacrosanct, the Compline and Address. Compline is the last monastic office of the day and can be sung, as we did, to the most hauntingly beautiful plainsong. To miss this was the one unforgivable sin of Westcott House, and permission to be absent scarcely ever granted. Afterwards the whole college was expected to observe the 'greater silence' until breakfast the next morning, a sort of weekly mini retreat. To me the silence was absurd, and I thought of it as a kind of perverse repudiation of what any healthy Cambridge student ought to be doing on a Friday night. The expectation was we should retire to our room and meditate on the words of the address, usually given by a visiting bishop or prominent priest. When they come to academic institutions, speakers often make the mistake of thinking they have to be clever or learned, and drag out their old college notes, instead of speaking directly from their own experience, missing the point of why they were invited in the first place. They rarely generated enough provocation to make you want to sit up mulling it over.

But I loved sung Compline, particularly when I was the cantor. The melancholy lines of the plainsong are not easy to sing, especially when you reach the words, 'Keep me as the apple of an eye': on 'eye' there is a neume of nine notes, falling and rising with a mellow modality. The congregation then sings, 'Hide me under the shadow of thy wings', using the same nine notes on 'wings', until they whirr away like swans into the distance. This musical beauty matches the poetry of the words, words such as: 'Brethren, be sober, be vigilant, your adversary the devil, like a roaring lion, walketh about seeking whom he may devour, whom withstand, steadfast in the faith', or the prayer that we may 'rest upon Thy eternal changelessness'.

Spiritual incarceration was never my scene, so I, and a number of like-minded friends, used to climb over the back wall of the college, across what was then a vacant lot used by Heffers Bookshop as a car park, to the Cambridge Arms, an unpretentious working man's pub, with a sprinkling of sawdust in the public bar, where we drank Greene King IPA, a true real ale classic, and reliable antidote to whatever dreary religious diatribe we had just been subjected to, rather like turning water into wine.

The sacrosanct nature of Friday Night was captured in an oral tradition of near canonical status concerning a former student, Simon Phipps, later Bishop of Lincoln. Phipps moved in elevated social circles and had been an occasional escort and confidant of Princess Margaret, particularly around the time when she had to break off her relationship with Group Captain Peter Townsend. On one occasion Phipps told the Principal, Ken Carey, that he had received a rather special invitation from Buckingham Palace, but unfortunately it fell on a Friday night in term. 'Well, you know the rules, Simon,' the Principal said. 'If I bend them for you...' Next day, so folk lore has it, a red-liveried flunkey delivered a royal dispatch saying that Mr Simon Phipps is commanded to attend Her Majesty at Buckingham Palace on the date in question – the lengths one had to go to be excused Compline.

Looking back, I see that the greatest and most systematic theological input came from Peter Walker. Scholarly, devout, and seeking enlightenment at the intersection of literature and religion, his guiding lights were Dietrich Bonhoeffer and Bishop George Bell of Chichester, the Scottish poet, Edwin Muir, accessibly buried in the churchyard at Swaffham Prior near Cambridge, W H Auden, to whom later he ministered when Bishop of Dorchester, living in lodgings in Tom Quad at Christ Church, and Dag Hammarskjöld, Secretary-General of the United Nations in the 1950s, and Nobel peace Prize Winner. His book *Markings* was deeply pondered by Walker who often preached about it, quoting memorably, for me, his great prayer: 'For all that has been, thanks; for all that shall be, yes' – gratitude for the past, embracing the future, whatever it may bring; in Hammarskjöld's case, death in a plane crash. T S Eliot was another source of inspiration and quotation, again with a local connection through Little Gidding, but at that time Eliot was so widely cited by preachers and spiritual directors, drawing on *Ash Wednesday* and the *Four Quartets* that it's hard to make him too Walker specific.

Researching the literary hero of Walker's later years, the poet Geoffrey Hill, I find his work described by one critic as 'terribly dense and allusive'. Dense and allusive might be the most apt description of Walker's own style of communication, including his sermons, which employed a convoluted, gerundive syntax as he grappled with the task of trying to squeeze into words the mystery he perceived around him and found in the work of others. I remember, years later, visiting him in his library in the Bishop's Palace at Ely and a conversation constantly interrupted by his taking books from the shelves and leafing through their pages to find a passage that hopefully would express what he couldn't quite say himself, this inevitably at the cost of eye contact, which made the communication even more remote.

In private conversation he had the easily mimicked trait of sucking in air between his teeth, with a hissing sibilance, while shaking his head minutely from side to side. It was a mannerism of mild, but amused, misgiving or disbelief. Many students, myself included, were able to give a fair impression of their master. Two examples, of the thousands that must have occurred stick in my mind. Walker was a classical scholar and had taught Latin to schoolboys before being ordained. We were visited by an American theologian who announced that he had left his car in the 'mult-eye' storey car park. You could see the imagined Latin misspelling running through Walker's mind. 'And do you know what he called it?' (Sucking sibilance, shaking of head.) 'The multae storey car park. That is what he said: the multae storey car park.'

On another occasion, one of the students had been interviewed in London by Tony Bridge for a curacy at Christ Church, Lancaster Gate, obviously before my time there. Bridge was known for his colourful language and the student reported that during the interview he had been asked whether he would like tea or coffee and when he said that he would prefer coffee, Tony called out to his wife, 'Brenda, get this poor bastard a cup of coffee.' Walker: 'Get this poor bastard a cup of coffee.' (Sucking sibilance, shaking of head.) 'That is what he said, that is what he said… "get this poor bastard a cup of coffee."' And the tears rolled down his face.

But if he was an aloof, diffident and uneasy bachelor (he later married Jean Ferguson, the head of the University's Counselling Service), we still loved him for it. When first he became Principal he had found it almost impossible to get through to the young men, and his predecessor, Ken Carey, subsequently Bishop Edinburgh, advised him to buy a crate of whisky and invite the chaps up for a night cap, a ploy that proved most effectual, since the lure of a free drink and the possibility of an injudicious revelation about Cambridge life was irresistible.

I had been dating the sister of a fellow student, Kate Morris, from Fen Ditton, a shapely and delightful girl who attended the Perse School, who had recently ended a relationship that had caused her parents some concern. They had therefore deemed it good that she should seek the more ascetic company of the theological college, where they presumed lust had been dulled by sanctity and the daily round of prayer. But she was an eager girl whose passion would not so simply be doused. Peter Walker invited me up for whisky.

'Did you, er? How shall I say… did you, did you, er, as it were…? Did you ever (sucking sibilance, shaking of head), did you…?'

'Have sex with her?' I said, to put him out of his misery.

'No,' I said.

'Well, that is a relief.'

It might have been for him, but it certainly wasn't for me.

Maybe this episode was not far from my mind when I was

asked to contribute a narrative describing a fictional event that might have been included in the synoptic gospels for the first of a series of seminars led by Denis Nineham, the Regius Professor of Divinity. The idea was that by trying to fill in some of the biographical gaps in the gospel narrative, we might gain a fresh insight into the nature of the text itself. I wrote a sort of courtship scene between Jesus and Mary Magdalene, in which a hesitant Jesus, knowing his divine commission and the restraints that that imposed on him, like so many lovers unconfident of their ground, made a hash of telling her he loved her. The memories of those who told the story of Jesus must have included knowledge of how he related to his close friends, yet that is information that scarcely peeps through the gospel narrative, possibly because, although one of the fundamentals of redemption theology is that the Son of God was tempted as we are, the desire to present him as incarnate God persuaded the gospel writers to airbrush out that part of the story. What a pity this seminar didn't happen forty years on when I might have written *The Da Vinci Code* and made my fortune. The piece served its purpose by provoking lively discussion, winning much approbation but drawing many criticisms, the worst being that I had portrayed Jesus as an 'Eton and Balliol' man – studied intellectual reserve, lacking passion, white upper-class toff.

*

From time to time we had visiting guests who might stay for anything from a few days to a sabbatical term. These were mostly academics, who Casaubon-like, worked on unfinished theological treatises, their equivalent to 'The Key to all Mythologies' in George Eliot's *Middlemarch*, from process theology to the life and times of Theodore of Mopsuestia. Still others were contacts of the Principal needing, as he would say, to recharge the batteries. In this latter category a fellow by the name of de Selincourt turned out a very peculiar fish. Since his interests were poetry and literature, I was introduced to him as a man of fellow feeling and he to me as one who might 'be of help' in my thinking about theology and literature, an interest I shared with Peter Walker. However, as I recall it now, his conversation turned almost entirely on the claim that T S Eliot and W H Auden, in their private correspondence, address one another as 'my dear Bumfarter', a fact I have never been able to verify. Turning up unannounced in one's room at any time of day or night, it soon became apparent that de Selincourt was a freeloader with a proclivity for young men, and he quickly earned the Audenesque soubriquet for himself: 'Mind your backs, here comes Bumfarter.' He was a huge and magnificent joke, who would these days be prohibited as a reckless homosexual predator treading clumsily across the boundaries of sexual harassment. We had no illusions and thought him a harmless old queer from whom we needed no protection.

In my naïveté it never really occurred to me that anyone in the college might actually be homosexual, the gentler term gay not having fully entered the English language in 1966, at least not with that meaning, and homosexuality not having been legalised until the following year. It wasn't until years afterwards, when they began to come out in the easier social climate of the 1980s and '90s (and in 2006 to enter civil partnerships) that I realised several of my greatest friends from Westcott days were in fact gay. One of them, John Slater, who became Vicar of St John's Wood and died prematurely in 2004, had actually competed with me for the affection of the eager Kate Morris. Was this a genuine love rivalry or a smokescreen? I suppose those gay men had learned to repress and hide their sexuality, the consummation of these natural instincts being illegal and certainly a bar to ordination. Interestingly, there was no public offer of pastoral care in the college for those who might be struggling with their sexuality, whereas the actively heterosexual, assumed to be the married few, were officially allocated to the Vice-Principal, Brian Cooper, for counsel and might, what with his being married himself and his wife exuding hormonal fecundity and three young children. The Principal and the Chaplain, Raymond Hockley, were both bachelors who assumed no knowledge of the conjugal state and gladly passed the buck to Cooper, who, pram-pushing and sandaled, showed wry amusement at their reluctance. I never asked for a consultation with him on this or related matters, but a clue to his approach lies in his nickname, 'Coop the Loop'.

I think there would be little ambiguity about the Chaplain's predisposition today; musical, effeminate, holding his cigarette between the tips of his fingers, and an ever so slightly camp way of beginning a sentence with a palatal 'tch', a sound which when repeated can indicate admonition, as in 'tut, tut', but in his case sweetly engaging. When I first met him, he was obsessively concerned for another student, David Thomas, absent on a six-month course in France, who in his view had been ill-treated by the 'wicked' Bishop of Willesden, intentionally mispronounced 'Williesden'. The nature of the Bishop's offence was a mystery, but it had to do with indecision over a curacy at St John's Wood Parish Church. Raymond was popular, a classic case of to-be-teased-is-to-be-loved: anyone might feign gentleness and say, 'Tch, poor David' and the persona of Hockley was immediately conjured.

Since we were to become clergyman, and therefore actors of a sort, it was important to learn the art of stagecraft and how to project our voices, so that we could be heard clearly when conducting services. To this end each of us received individual instruction from Mrs Barrow, a formidable widow woman, stout, broad-hipped and a gammy leg necessitating the constant support of a silver-handled cane and the arm of a willing young man. To see Mrs Barrow waddling through the court towards the chapel was enough to strike fear into the most confident would-be bishop. One of her favoured techniques was to hold the student's diaphragm to check his breathing as he spoke, in order, as she said, to facilitate the smooth reading of the collect. It was a moment of generally unwelcome intimacy and she was only once denied, by a princely youth, named Giles, who was heard to shout through the chapel walls, 'Unhand me, woman.' For my part, I was her favourite. I do not boast of it, but it is true. At the time I was trying to perfect the gravely voice of my hero Richard Burton by listening to his recording of Dylan Thomas' *Under Milk Wood*, which I tried to imitate, but my vocal equipment was as yet young and uncorrupted, and it was impossible to get the timbre, so I had to be content with my lighter tenor. Mrs Barrow liked it, however, and invited me to her small house on Parker's Piece to read poetry, along with another student, Hector, more her own age and a writer of poetry himself. I purposely avoid the word 'poet' in relation to Hector because I was his severest critic in that department and on one embarrassing occasion, when it was his turn to read his sermon to the sermon class, he quoted several stanzas of sentimental poetry, which, in the discussion that followed, I criticised for its slushy inappropriateness and said that I couldn't identify the poet, but wondered if it were Mrs Alexander, of 'All things bright and beautiful' fame. There was a blushing silence in the room, only broken when Jeremy Davies reprimanded, 'Hector wrote it, you fool.'

After the theological desert of the Department of Divinity at Newcastle University I found myself at Westcott faced with new theological questions, not simply those on the curriculum, but those raised in conversation with men who had already thought more deeply about God than me. For example, there was the whole field of ethics, of which there had not been the merest sniff at Newcastle, and the problem of evil and suffering – how an all-powerful and all-loving God can allow such suffering in the world? This wasn't just theoretical. Each week I visited twenty-five-year-old Sammy in Chesterton Hospital who, as a result of a motorcycling accident, was quadriplegic except for a radial movement of the left forearm. He couldn't speak, but could hear and understand, and in response would blink his eyes. To keep the conversation flowing, visiting him was best done in pairs, and as far as Sammy was concerned the cruder the talk the better. When he found something particularly amusing, he would emit a violent, fortissimo shriek that caused other more decorous visitors to turn accusingly, as if we were abusing him, and sometimes, looking only at him, to come over to ask if he was okay. We would reply, with the smug moral authority of extreme do-gooders that he was merely laughing at a filthy joke. Getting a balance between coarse humour and propriety was difficult and we knew we mustn't excite him too much because with his left arm lever he was capable of trapping the bottom of an unsuspecting female nurse in a vice-like grip from which it was difficult for her to extricate herself. Gerald Broadbent and I made a good double act, each having music hall genes, and we performed both for Sammy and to the ward. But it was impossible to return to the athletic, youth-centred culture of Cambridge without feeling a degree of anger on Sammy's behalf, who must spend the next fifty years of his life in bed, tormented by a libidinous chemistry that cannot connect with his limbs, like the roaring engine of a car you can't get into gear.

This theological collision between theory and reality occurred again when I gave my first sermon in Addenbrooke's Hospital, still then at the old site in Trumpington Street, just beyond Peterhouse. The 'Chaplain General', a particular man with a goatee beard and a sartorial taste for clerical chic, by the name of Bernard Chalklen, had allocated me the maternity ward and the Gospel for the day, John 16:21, where Jesus compares the sufferings expected to precede the second coming of Christ with the labours of childbirth: 'when her child is born, she no longer remembers the anguish because of the joy of having brought a human being into the world'. It seemed a gift and I prepared my address accordingly. As I spoke some of those present, I could see in the corner of my eye, began to weep. I suppose many of the women were scarcely older than me and I couldn't understand the effect of my words. Then the penny dropped and I saw that not one of them was holding a baby. These were the women for whom this attempt at maternity had gone badly wrong. I felt such a fool, such an insensitive idiot, to have eulogised the joy of motherhood to those so recently denied it and I realised the rosy Christianity I had learned from childhood contained a gaping hole at its centre. The usual theological escape is to say that God became human in Christ and in the crucifixion suffered as humans suffer, thus showing divine solidarity with the human condition. This of course doesn't always convince, especially those *in extremis*, but it does suggest that to suffer is part of what it is to be, even though there remains what seems a very great injustice, that suffering is spread randomly and unevenly. It is part of a mature Christian insight to be realistic about suffering and not to think that if you have faith it shouldn't ever happen to you.

The curriculum, as I have said, was not demanding. Putting a positive spin on such freedom, one might say it was intended to allow us to pursue to some degree our own theological and social interests. When Trevor Williams and Jim Sykes mentioned they were planning a visit to the Borstal at Hollesley Bay, in Suffolk there was no doubt in my mind that this was a venture I wished to join, particularly when it was made clear we were not to be observers, but to live for a week as inmates, under the same restraints as the other detainees, the only concession being that each of us would be given the status of 'senior boy' and therefore a private cell. Borstal life was not intended to be a breeze; the regime was tough. The inmates, boys between 16 and 21, were hardened law breakers, social misfits, many of them trained, through years at approved school, into the kind of emotional coldness that takes the harshest punishment without flinching.

Their first reaction to us was less suspicion than incredulity. Why the hell would we volunteer to spend time 'inside', when all they thought about was escape or 'having it away', in prison speak? Our presence aroused in them not only astonishment, but disrespect. 'Look, you don't have to be here; you could have it away any time you like,' said one boy to me. 'So why don't you just get the hell out of here? If I was in your shoes, I'd be right out of here, nick a motor from the screws and be down the Bush by opening time.' By the 'Bush' he meant Shepherds Bush, a part of London where many of the inmates came from. But his flight of fancy, his fancy for flight, was not farfetched. Before leaving their vehicles in the prison car park, the prison officers disabled them by removing the rotor arm. Even that wasn't an absolute deterrent to the enterprising car thief, who on the outside was able to break into a car and drive it away in less than a minute. With a cork and a couple of pins, boys had successfully made makeshift rotor arms capable of running for as much as three quarters of a mile. There was an ongoing competition, a kind of championship, to see who could get a screw's car furthest from the colony, a laurel worth achieving even at the cost of days added to the sentence.

Although this was early April, a cold east wind cut across the fields as we spent our days, icy-fingered, lifting turnips. We had been provided with fingerless gloves of the sort worn by Ron Moody as Fagin in *Oliver*, but they did nothing to allay what felt like frostbite. The days were monotonous and bleak and even I thought of running across the brown fields. The supervising screws carried flasks of tea, and I remember pausing in clusters for refreshments and rolling up a cigarette while we talked in whispers of escape. Each boy had about 3/6d (three shillings and six pence) pocket money per week, enough to buy half an ounce of 'snout', usually *Old Holborn* or *Golden Virginia*, which would be rolled into very thin cigarettes and, after smoking, the stub ends emptied of the remaining scorched strands of tobacco into the owner's tobacco tin. Being the currency of the institution, tobacco was extremely precious and none of it could be wasted. I cheated the system by having more than 3/6d in my pocket, so was able to buy extra tobacco and get alongside the boys by offering them a roll-up.

I had recently taken a £40 loan from a shady car dealer in Maida Vale to buy a clapped-out three-litre Humber Supersnipe, absurdly pretentious for a student, and, feeling the pinch somewhat, saw the economic sense of rolling my own cigarettes. I enjoyed them much more than tailor-mades and rolling my own became a habit I kept up until my last nostalgic gasp in Balliol College in 1997. When a curate in Westminster, I rolled my cigarettes in brown *Rizla* liquorice paper which fascinated the ladies of Rochester Row. It amused me to tell them it was a habit I had picked up in Borstal. 'Oh, his cigarettes are like little cheroots,' they said, as if that made the filthy habit acceptable.

On the Saturday night of our short incarceration in Hollesey Bay, the governor gave special dispensation to all boys to watch the Eurovision Song Contest on TV. It was 1967, the year Sandie Shaw won with *'Puppet on a String'*. The music begins with an oom pah, oom pah bass as the slinky, bare-footed sylph descends the stage stairs, pretty face peeping through bobbed hair, and sings in harsh mezzo tones with a touch of tenor, more dominatrix than girlfriend. Thus, a sixties icon is born and the boys shout and whistle and cheer as if QPR had just won the FA Cup.

On the student preaching circuit organised by *Episcopus Vagans* there was a regular slot at evensong in St Edward, King and Martyr, in Peas Hill, in the centre of town opposite David's Bookshop. It is a beautiful old church dating mainly from the early fifteenth century and contains a pulpit from which Hugh Latimer, one of the Oxford martyrs, preached in the early part of the sixteenth. I took advantage of the opportunity to preach there whenever I could because I was captivated by the numinous of this historical link with Latimer, the sense of fragile privilege exacerbated by the rickety, top-heaviness of the pulpit. Curiously, being in 'Latimer's pulpit' meant more to me in this quasi spiritual sense than occupying 'Newman's Pulpit' for thirty years in St Mary the Virgin, Oxford. Was it the time span or the character of the men themselves that made the difference?

In May 1967 Trevor Williams and Jim Sykes came bounding into college one day brandishing a copy of the Beatles' *Sergeant Pepper* LP, hot off the press, wrapped in its astonishing psychedelic sleeve, the artwork itself a revolution, and we retired to Trevor's room to listen. There we were, conventional young men, in grey flannels and pullovers, being blown away by 'Lucy in the sky with diamonds', 'She's leaving home' and 'Within You Without You'. It was the utopian promise of this last track, 'with our love, we could save the world', that inspired me to preach on *Sergeant Pepper* at St Edwards. Did I disturb the sleepy evensong of that sweet place? Maybe I did briefly that night, but, sensitive to changing times, the elderly congregation wanted to let the young have their voice. Despite the Indian sitar music and George Harrison's inspiration having derived from the Hindu Vedas, the message of the song was lifted straight from the gospels:

We were talking about the love that's gone so cold
And the people who gain the world and lose their soul
They don't know, they can't see, are you one of them?

What excited me was the fact that in the chaotic imagery of this drug-inspired album, immediately recognised as an iconic emblem of its own generation, there should be a text summing up the core message of the Christianity I was training to promote.

Even in 1967 we were feeling overwhelmed by secularisation and out of sync with a changing culture, so to find a key teaching of Jesus implanted in a rock album, admired by millions, was both a relief and an opportunity. From time to time there have been eruptions of popular culture giving hope to preachers who feel they've been banging their head against a brick wall of secular indifference. In 1971 the London production of the musical *Godspell* (meaning God's Story) did just that and some clergy stood outside the Wyndham's Theatre, accompanied by members of their congregations, engaging with people as they came out, particularly those who had been obviously moved by the retelling of the story, and trying to persuade them to join their local church.

We had to have our sermons vetted by a member of staff and having read my *Sergeant Pepper* homily to Peter Walker, he made no revisions and declared it remarkable. He hadn't thought the same, however, of a sermon I had previously delivered in his sermon class, a weekly seminar in which ten of us would sit round and take it in turns to give a sermon to an imagined church congregation. So long as I can remember I have thought Christ cannot be imprisoned in churchy metaphors – he didn't use any himself – and that the incarnation requires the widest frame of reference. On this tumultuous autumn afternoon, I took for my text a passage from the opening of D H Lawrence's novel *The Rainbow*. I began to describe, in Lawrence's words, the earthborn life of the Brangwens on Marsh Farm on the northern border of Nottinghamshire. 'They knew the intercourse between heaven and earth,' I began, 'sunshine drawn into the breast and bowels...They took the udder of the cows, the cows yielded milk and pulse against the hands of the men, the pulse of the blood of the teats of the cows beat into the pulse of the hands of the men... But the women looked out from the heated, blind intercourse of farm-life, to the spoken world beyond.'

When I ended there was a prolonged silence. I could see in the

Principal's face that something tectonic had shifted and when the quake came, he exploded and said it was the most sensual sermon he had ever heard, and he uttered the word *sensual* with a splutter of disdain. I began to shift apprehensively in my chair. I had only been trying to illustrate my understanding of the incarnation, but I was left in no doubt that this kind of sermon, if preached in a parish, would lose more souls than it would win. If only I had known then that Martin Luther had once declared, 'you can milk cows to the glory of God,' because to say so would have been a counter to the tirade of shock and, I think, real disgust that poured from Peter Walker. He was not a sensual man; his religion was cerebral, at a time when the mind was thought of more in spiritual than electro/chemical terms.

The sermon must have been very gauche (I no longer have a copy), but I was not trying to shock or be clever. I was trying to say that the whole of life is a proper subject for theological reflection, and that Lawrence's description of the farmer's relationship with the environment, albeit in deeply sensual and sexual language, is not only honest and innocent, but enables us to see the creation in a way that perhaps we had not seen it before. Besides, Jesus himself frequently used farming metaphors to make a theological point: ploughing, sowing, harvesting, separating the wheat from the chaff – not quite the heated, blind intercourse of farm life, but famously Christ located God in places the religious conservatives considered out of bounds, not least in the act of the woman who wiped his feet with her hair.

Twenty years after that sermon I wanted an altar piece for the University Church in Oxford, and discovered that in the basement of the Ashmolean Museum there was a store of paintings never seen by the public. One of these, by a sixteenth-century Italian, Francesco Bassano, depicted the angels appearing to the shepherds near Bethlehem. Dominating the foreground of the picture is a massive brown cow. She is being milked by one of the shepherds, while the other shepherds and their sheep are relegated to the left and right sides of the painting. In the top left-hand corner, minute and bathed in light, stands Bethlehem.

When the diocesan Advisory Committee met to decide whether they could approve the hanging of the picture in the University Church, one of them said what a pity I couldn't find a more religious painting, by which, I suppose, he meant a crucifixion or a resurrection. But I remembered then that 'the pulse of the blood of the teats of the cows beat into the pulse of the hands of the men', and all the incarnational vigour I had felt on that particular day of sermon judgement. So, I managed to win over the Committee by arguing that the Word becoming flesh *was* the centrepiece of Christian belief, on which all subsequent understandings of Christ depend. What, for example, would the crucifixion mean if it were not for this picture, this prior picture which qualified all subsequent theology? Here God enters the lives of simple people as they work at their ordinary tasks, and his presence arouses astonishment and hope. It was a hard argument to trump.

But there was one other compelling image in my sermon text: the women of Marsh Farm knew the instinctive sensuality of farm life, yet it wasn't enough for them; they strained to reach out to the world of 'speaking' and 'utterance'. They wanted culture. They wanted the flesh made word. This applied not only to farm life, but to religion as well. Later in the novel Will and Anna Brangwen visit Lincoln Cathedral so Will can show his wife the place that fills him with instinctive spiritual awe: 'he pushed open the door, and the great, pillared gloom was before him, in which his soul shuddered and rose from her nest... Here in the church the "before" and "after" were folded together, all was contained in oneness.' For Will Brangwen the Cathedral symbolises the possibility of fulfilment in an unfulfilled, frustrated life. But for Anna, while the experience is impressive, the cathedral represents an imprisonment of her feelings. As she looks at the roof, she would rather see the sky above; she doesn't want to be contained or limited by religion. So their responses to the same religious symbol are in stark contrast to one another. Anna insists that a symbol cannot be all in all. It is to be an introductory experience, not a consummatory one, as it is for him. Will is disillusioned by Anna's dissatisfaction. She is trapped and wants to be free. They had both had their eyes drawn to the altar, but while Anna was moved, it was for her nevertheless 'barren, its lights gone out. God burned no longer in the bush.' Anna drew his attention to the imps and gargoyles which 'winked and leered, giving suggestion of the many things that had been left out of the great concept of the church. However much there is inside here, there's a good deal they haven't got in, the little faces mocked. He was forced to admit that there was life outside the church.'

The same argument is made in the chapel of New College, Oxford, where by the West Door there is a statue of Lazarus by Jacob Epstein. Lazarus is in the process of tearing away the bindings with which his body was preserved in death, but as he does so he is pushing his way forward out of the church as if the church were his *tomb*.

Subsequently, Lawrence's story tells us, Will would go to his little local church, and play the organ, and train the choir, and do practical jobs, preserving the fabric and attending to its upkeep. He settled for a humdrum life, 'If only there were not some limit to him, some darkness across his eyes! He had to give in at last to himself. He must submit to his own inadequacy, the limitation of his being.'

Here is the universal human anxiety about self-worth, the cry for personal identity and purpose within the mind-bending scale of things. It is what you might call the incarnational ache, the yearning for God, and the uncertainty of whether God is really present. In the list of those things from which people believe they need to be saved, this is perhaps the greatest, the incarnational ache. The Word needs to be made flesh, but the flesh needs to be made word, articulated and given meaning.

*

When in 1999 we moved into a new Victorian-style vicarage in Norham Gardens on the North side of the University Parks we entered the privileged world of Oxford's wealthy elite. The houses are amongst the most expensive in the country, their occupants being movers and shakers. Quickly we got to know investment bankers, private equity directors, BBC correspondents, TV company owners, film makers, publishers, famous authors and property developers. Many were intrigued to have a clergyman in their midst and even mildly resentful that my stock in trade was the *meaning of life* – it's a powerful key. Others were hostile and didn't get it at all. What would I have been had I not been a clergyman, they often asked and I would tell them how, while at theological college, I very nearly chucked in religion for a job like theirs.

My attitude to money is ambivalent. I desire it and am frightened of not having enough of it, so I am something of a camel trying to get through the eye of a needle. I hate spending it, especially on what I regard as trivialities – meals out, designer clothes, taxis. I would much rather eat at home, get a bargain in the sales, or travel by bus. Having not had much of it in childhood has made me a hoarder, a miser, laying up for myself treasure on earth where moth and rust doth corrupt. And this despite my most successful wedding address which culminates with the words, 'Where your treasure is, there will your heart be also.' I had once married a bride who, when it came to the rehearsal of the marriage vows, got in a terrible tongue-twist over the words 'to love and to cherish'. She just couldn't get it right: instead of to love and to cherish, she kept saying, 'to love and to tweasure'.

'Look, why not think of cherries,' I said. 'Just say to love and to cherry, then add a little sh on the end, like this: to love and to cherry-sh.'

Next day when she arrived at the church door with her father, she said to me, 'I've been practising, and I've got now – to love and to cherry-sh.'

'Marvellous,' I said. 'There's no need to be nervous. I'll take all the responsibility for getting it right.'

So we reach the dreaded moment, and I say, 'In sickness and in health, to love and to cherish,' and she says, 'to love and to tweasure – Oh, my gawd, I've done it again.'

While I was at Westcott House I was joint Director of *Heritage Tours*. My partner was Terry Ellis, who with Chris Wright founded the record label and music business *Chrysalis*, a brilliant title that had serendipitously emerged from combining their names, Chris and Ellis. During the long vac after my finals I had worked for a company called Undergraduate Tours. You had to have your own car – I had a clapped-out Ford Consul – and the basic work was to drive two or three Americans at a time around London showing them the sights. The most lucrative work, if you could get it, was to take your passengers on a week's tour of Britain. Twenty-five per cent of the fee went to the hotel porter who had procured the booking, twenty-five per cent to 'Undergraduate Tours', and the rest you kept. I only ever did one such tour. It was the summer of 1966, when England won the World Cup Final, a match I didn't want to miss, but could do no more than glimpse through a TV shop window in Kendal in the Lake District. My clients were three American ladies, thirty somethings, spinster nurses, with little hope of, or perhaps interest in, matrimony it seemed. At the end of the week, back in London, they paid me cash and that night I swaggered into a pub in Queensway with a wad of two hundred pound notes in my back pocket, the equivalent

of two thousand pounds now. Terry thought this car tours
formula a winner. One evening he drove to our suburban semi
in Loughton in his new Austin Mini with a proposition. In the
orange-ceilinged, green-walled living room (my mother's bid to
be modern) we planned the future. First 'Heritage Tours', then
package holidays, then apartment blocks on the *Costa del Sol*.
Of course, if the music business really took off, we'd have to
prioritise that, but we could run both in tandem. Overhearing
the conversation, my mother looked sheepishly suspicious and
thought Terry a fantasist whom I would do well to avoid.

In the Cambridge vacations I stayed with Terry and Chris
in their flat in Blythe Road, Shepherds Bush, running *Heritage
Tours* from the front room, where I also kipped on the sofa. At
university they had networked with bands and artists to promote
student bops and pop concerts and in London had cornered the
market as agents with universities all round the country. At
first, this was their core business, but they soon branched out
into management. Terry once told me that he looked after artists
like a father confessor, like a young priest, and several came to
rely on him to organise their chaotic lives. His career took off
when he became agent for the highly successful Jethro Tull, and
it soon became clear *Chrysalis* was going to be big.

On one occasion while staying in Blythe Road, I went with
Terry to one of his gigs to hear some nascent pop-failure. Not
ever having really been into pop culture, I didn't know what
to wear. I chose a blue and grey striped cotton jacket, like a
Cambridge sports blazer, but lighter in weight. I thought this
looked suitably trendy even for the Edgware Road. The boys in
the band were down to earth and didn't stand on ceremony. One
of them eyed up my jacket and said threateningly, 'I wouldn't
look like that if I were you, you don't arf look a cunt.' A few
days later I returned to Westcott House and regaled my fellow
trainee priests with this story, which caused so much mirth the
punchline became a code-saying in the college for anything one

might disapprove of. They would say, 'I wouldn't look like that if I were you...' and the remainder of the sentence would be supplied in the knowing mind of the hearer.

Chrysalis made its founders multi-millionaires and Terry wanted me to be part of it. I will not pretend I preferred the way of the cross but having spent five years preparing to be a clergyman I couldn't persuade myself to give up. In any case, I knew deep down the religious leader can also play for high stakes and build empires. There's opportunity for glory and power in religion; people invest their hope for eternity in you and look to you for the secret of salvation, supposing you have special access to the divine, however much you protest your faith is no more privileged or sophisticated than theirs.

Edge of Metroland

1978

The elderly parishioners of Southgate were immensely proud of their parish magazine, which had had the same cover for a decade: a black and white photograph of the church, sober, decorous, and dull. It had a wide circulation, well beyond the people who regularly attended the church, and was delivered by a dedicated team of those of riper years who made an afternoon of it on the last Wednesday of each month. I wanted to make it snappier and more up to date. Amongst the newcomers to the congregation were a couple of art students from Middlesex Polytechnic (now Middlesex University), who asked me what they could do to help the church. I suggested they design a new magazine cover. When they turned up at the vicarage with their artwork it was a cartoon of David Jenkins, Bishop of Durham, who had recently become notorious in the press for claiming not to believe in the virgin birth and saying he thought the resurrection of Christ should not be thought of as 'a conjuring trick with bones'. The cartoon was so different from the sombre photo of the church, I blenched at the thought of publishing it. But I had asked these students to help and hadn't imposed any restrictions in advance, so I felt I should have the confidence to run with their idea. Not only was their picture brave, a word I subsequently heard in the mouths of senior clergy as a circumlocution for *reckless*, they insisted the page size should be A4 instead of A5, so it was to be in-your-face tabloid. When it arrived on the newsstands, the ancients of days were aghast and refused to deliver it. Their respectability had been threatened; no, worse than that, it was mocked.

I kept forgetting my predecessor had been there twenty years and had died, you might think with some panache, in St Paul's Cathedral where he was a Prebendary. It was hard for the

121

many who still mourned him to take me to their hearts. Thirty-three was far too young they thought for a person to be vicar of a suburb that advertised itself as 'Queen of the Boroughs'. I pointed out that our Lord was only thirty-three when he redeemed the world and nobody complained he was too young, but they were not convinced.

Behind the trivial round of church services, mothers' meetings, bazaars, barn dances, pearl necklaces, and the advertisement of these values in the monthly magazine, was the affirmation of a lifestyle so satisfactory it ought not to be disturbed for fear of something more dangerous taking its place. I recognised the cartoon was both anti-suburban and bore the mark of student politics, idealistic, if a bit raw and silly, but then the congregation was for ever complaining the Church needed more *young people*. If only we could draw more young people in. But on whose terms? Were the young simply to become young fogeys or might they be allowed their say?

It was the dilemma of T S Eliot's 'Love Song of J Alfred Prufrock', which I had sometimes used in talks given in school chapels. Prufrock is bored and frustrated. He says of the drinks parties he attends, 'the women come and go talking of Michelangelo.' He worries he has wasted his life and repeatedly thinks to himself, 'do I dare, do I dare?' Do I dare be other than predictably dull and boring? 'Do I dare disturb the universe?' Do I dare to be different or will I always go with the crowd, like a fashion slave? Or am I condemned to regurgitate other people's ideas, always trying to tell the examiners what they want to hear instead of what I actually think myself. Isn't everything there to be questioned, shaken up, disturbed? In those early days in Southgate, I was willing to disturb the universe, if only to stop the Church of England from falling asleep. The Bishop of Edmonton (*Bishop Bill* as he alliteratively liked to be known) had said to me before I started, 'If I haven't had five or six letters of resignation during your first three months, I will know you're not doing your job properly.' It was the best, and pretty well only, piece of advice ever given me by a bishop. Plenty of 'blessings' and earnest hopes that the Lord would prosper my work, but few practical tips.

By a stroke of luck, or some might say divine intervention, the reading for the Sunday after the magazine crisis was Jesus' story of the labourers in the vineyard, about loosely held assumptions being turned upside down (Matthew 20:1–16). Desperate to get the harvest in, the farmer takes on workers at different times during the day. In the evening he pays each of them exactly the same wage. It seemed quite extraordinarily unfair to those who had done a full day's work that those who had worked only one hour at the end of the day should be paid the same as them. They thought they'd been cheated even though they had been paid what they had contracted for. They could not understand the generosity of the landowner who dared disturb the social pattern they expected. Stories like this are not intended to be read as allegory and it would be clumsy to try to say who the landowner and workers represent. Much better to let the controversy, which is the dynamo of the story and which anyone can immediately identify with, force the readers to ask themselves what it means for them. The gospels have a blunt, but engaging, expression about the proper response to parables: 'Let anyone with ears to hear listen!'

Jesus challenged the things people take for granted, which is why I admire him. He broke the religious law by healing the sick on the Sabbath day, because he put compassion before petty rules. He praised a poor widow who put tuppence in the collection plate, because it was all she possessed, and criticised a flash Pharisee who made a great show of stuffing a wadge of notes into the collection box. He outraged the religious types by going to dinner with social outcasts such as tax collectors and prostitutes, and the fogeys tutted and whispered about it in the synagogues and over whatever they drank in the middle of the morning.

Despite these attitudes, I wanted to see the positives of where I was living and to affirm the community I had come to belong to, but I admit I found it in many respects soulless, and when I went out in the morning across the Green it felt more like Toyland than real life, with faux stocks and so-called 'village gates' as you came up Cannon Hill from the North Circular. This was no village, yet many residents thought of it in those terms.

I got another perspective on suburban values when the Bishop of Edmonton asked me to take on a difficult-to-place young clergyman, who in 1981 had gained notoriety by producing a spoof of the *Church Times* which sold 30,000 copies through WH Smith. The front page led with a piece on the enthronement in St Paul's Cathedral of The Rt Revd Graham Leonard as Bishop of London, who is referred to as the 'Madre' – so you get the general flavour. At Cambridge, David Johnson had been President of the Union and famous for his hilarious speeches. Now he possessed that intelligent, gossipy, camp humour which made him a favourite at the tables of London hostesses. We discussed how it would work out were he to join the staff in Southgate and at the end of the conversation I was touched when he dropped his guard and said he'd spent his life trying to escape suburbia and couldn't face going back to it. It was as if being sent to Southgate was a punishment for having been so provocative and interesting. Get back in your box! But he was not so easily tamed. A few years afterwards, posing as an eccentric bigot with a nose for theological dissimulation, he wrote to a number of Church of England bishops with preposterous stories and requests for pastoral advice to see how they would respond. To the Bishop of Lichfield he proposed that an aunt had recently died leaving, in a brown envelope, a mummified finger, with written authentication from the Pope that this was the digit of St Chad, and her dying wish had been that it be returned to rest in Lichfield Cathedral. A mysterious Latin tag, which he pretended not to understand, actually asserted that this was not a finger at all, but the 'male member' of St Chad. In another sting he tried to persuade the Bishop of Norwich to cooperate with him in the production of a TV drama series entitled 'Beach Mission', based on the very successful *Baywatch* series, starring Pamela Anderson. At the time it was common for enthusiastic evangelical undergraduates to go on beach missions during the summer holidays and try to convert other young people to Christianity, sometimes by 'flirty fishing', i.e. using their sexual attraction to entice their peers into conversations about Jesus. Besides, Jesus had said, had he not, 'I will make you fishers of men.' Johnson wrote to the Bishop of Norwich, explaining how the programme might unfold, 'The young evangelists could patrol the beach in their skimpy costumes, attracting young viewers, then when they had got their interest, they could slam home the gospel message.' In both cases, although clearly suspicious, the bishops took these letters seriously enough foolishly to enter into correspondence with Johnson. It was clearly a hoax. The letters were published as *The Spiritual Quest of Francis Wagstaffe* and there were many red faces as a result.

Years later I often met Johnson in Oxford. He was funny, but his schoolboy humour was mean, and he tried to make you look a fool. His health withered, he hung around the Oxford Union Society and was to be seen driving around Oxford in a personal mobility scooter wearing a *cappello romano*.

Religion in Southgate

Suburbia has proved rich soil for religion and despite the fact we already had seven hundred and fifty people on the Roll, I was expected to grow the community more. But these were the Thatcher years and her administration promoted individualism and materialism, summed up in her famous adage, 'There is no such thing as Society'; an attitude inimical to Christian principles. It fuelled secularism. And the demographic was changing too. Jews were moving to Southgate from Golders Green and, after the Turkish occupation of Cyprus in 1974, Greek Cypriot refugees began to settle in Palmers Green and Southgate. I had six Cypriot girls in my A Level Religious Education class at the local Minchenden School. My students were thoroughly modern young women, but occasionally on Sundays they were taken by their parents, or more likely their grandmothers, to the Greek Orthodox church where they heard the Gospel read in an old Greek they could scarcely understand, the equivalent of us hearing the Bible in Chaucerian English, had there ever been such a version. But the important thing was that this ritual preserved their cultural identity in a foreign land. They were being asked to remember that above all they were Greek Cypriots and their religion was from the Orthodox East, not the Catholic West. I said to Bill Westwood that with all this cultural diversity, I could not see how I was going to make much progress and he snapped back that in that case maybe none of us should bother.

In one sense religion looked after itself: services happened every day of the week and people attended. This was church going on a grand scale. On Sundays there were services at 8.00am, 9.30am, 11.00am, 12.15pm and 6.00pm. After eighteen months we abandoned Choral Matins at 11.00am 'because only forty people attended.' For most churches today, forty would seem like Kingdom Come. Instead we introduced a monthly Family Service which grew and grew until we had as many as three hundred people present. It was informal, short, and involved the congregation in leading the worship and making presentations, and we formed a band of instruments to accompany the music. I even involved my dear old golden retriever, Leah, who was to demonstrate obedience and relational trust. In rehearsal it worked perfectly, but on the day, with the sound system on, she couldn't tell where my voice or whistle was coming from and became completely disoriented, to the delight of the parents who knew this was what parenting was like and were glad not to be patronised by one man and his dog.

The dividing line between religion and social life was indistinct. There was no border between worship and community, each was part of the other, just as historically every citizen of England had belonged to a parish and was entitled to the ministrations of the Established Church: this was part of the genius of the Church of England. It didn't matter if people came to church for the prayers or the coffee afterwards, or matter what they believed or whether they turned up only for a daughter's wedding or to give their grandmother a decent send-off. It is an ideal effectively now lost as a dwindling Church ironically finds it harder to be inclusive.

I could see suburbia needed community, and a focal point for community, more than anything else. Otherwise it was a barren land: no effective town centre, no great public building other than the church, a dormitory, a grid of maze-like roads indistinguishable from one another, a culture vacuum, which I do not say condescendingly, but merely as a sociological observation. Sometimes people can only discover their 'hunger to be more serious' when they are presented with opportunities for seriousness, when they are shown the menu.

Nevertheless, my first great change had little to do with seriousness, at least in an obvious way, and more to do with having a good time – although the two are not mutually exclusive.

A wealthy spinster of the parish wishing to encourage me offered to finance a new venture. I could choose. It didn't matter what it was. Above the entrance to the splendid hall complex was a semi-redundant space kitted out as a sort of boardroom. Tentatively I asked her if she would countenance paying for it to be turned into a parish bar. Well, she had got her money from the family's estate agency business and they weren't averse to a gin and tonic, she said, rubbing her hands together. We sold Greene King IPA to remind me of Cambridge days, put up a dart board and furnished the room with sofas. Success was almost immediate and then I began to worry that some people who used the bar three or four times a week never darkened the church door. Should there be some sort of condition that you couldn't have one without the other? But if there was 'no border between worship and community', as I have argued, I had to accept that this philosophy, which I so absolutely believed in, would create many loose connections. The realisation led me to initiate other community projects which had no overt proselytising agenda, indeed no covert proselytising agenda either. I had seen that the best kind of 'mission', to use a churchy term I otherwise shun, is sheer openness: try to be yourself and if others are drawn, so well and good. Dioceses waste hard-earned money on 'Missions Officers' and outreach programmes in an attempt to advertise the Christian Church, but only succeed in making religion look dull compared with church communities that have learnt to be interestingly themselves.

Southgate's Green is its best feature, with the church at one end, *Ye Olde Cherry Tree* pub at the other and a village pond. No surprise then to see maypole dancing on May Day. But since few people other than the children's parents turned out to watch, it was a measly occasion. My wife, Annette, decided we ought to stage a comprehensive fair, with stalls and coconut shy and tug-of-war. First time round the riper-years-brigade foresaw endless obstacles – until the money came rolling in, money which was going to be given to charity, by the way, not for the church coffers. The bar did record trade and all sorts and conditions of men and women were brought together, regardless of race or religion. It is an event that has now been going over forty years.

Despite the fact some of the finest concert halls in the world were half an hour away in Central London, I wanted good music on our doorstep and inaugurated a concert series of classical music in the church hall, under the banner 'Music at the Green'. The church's hall complex was the best I have seen and certainly exceptional for the period. The backstage dressing rooms had illuminated mirrors to rival anything in the West End. We had a very good piano and the operatic bass, Christopher Keyte, helped me invite leading professional instrumentalists to give recitals.

In the school holidays we ran a five-week summer camp for children and at Christmas, together with the Southgate Rotary Club, provided a Christmas Day dinner and entertainment for one hundred needy or lonely people.

The magazine hullabaloo died down, but the barrier to change had been breached. We kept the A4 format, didn't flinch at tabloid influence, persuaded the local newsagents to stock it, and included community news, while still covering and advertising church events. It meant we needed to print more copies at a time when home printing was still in its infancy. Richard Cox, born and bred in Southgate, who went on to found *Key Publications*, specialising in aviation, brought a can-do attitude to the project. We bought an offset litho printer, a nightmare to operate, and one evening a month he and I stayed until the job was done, before having a fry-up and a bottle of wine in the vicarage. We also went on to leaflet every house in the parish three times a year with comprehensive information about what the church had to offer. In his 1974 book, *Built as a City*, the Bishop of Liverpool, David Sheppard, had said the clergy should spend half their working time on the needs of the church and the other half on the needs of the community. This was the policy I adopted, and it drew people in. I think they found the so-called can-do attitude attractive, even if it had something in common with a wide-boy approach to cutting corners and by-passing authority. In any case these were the days before the onset of church-speak and central managerialism when the parish enjoyed almost complete autonomy. Apart from being on the Diocesan Education Committee and a personal advisor to the Bishop of Edmonton, I had little to do with the Diocese of London and was untroubled by central diocesan administration. We were left to get on with it. Twenty years later the internet would put an end to all that.

I don't think you have to have a 'theology' for everything, but I find it hard to read the gospels without thinking there was an element of maverick leadership in the life of Jesus of Nazareth. No one gets crucified for being uncontroversial and keeping their mouth shut. Jesus broke the Jewish law by healing on the sabbath, he upset the Temple authorities by turning over the tables of the moneychangers, was happy to let a woman anoint his feet and wipe them with her hair, ate with tax collectors, touched lepers and told the wealthy to sell everything and give the proceeds to the poor. He also told a story about an unjust steward who, threatened with the sack, did a deal with all his master's debtors in order to buy their support in the future. Luke says, 'the master commended the unjust steward because he had dealt shrewdly. For the sons of this world are more shrewd in their generation than the sons of light.' As I have already suggested, parables are intended to spawn ideas not limit them. But what I take away from this is that religious energy can be generated at least as well by creative risk-taking as by stolid respectability.

Had those feet in ancient time walked upon Southgate Green there might have been a parable in the action of my neighbour, who owned five garages on the North Circular. When the organ was being renovated on a tight budget, the metal pipes in the front of the case were looking very dowdy, but they were large and the organ builder prevaricated, so Roger sent an open backed lorry, took the pipes to his nearest garage and sprayed them with Volvo silver paint. He was shrewder than the sons of light and certainly quicker.

For all that, the backbone of the church was held together

by the ligaments of voluntary, salt-of-the-earth administration, undertaken independently with only occasional consultation with me: the running of a three-department Sunday School, the management of the halls complex, church finance, the uniformed organisations of cubs, brownies, scouts and guides, visiting the sick, the church tennis and badminton clubs, and cleaning the church building. We employed an organist and a choirmaster, a part-time youth worker, a full-time halls caretaker, parish administrator, and two full-time curates, paid for by central Church of England funds.

*

It is difficult to interpret the past through the lens of the present. I was much more theologically conventional then than in retrospect I imagine myself to have been, and my vocabulary was more orthodox, as I shall show in a moment. The radical questioning was there beneath a façade of theological correctness. When a particularly outspoken Scottish curate said to me of life after death, 'Surely you don't believe all that nonsense, do you?' I found myself defending a traditional view. It was almost certainly a pastoral judgement made in the light of having sometimes to conduct as many as four funerals a week.

Very soon after I left Southgate for Oxford, I wrote a book of short stories, *Changing Faces*, several of which were based on my experience in Southgate. 'Quite a Chat' describes a visit made to a dying man who wanted to discuss death and make arrangements for his funeral.

Henry Crimond died of cancer. He had been a pillar of the church for forty years: sidesman, financial guru, member of the church council, and encourager of harassed vicars. Genial in life and practical about death, this ripe apple had left £250 to pay for a 'good old knees-up' after his funeral. Henry's shot at life after death, his own Messianic banquet – a binge in the parish hall.

The pin-striped funeral conductor gave an exaggerated but oddly inappropriate bow to Henry's mortal remains and the bearers, hurriedly forsaking cigarettes, took up the coffin with professional propriety.

I had spoken to Henry about this moment two weeks previously, when the surgeon had told him he had only a short time to live. Cancer of the pancreas is insidious and difficult to treat effectively. Henry lay in bed propped up by pillows, his hearty features having shrunk, his eyes sinking into grey sockets. 'Well, Vicar, the quack's given me my marching orders,' he said in an attempt at defiance. We looked at each other hesitantly. I took his hand which he gave willingly, not in the hail-fellow-well-met muscular manner I was used to from him, but softly like a woman, and through that intimate contact devoid of all client-greeting and deal-clinching, a new language of care and vulnerability was spoken.

'I'm sorry, Henry,' I said. 'Are you afraid?'

'I'm worried about Connie... she's been... she's been...' he began to weep. I knew what he meant: his helpmeet, his lover, mother of his children, his sense of proportion.

'A good wife,' I said.

'She's a wonderful girl I couldn't ask for better.' He paused. 'I hope one day we shall meet again in heaven. Do you think we shall?'

'I don't know any more about heaven than you do, Henry.'

'But you're a priest; you're supposed to know.' He sensed my evasion and at a time of crisis wanted comfort, not a philosophical discussion. Even if he had intellectual doubts about the possibility of personal contact after death, he wanted to hear me say that of course we shall. He needed me to conspire with him in any way I could to ease the pain of being forced by the inexorable progress of terminal illness to part from his loved ones. And I was ready to do that because I wanted him to be at peace in his soul. But he had always called a spade a spade. He once told the church council they were hypocrites for refusing to give money to an international charity because it would 'end up in the hands of freedom fighters.' He said they were using a half-baked political excuse to justify their basic selfishness, hidden under that great escape clause, *charity begins at home.*

'St Paul says our bodies will be raised as spiritual bodies.'

'But shall we recognise each other?'

'Perhaps we shall recognise each other by our personalities rather than our physical characteristics. I mean, will the physically disabled person be disabled in heaven? Or the soldier who's had a leg blown off go around on crutches?'

'I see your point,' he said, examining the back of his hands, now resembling a textbook illustration of skeletal metacarpals and phalanges. 'I'm beginning to think it might not be such a bad thing to get rid of this worn out old body and swap it for a new one.'

'St Thomas Aquinas, who was a very fat man, believed that at the resurrection everyone would be medium-sized and aged thirty,' I said.

He smiled. 'Thirty was a nice age to be.'

He seemed drowsily to gaze into a haze of memories circling the yellow light of a table lamp burning unnecessarily in the spring sunshine. Letting go of my hand he reached for the bedside table, knocking over a teacup. 'Somewhere there you'll find an envelope,' he said. I wiped off the drops of tea that had blurred my name. 'Those are the instructions for my funeral. Don't open it now. Wait until I'm... until I've gone.'

Henry needed to say out loud: I am dying. I shall soon be dead. Friends and relations had visited and looked on the bright side and said he would be out and about in the better weather and he'd put on a brave face, but had really wanted to shout out, I shan't bloody well be here.

'I want to be cremated. I suppose you think that's wrong.' There was a pale glint in his eye as he tried to spar in his old jovial way.

'It's perfectly legal.'

'What?'

'Cremation. Anyway, it's the essential you that matters. Our bodies are made of recyclable physical atoms and they need to be recycled... we are dust and shall return to dust.'

Our half hour together had clearly been an effort for him, fighting off physical discomfort and the soporific effect of the morphia. He now began to sink more heavily into the sheets and pillows.

'Shall we say a prayer before I go?' I asked. He nodded. I struggled to find the words but thought to myself that God copes where human resources fail. 'O God, we pray that Henry may be surrounded by your healing love and power. Give him courage as he approaches death... We give thanks for all the support and love he has received from Connie over the years and especially in recent months. We commend her and Joyce to your fatherly care...'

'And my grandchildren, Mark and Samantha,' whispered Henry. His head lay back in serious contemplation, like an effigy on a tomb. I made the sign of the cross on his forehead with holy oil, drawing the marks slowly over the crevices and cracks of his skin which I saw as through a magnifying glass trying to give all my attention to this real slogger of a Christian pilgrim.

Downstairs in the neat living room, verdant with indoor plants as pampered as the Yorkshire terrier, Connie had sat pretending to be reading a magazine, listening, waiting for the stair to creak because as soon as I reached the hall she was up, looking enquiringly, already having boiled the kettle. 'It was so kind of you to come,' she said. 'I know how busy you must be, but he especially wanted to see you.'

'How are *you*?' I asked. I could see her hand shaking as she poured the tea.

'Oh, I'm fine. The doctor's coming at 4 o'clock. He gave me some sleeping pills, but I haven't used them. Did Henry talk? He's hardly been with it the past few days.'

'Yes, we had quite a chat.'

She looked relieved. Obviously, she had hoped, as she thumbed through her magazine, that in the room above there had been an unravelling of mysteries, a spiritual reconciliation that went so far beyond anything consultants, solicitors, or neighbours could offer. I experienced a dazed sense of platitudinous incompetence, but maybe she was right: an effective steward of the mysteries of God rarely knows themselves to be such at the time. I hoped that in this case love had triumphed over reason and the peace of God which passes all understanding had been. mediated through the sacrament.

Henry died three days later.

*

I took particular care in telling that story because it stands for many others. In the early 1980s cancer treatment was still relatively undeveloped and the 'C' word struck fear into many, including me. I was so involved pastorally with people, particularly women in their sixties, who were dying of the disease, every time I found a bump in my skin or felt an unusual little pain I thought I had got it and went rushing to the doctor. Many of those I ministered to were desperate and tried every treatment going: beginning with their GP, Harley Street if they could afford it, religion and church, anointing with the oil, secular faith healing, acupuncture, diet and herbal remedies – often all at once, there being no time to lose. My mother had taken ginseng, she said for *long life*, but knew she had something radically bad going on inside.

These rites of passage – births, marriages and deaths – were a key entrée into the lives of parishioners. Infants were sometimes baptised four at a time on Sunday afternoon at the request of parents who didn't really believe in God but valued the Christian moral compass and wanted their children 'to be able to choose for themselves when they grew up'.

There would also often be four weddings on a Saturday afternoon, on the hour, lasting exactly half an hour, with choirboys, misleadingly innocent in white ruff and surplice, thrusting the collection plates at people as they left the church and laying bets on which ceremony would yield the richest pickings. With that on-the-hour timetable lateness for the bride was not an option, although one or two, working on Greek Cypriot time, were so late they spent the afternoon being driven round the North Circular until a new slot became free. I make it sound like a wedding factory with no spiritual content, which is to denigrate a sacramental ministry I greatly cared about. The clergy met with all couples and prepared for each wedding with care, and once again it was surprising how often couples discovered in these meetings a seriousness they didn't know they had. About one in five couples continued to come to church after they were married and, if they fell away, returned when they had children.

The Church of England's censorious and exclusive attitude towards divorcees at that time caused widespread alienation and ill feeling. You only had to refer to divorce in a sermon for the letters to pile up on the vicarage doormat from people with a sad story of resentment and injustice. The annual divorce rate in England and Wales peaked in the mid-eighties: in 1940 it was 7,755, in 1960 23,868, and in 1985 160,300. I decided, contrary to the will of the Church, to allow the marriage of divorced persons in Christ Church. I advocated the ideal of lifelong commitment, but not lifelong misery. Besides wanting its adherents to be perfect as their Heavenly Father is perfect, didn't Christianity speak also about repentance, forgiveness and new beginnings. Marry in haste and repent at leisure is not a quotation from the Bible. I wasn't indiscriminate: I drew the line at solemnising the union of serial divorcees, and I tried to be understanding and helpful wherever I could, which resulted in even more weddings and much good will when the Church was experienced as the inclusive place it claims to be.

Energy e = mc2

Whenever the Rector of St Aldate's, Oxford, stood up at a meeting and declared that the previous Sunday he had had over a thousand people in church, as if that validated what he was about to say, a wave of mild nausea, tinged with jealousy, swept over the other clergy in the room. No need to rub it in. In Southgate I could have played the same game. Our combined church attendance was very high and, had I wanted, I could have stood up at the next meeting with my fellow clergy and boasted that last Sunday I had over 600 people in church. I think the secret was energy, part of the can-do attitude so admired in the suburbs. We were a young team: we worked hard, set ourselves goals, didn't flag, reached out to people on the fringe of religious interest and made traditional stuff fresh and compelling.

Secure in my five-bedroom vicarage on the Green, I didn't wholly recognise what a tough ride the population as a whole was having in Thatcher's Britain; how divided society was, and how close we were to the breakdown of law and order. There was a need for durable values and something you could trust at the core of life, a need for a perspective beyond material concern. The church was able to provide that. Ironically, as the Thatcher era unfolded, extreme materialism became characteristic of the age as yuppie traders in the City of London earnt obscene amounts of money, much of which they spent on champagne, cocaine, and Porsche cars – it became a distasteful symbol of divided Britain.

On election night in 1979 there was a party in the parish hall. I don't know who had organised it; certainly not me. But I was there talking with Sir Anthony Berry, the Tory MP for Southgate, who told me with stars in his eyes there had been a wonderful victory in our neighbouring constituency of Finchley. 'Who's the candidate there?' I asked. He looked at me with astonished disdain. I had no idea it was Mrs Thatcher. I had voted Labour.

Thatcher's monetarist policy of high interest rates and reduced taxation helped reduce inflation but led to a fall in output and unemployment rose to three million. Heavily populated by ethnic minorities, the deprived inner-city areas felt the economic injustice most keenly. One summer night we were driving back from the English National Opera at the Coliseum, having seen the *Magic Flute*, and as we came along Green Lanes through Haringey were suddenly confronted by very agitated police and diverted up a side road away from a riot that had flared up near the Wood Green Shopping Centre. This was a spin off from the Toxteth and Brixton race riots. Our leafy suburb enjoyed a degree of immunity from the social upheaval going on around us, although we had a substantial number of police families living in the parish in Metropolitan Police housing. Many of those residents were in the front line.

Then came the Brighton Bombing in 1984 when the IRA failed to murder Margaret Thatcher, but succeeded in killing our MP, Anthony Berry, the only sitting member of parliament to die in that grim event.

When the radio announced we were at war with Argentina over the Falkland Islands in 1982, a shiver ran down the spine of my generation. We had been brought up the immediate shadow of World War II and reared on stories of its suffering and bravery. In one of the early news reports Brian Hanrahan described the first raid by Harrier jets with the words: 'I'm not allowed to say how many planes joined the raid, but I counted them all out and I counted them all back.' We knew this meant lives were at stake. At Southgate Cricket Club, so-called educated members fired off unsavoury racist tirades against the 'Argies' and the 'Dagoes'.

When the communist Arthur Scargill whipped up the anti-Thatcher miners' strike in '84, the insulated metropolis could kid itself these were problems belonging 'oop north', that mythical, alien kingdom beyond the Watford Gap. That was the political backdrop for my ministry in North London.

But what was its theological energy? I know very few Christian communities that are self-definingly theological. Theology is for the professionals, which may or may not include the clergy. The energy of a community is usually practical rather than ideological – loving your neighbour as yourself, going the extra mile, looking out for those in trouble and caring for the sick. Of course, there's theology in that, but essentially it is about community and social survival. I suspect the rationale I gave to it all from the pulpit was the natural, and possibly artless, conviction theology of my childhood. I was assured without being stuffily neo-gothic, religious without being sanctimonious. I was in my prime and enjoying life. And that exuberance was key. Once the Southgate community had seen the potential of an extended vision to their church life, they wanted it to succeed and were prepared to break the rules to do so.

I saw a similar popular charisma in the Bishop of Edmonton, Bill Westwood. He was a humorous cove who people could see wasn't the very definition of a clergyman; he could easily have been something else, one of us, even. He was popular on the radio, in touch. He explained to congregations how easy it was to get held up in London traffic. If I'm late, just start without me. To save him embarrassment on the underground, his episcopal crook unscrewed into sections like a professional snooker player's cue. At confirmation services (an admission ceremony for those wishing to join the church) he told the congregation he realised many of them were there out of duty to a nephew or niece, or because it was raining outside, or someone present owed them money. Always got a good laugh, that one. He knew about money, human weakness, the way of the world, and likely something of sex, drugs and rock 'n' roll. People emerged from these occasions with a smile on their face, concluding the church had more fire in its belly than they had supposed when they went in. It was a simple incarnational theology of identification: accessible, meaningful, we get it. Week by week, I aimed at the same outcome, adding the spice of opening up the raw questions of faith: how was Jesus God? Did God allow suffering? Are we *saved* and if so from what? Did miracles happen? How could we apply 'sell all you have and give to the poor' or 'be perfect as the Heavenly Father is perfect' to the compromise of our everyday lives?

The first seventeen years of my ministry was characterised by this youthful confidence in the rightness and inevitable progress of the religion I represented. When I moved to Oxford, I immediately felt a shadow fall across this exuberance as I was weighed down by opposition to change of a quite different order. For some in Oxford the parish had become a little haven of self-identity, a way of being associated, however obliquely, with a University that otherwise kept them at arm's length. For the University itself, the church was all heritage and tradition, a museum item to be conserved.

*

There was another energy at play in Southgate, that essential survival instinct which delights and enhances us, and yet is so volatile it can easily sputter and boil over in a dangerous chemical reaction – sex, in all its fifty shades.

I received a request from Westcott House asking if I would

accept as a curate a particularly talented young man, learned in religious studies, knowledgeable about the arts, with great entrepreneurial skills, popular amongst his peers, but in an open homosexual partnership. A clandestine relationship was okay, it seemed, but a brazenly open celebration of love was like raising two fingers to the Church. I said I would take him. Bishop Bill Westwood said he would licence him but would have to clear it with the Bishop of London, Graham Leonard. In an act of monumental hypocrisy Graham Leonard declared he had no homosexual clergy in his diocese and therefore the young man may not be licensed. I knew, Westwood knew, and Leonard knew, the London clergy were the gayest in the land. The prejudice ran deep, even into the fibre of those who most wanted liberation.

My brother-in-law was one of the early victims of AIDS. He was a manager in the Strand Palace Hotel and shared a flat with Diana, a front which allowed his mother to pretend he was straight. Neil was the love of his life. Alastair sported a droopy moustache like Mexican Pete and was a good sailor and horseman, skills learned in Cornwall on the family farm and in the sailing paradise of Mylor and the Carrick Roads in Falmouth. It was out sailing one afternoon that his legs gave way and from Truro Hospital he was flown to St Mary's, Paddington. I officiated at his funeral. Normally the undertaker's team of coffin bearers josh and chat about football and the like, but on this occasion they cold-shouldered me completely and huddled together at a distance as if I were contagious. Not only was the body in the coffin a social outcast, so by association was I. It was the politics of fear, just as the Bishop of London's dissimulation was the politics of fear.

I am aware that Christianity's love/hate relationship with sex is becoming a major theme of this book. I didn't set out with that in mind; it has emerged as an elephant in the room demanding to be acknowledged. Whether you celebrated sex or repressed it depended on the politics of the moment. Evangelicals never owned up to being gay, but they lionised heterosexuality (along with the Word of God) so long as it was within marriage. They say the evangelical Trinity is 'Father, Son and Holy Scripture', but it could equally be Father, Son and Holy Matrimony. I was once invited to preach in St Peter's, Arlington, in Washington DC and Annette and I were accommodated in the curate's house, since he and his wife were conveniently away that weekend. Carefully placed by our bed was a manual of what Christian married couples might get up to in the privacy of their chamber. No holds were barred, no flight of fancy out of bounds, it was a positive porn site of married bliss. But that's America for you and I'm not suggesting evangelical bedrooms in England's green and pleasant land are thus equipped – not that I've been in many. Come to think of it, I haven't been in any.

Then one August Saturday a scout leader came to the vicarage, tense and very earnest, to say there was something I ought to know. I had no inkling what was coming and could see my potential informant shifting uncomfortably from side to side. Eventually we got to the nub of it: during the summer camp there had been wife swapping amongst the officers of the Baden Powell set – easily achieved, I imagined, going from tent to tent in the dark. a) I had no idea whether I had any responsibility for what went on in the 'uniformed organisations', even though they were nominally associated with the church. b) Had these shenanigans, assuming the story was true, had any deleterious effect on the children? c) Did I find the whole business as shocking as my informant?

When the facts unravelled, it emerged the message had not been lost in translation, and to put a respectable gloss on the whole affair(s), Akela was going to marry Skip and the Quartermaster was going to marry the Guide Captain. Whereas hitherto Skip had been wed to the Guide Captain and the Quartermaster to Akela. Sometime after I left the parish, the

Guide Captain became churchwarden.

Quite unrelated to this event, Tracey (not her real name), a sixteen-year-old Ranger in the Girlguiding Movement, became pregnant by a randy senior scout of similar age and the rumours soon began to spread. She had already left home because things were rough and, now petrified of returning, came to live in the vicarage. Not much more than ten years older than her, Annette mothered her, encouraged her, and talked to her late at night. She decided to have her baby adopted, took stock, and got her life back on course by getting married to a different man and becoming a policewoman. As she patrolled the streets of North London, she'd see small children at play and wonder if one of them was hers – so easy to see your likeness, or that of your lover, in any of those faces if you look hard enough.

We still had an all-male choir of men and boys. As parish church choirs go, they sang well, and what would choral evensong have been without them? Several of the men had been Oxbridge choral scholars and could easily have been lay clerks in a cathedral choir. The commitment of the boys was greatly bolstered by a weekly youth club run by two choirmen after choir practice. It helped the boys to bond with each other and with the adult leaders, which pleased the parents because these were able and intelligent men who gave those boys a real educational boost not only in music but introducing them to new ideas and helping them with homework. The men were welcomed into family homes, sometimes sharing meals. And then one morning my PA, the mother of one of the boys, said to me casually, 'You know something odd happened last night. After supper, Rhys said Chris had been such a good boy, could he go and tuck him up in bed. My husband and I looked at each other for a moment… and then said it would be fine. Of course, we absolutely trust him, but it did seem a little weird.'

Only days later I received a phone call to say Rhys (not his real name) and another man in the choir had been arrested and were in police custody. The alleged offences were not against boys in the church choir, but against another boy who lived locally. At the Old Bailey the judge instructed the jury, in summing up, that they must keep in mind that the boy who had been buggered (a technical legal term) was only eleven years old.

In the past thirty years attitudes towards child abuse have become much more severe and the law has changed accordingly. Rhys got three years, which today would have been ten, and his accomplice six months. I visited them in Wormwood Scrubs, driving down the Marylebone Road, across the rooftops of Paddington, through its steeples and the stucco facades of my old haunts in Lancaster Gate, to be met by the Prison Chaplain who led me through a procession of clanky gates with forbiddingly efficient locks. Rhys was full of excuses. He loved (his word) the boy he had defiled (my word) and, since the boy had 'gladly consented', didn't understand why a sexually consummated relationship between a thirty-five-year-old man and an eleven-year-old boy wasn't acceptable. Oh, the delusions of body chemistry. He was released on licence after eighteen months and dared to show his face again in Southgate. To my amazement the choir families were surprisingly accepting, including the tough guy father whose job it was to put derailed trains back on the track; I had expected him to sort the matter out in a dark alley. Was this an eruption of Christian love and forgiveness? No, I think it was a kind of embarrassment at their own gullibility in allowing these men so dangerously close to their own children. And it was partly our old enemy, the banality of evil: it was catastrophic for the child who had been abused, whom no one knew, but for the rest the dull, mucky, delusional path of sin was too banal to dwell upon, a reality uncomfortable enough to be suppressed, but not unbearable enough to rise up in arms against it. Had a child been murdered, it might have been different.

I am trying to convey how things were in the early eighties. Maybe, however, my reflections are not time specific. In 2020 the national 'Independent Inquiry into Child Sex Abuse' reported on the Church's lamentable record in this regard: it pointed out how the Church's failure to respond consistently to abuse victims added to their trauma and concluded, 'The culture of the Church of England facilitated it becoming a place where abusers could hide,' adding that alleged perpetrators were often given more support than victims. Was this also our failure in Southgate?

In the aftermath of these events, we achieved what I had wanted for a long time, the creation of a mixed voice choir with women and men, girls and boys under the direction of a new choir conductor, accompanied by a brilliant, if eccentric, young organist who had been organ scholar at Exeter College, Oxford.

At 6 o'clock one evening in the dark days of winter, a ring at the vicarage door and there before me a young couple with ashen countenance. The woman I had known since childhood; she was the daughter of one of my father's tennis partners. They sat down in the study, I enquired what was troubling them, and then the man blurted out, 'I have just returned home from work and found my wife in bed with your curate.' As I tried to compute this message, he held me in his glare. So, *she* wasn't such a shrinking violet after all. *My curate* was a Scotsman, married with a baby, and I remembered how at the Burns Night Party there had been the usual banter – what are you wearing under your kilt, Jimmy?

After an hour's cautious mulling over of this new reality, as much between the couple themselves as with me, I asked how they thought the situation might be resolved. Did they need more time to think? But, no, they were clear; the matter must be referred to the Church of England authorities. By then Bill Westwood had been made Bishop of Peterborough and the new Bishop of Edmonton was Brian Masters. When I phoned, he floundered, clearly out of his depth, heterosexuality not being his forte. Should we send my curate on holiday for a couple of weeks to let things die down? I said that a holiday would scarcely see justice done or placate the offended party. I had already asked the curate if there were any other offences to be taken into consideration and discovered there were. He had developed what you might, in an undiplomatic moment, describe as a 'ministry' to lonely and disaffected women of the parish. Apart from the daughter of Dad's tennis partner, there was a woman getting her own back for her husband's infidelity and another who was simply flattered by the attentions of a man of the cloth – and each knowing perfectly well the man was married, which possibly, I suppose, in their eyes made it more acceptable, in the manner of female adultery in a Tolstoyan novel.

The Bishop decided he must refer the matter to Lambeth, which is churchspeak for blacklisting a man (we were all men then) on a register in the Archbishop of Canterbury's office, and that my curate would then be moved to another parish as soon as a suitable post came up, but for the time being he would continue to serve in my parish. The gossip was far too electric not to spread round the community in days. And once again the response was far less morally indignant than one might have expected or hoped. One intelligent member of the congregation stopped me in the street to say he thought the curate's sermons had improved enormously since the crisis began, as if the suffering of his wife and all other parties involved might be an acceptable price to pay for marginally more profound soul-searching from the pulpit. Just as with the response to Rhys when he came out of prison, people now found infidelity sufficiently banal to be here today and gone tomorrow. I was troubled by this moral laziness and my wife even more so, especially when some years later it was reported in the press that the same priest had been accused of the same offence in another diocese, but had been acquitted on the grounds of his accuser's alleged mental health disorder. In today's managerial church, which on the whole I find life-sapping, a situation like this would not be swept under the carpet and far more radical disciplinary measures would be taken.

Another teasing ethical question during these years was IVF – *in vitro* fertilisation – relevant to me because Annette and I had received treatment at the Royal Free Hospital in a recurrently unsuccessful attempt to have a child ourselves. The clergy attended seminars and meetings on the matter, as if the moral world turned on it. The Catholics, with their fundamentalist pro-life obsession, were set against it. God had invented sexual intercourse and that should suffice. Any artificial manipulation of sperm and ova risked destroying potential lives, which was anathema. What they hadn't grasped was that, just as a sycamore tree casts off thousands of flying seeds to create two or three saplings, so in God's amazing invention millions of sperm and a multitude of embryos fail to come to fruition, reproduction being naturally and necessarily a wasteful and prodigal process. One has only to think of the parable of the sower, where the farmer open-handedly broadcasts seed across the path, on rocky places, among thorns, as well as the good soil in the confidence that a good proportion will germinate.

In the best tradition of showbiz Evensong, which I had pioneered at St Stephen's, Rochester Row, I decided in place of the sermon to address the matter of IVF fertility treatment in Christ Church, not least because one of the Royal Free Consultants was a member of the congregation and willing to lead the presentation. On the night I realised the discussion broke unwritten taboos by necessitating the naming of parts of the reproductive system. Afterwards, some of the older women told me they were glad to think about important ethical issues of the day, but were uncomfortable, in truth completely discombobulated, about hearing of semen and ovulation and fallopian tubes so close to the altar from whence they received their Holy Communion. It was the equivalent of saying: can we not talk about this while we're having our supper. Sex – even objective, scientific sex – and sacred space do not go together.

While you might wish for a less anecdotal theology of sex than this, what this set of stories illustrates, from direct experience within the Christian community, is how traditional Church teaching on sex has been overtaken by a post-modern discourse on sexuality which is also essentially post-Christian. People no longer accept being told by the Christian tradition how to behave. We see this most evidently in the bewildered faces of the young when confronted with Christian agonising over the ethics of homosexuality; faces that ask, what's the problem? Or on the nature of marriage, which until very recently was generally accepted as being, by definition heterosexual, for the procreation of children, and ideally lifelong. Now marriage is principally understood in terms of committed relationship. Why, for example, should couples who have lived together for a long time without marrying, have fewer legal rights than those who have?

Without being reductionist about this, or suggesting the sexual mores of Southgate was in any way admirable, I am simply saying it was a product of its time. Watching the Church wrestle with these moral dilemmas, I came to see Christian social ethics as culturally relative. A major social institution cannot be totally out of gear with the society it exists in. It can be in critical dialogue with the spirit of the age, but not alienated. And the contemporary Church in a multi-cultural society must recognise and acknowledge that it does not possess exclusive rights to determine what is right and wrong. One of the most galling experiences for anyone looking in on the Church from outside is the feeling they are being judged, often hypocritically, and that their secular ethical position, however altruistic, is somehow second rate. Christian social ethics adapts, and the

Church can easily kid itself it doesn't, simply by lagging twenty years behind the times. In any case all ethics has to adapt as new moral conundrums present themselves: at that time IVF was a classic example; a good 2020 example is gender fluidity.

I do not think the integrity of Christian ethics is undermined by this analysis. While it is true Christian ideals often coincide with secular ideals, there is nevertheless a vision of a Christian moral imperative, the sovereignty of Love, specifically the *self-giving love* exemplified by Jesus in the gospels. The imperative of Love is the yardstick for what is known as 'situation ethics': in whatever moral dilemma or situation you find yourself, it is important to make an ethical decision in terms of what is the most loving thing to do. In those terms it appears deceptively simple – do the loving thing and all shall be well. Broadly speaking I adhere to the principle of simplicity in ethics, but equally I know there are many nuances in any ethical situation which can bring like-minded people to different conclusions on the same issue – war and peace, crime and punishment, sexual love and infidelity, to name but few.

Furthermore, there are odd paradoxes and puzzlingly abrupt disconnects. Take Donald Trump for example, a self-confessed, self-admiring, pussy-grabbing, chauvinist, adulterer, who has the votes and hearts of millions of Bible-believing evangelicals in America, for whom you would think his attitudes would be both an anathema and an abomination. His supporters overlook his immorality in favour of what they see as decisive leadership. Maybe, because of their fundamentalist mindset, they have assimilated the middle eastern attitude to sex and sexuality, evident in the culture of the Bible, and accepted the male-dominated social foundation of it: the chattel status of women, the right of men to objectify women, to 'put away' their wives and take to other women.

*

As I look back and imagine having a second shot at life, I always think being Vicar of Southgate is the one job I would never take again, yet I was happy there and, ironically, perhaps at my most successful. Compared with the self-contained bubbles of Cambridge and Oxford (where I would work next) this was the 'real' world, if you'll pardon the cliché. The suburbs are where most people live, and certainly where most people sleep; the cultural tone is different, the buzz is elsewhere, and I must acknowledge I often found it boring. It was *Metroland*, the land of commuters. While others boarded the London Underground from Southgate or the Great Northern overland train from Palmers Green to work in Town, I stayed behind in the *Dormitory* suburb, with the words of St Paul's *Letter to the Romans* in my mind: 'it is high time to awaken out of sleep; for now is our salvation nearer than when we first believed.' Despite the many signs of new life and fresh vigour I have described in this chapter, I always knew the structural social conditions of suburbia would frustrate my ambitions. But for all that, the people were the salt of the earth, and that's no condescending jibe; the Christian Community was as strong there as I have known it.

The Parson's Wife

In 1998 we bought a tumbledown house in the Andalusian village of Chite on the edge of the Sierra Nevada halfway between Granada and the coast. In the late spring you could ski in the morning and swim in the Mediterranean in the afternoon. The house needed renovation and reinforcement against earthquake tremors, and as work progressed we pondered what name to give it, only to discover the locals had beaten us to it: they called it *Casa Del Cura*, the house of the priest, and every time they said those words they nudged each other and began to giggle. In Catholic Spain priests never marry, but here was one enjoying full family life.

It reminded me that a parishioner in Southgate had given me a faded, second-hand book titled *A History of the Parson's Wife* by Margaret Watt. It is a serious work which begins at the English Reformation in 1533 with the dilemma of whether priests in Henry VIII's new Church might marry or not, and specifically with the case of Archbishop Thomas Cranmer's German wife, Margaret, his second, his first having died in childbirth ten years previously. Watt tells the dubious story of how, because of the need for discretion in a world of dangerously unpredictable Church politics, Mrs Cranmer sometimes travelled *incognito* in a box with ventilation holes in the lid.

Later in her book, Watt turns to parsons' wives in literature, with the redoubtable Mrs Proudie in Trollope's *Barchester Towers* coming out on top. Mrs Proudie is a domineering wife who rules over her household, and her husband, with a rod of iron in all matters both temporal and spiritual. She is of the Low Church Party and has absolute belief that she is right.

I tell you all this by way of introduction to Mrs Mountford, not the daughter of a German theologian like Mrs Cranmer, and certainly not a tyrant of the Proudie school, even if she knows

151

her own mind. You have already met her as the alluring Nurse Rowe in Chapter One, but not specifically as the parson's wife. She's enough of a libber to object absolutely to being defined by her husband's job, but once that caveat is out of the way, there are aspects of being a vicar's wife that she loves. For a start she attends church, which some of the more dissident clergy spouses these days pointedly do not. It has, of course, been *spouses* since 1994 when women first became priests; and were there to be a book, 'A history of the Parson's Husband', it would be interesting to see which character type predominates. Although, 'parson' is an archaic enough word for me never to have heard it used of a woman, despite the fact most dioceses have a *'parsonages* committee' to oversee clergy housing. Thus, many female vicars live in what is technically a parsonage i.e. a vicarage or rectory.

Annette and I were married while I was a curate at Christ Church, Lancaster Gate, and she was still a student nurse at St Thomas' Hospital. I am sure we didn't see ourselves then as a husband and wife team or that we had any special pastoral responsibility for the large group of young people at the church; we were simply part of it. But there was one factor which did set us in a special relationship with the others – our flat belonged to the church and this made our home a semi-public space. People expected to drop in, to be made welcome, and frequently on a Sunday night after Choral Evensong the whole crowd came round for coffee and treated it like a second home. I mentioned ealier I had bought a seven-foot Broadwood concert grand piano from a lady in Hampstead which fitted into one corner of our enormous living room where we held occasional concerts. There had to be refreshments and we had deliberately made hospitality the key to our parish theology. Annette embraced this doctrine with zeal, and when a loopy young parishioner ruined our new electric kettle by lighting the gas underneath it she laughed it off, and when we invited two old ladies for Christmas dinner and Annette presented a single roasted duck between us, I carved it as if it were Bob Cratchit's Christmas goose and everyone had their fill. We were poor, but never thought of ourselves as such. We quickly learned that hospitality can pour from the poorest pockets like oil from the widow of Zarephath's cruse after it had been blessed by the prophet Elijah. The more you give, the more you have to give. That was Annette's motto and she applied it unwaveringly throughout our marriage, whether feeding undergraduates at home, making pancakes for Shrove Tuesday, or entertaining the many famous visitors who came to our home.

The one homely thing we were unable to do was provide children for the vicarage. Not for want of trying as I have described. Our infertility was caused by auto-immune problems which at that time were untreatable. To both of us this deprivation was visceral, worse for Annette than for me no doubt, but once, during the humiliating process of IVF, an implanted embryo split into eight cells, which meant LIFE, and I walked around the streets of Southgate, already a father, with such bounce in the soles of my feet the surface of the earth had become a trampoline.

Annette's sister Sally had not found conception difficult and had a bright five-year-old daughter, Zoe, who often came to visit us in Southgate. Sally was married to Bill whom she had met at the Royal College of Music and now they earnt a sort of living depping in London orchestras, Sally on the double bass, Bill on the clarinet, and doing a bit of teaching on the side. Money was always in short supply, but that didn't stifle their grandiose plans for the future, sending Zoe to the exclusive Lady Eden's School in Kensington where she would meet the right sort of people. When it came to the prospect of a second child there was the question whether they could afford it. Sally was in favour, Bill apprehensive. Very soon Charlotte was on the way. We all dutifully brought presents for the baby, cooed over her, and said how cute she was, but Sally seemed fragile both physically and emotionally. After four or five months it was clear she was suffering from puerperal psychosis which became so bad she was admitted to St Mary's Hospital in Paddington. Her hormones were playing with her mind and the financial problems were so bad, Annette gave her money to buy a pair of shoes and then we discovered she had sold her double bass to pay off some debts.

On Shrove Tuesday 1984, we held the *Annual Revue* in Southgate parish hall. The clergy, assisted by a few other stage-struck types, put on a show satirising themselves, leading church figures, and any absurd religious posturing prevalent at the time. It was popular, funny, and cathartic – a very appropriate prelude to Lent. Prior to the show we ran pancake races and Annette had discovered pancakes froze very well and therefore large numbers could be made in advance. Afterwards, she helped clear up the hall and I got home ahead of her. The phone rang and it was one of our resident, churchgoing police officers saying that Sally was missing, having discharged herself from hospital, and they had reason to think she might have walked to Paddington Station and taken a train to Cornwall. If only she could get back to her native surroundings, to her roots, she thought, maybe things would be alright; she could be looked after and perhaps see life again from the perspective of the carefree days of her youth.

I rushed to fetch Annette and we drove immediately to the basement flat in Inverness Terrace in my old parish of Lancaster Gate where they lived. Zoe was in bed, Bill paced about, Annette's mother, Clara, who had come up from Cornwall to look after the children, rocked the baby's cradle. Then the phone rang. It was the same policeman, our friend, Mark. 'I'm afraid the worst has happened,' he said. Sally had indeed boarded the train to Cornwall and soon after it had crossed from Devon into Cornwall and gathered speed, she had opened the carriage door and fallen onto the line. I just thought to myself, 'Those poor little bastards.' Annette's father had to travel from Falmouth to identify her body, an experience he could never speak of, but at least we learnt that her face was uninjured and peaceful in death.

*

Not very long before this tragedy occurred, Sally had asked Annette if anything were to happen to her, she would look after the children, wouldn't she? Now decisions had to be made. Charlotte had been taken to Cornwall by her grandmother, but everyone thought that could not be a long-term arrangement. In any case, her other grandmother objected and wanted to look after both children in Inverness Terrace. Bill was bereft and felt he couldn't cope. In time, Annette and I offered to bring up Charlotte, but only on condition that we adopted her, because we feared if we bonded with her over a period of years and then had her taken away, the wrench would be too painful. Emotionally, too, it made sense for Annette at the age of thirty-five to mother this child, who was after all partly of her own blood. But what about Zoe? Zoe had a father, a home, a school. We would gladly have adopted her too, but she and Bill had other needs.

The adoption went through and Charlotte, at six months, became the Vicar's daughter, baptised in the church, and a feature of many church occasions from the family service to the Pensioners' Christmas Day dinner when, in a cloth cap, she gave her impression of Arthur Scargill, the notorious leader of the National Union of Miners. Zoe came to stay every weekend. People in the diocese as well as the parish said the experience of parenthood had mellowed me and I now suffered fools more gladly.

The greatest ambiguity was for Zoe and me. Zoe wanted me

to treat her with the same uninhibited fatherly love I showed to Charlotte, but I always held back for Bill's sake. He had lost so much. Zoe was all he had. I never felt free to trespass on their relationship however much I wanted her to be my daughter too. It was clearly a confusing and distressing dilemma for a child to have to cope with and Annette and I could not find a way round it. Even so Zoe spent more time with us than she did with her father and, when at boarding school, nearly all her school holidays. In public we presented as a family. It was much easier to live *as if* than constantly to have to explain our situation to people who, once let in, could become super inquisitive and sometimes unhealthily infatuated with the story. Those who only ever saw our family from the outside made assumptions we just went along with. 'Oh Vicar, Charlotte has got your eyes and her mother's nose.' Women chatted conspiratorially to Annette about the first trimester or breastfeeding, which since she was a qualified Health Visitor and midwife didn't faze her. In these sorts of conversations I felt uncomfortable about the implicit lie of our failure to say, *yes, but,* and eventually, when the assumptions became embedded in longer term friendships, to dread the day when led down some conversational *cul de sac* one might have to untangle the whole blessed business and be exposed as a deluded liar.

Our children, if I may now (thirty years later and in the light of Bill's death in 2012) use that term, were undoubtedly deeply scarred by the death of their birth mother, but they flourished. Zoe read English at Cambridge and a Master of Fine Arts (MFA) postgraduate degree at UCLA before becoming a film writer in LA and marrying an American film writer. Charlotte read English at Edinburgh and after a few years working in finance an MSc at the Cass Business School. Both now have children of their own.

At the age of thirty-eight Annette also read a degree in English and was taught for part of the course by the author

Philip Pullman. She had intended to become a teacher, but, as that reality approached, realised her natural talent was the care of people, so she founded the Charity *Family Links* instead, specialising in nurturing relationships between parents and children, teachers and children, children and children, and in special situations such as the families of military personnel and women prisoners. The secret was affirmation: finding the good in other people and praising them for it. Also, the setting of boundaries to help people – adults and children – recognise what behaviour was acceptable and what was not. In *Circle Time* school children were given equal opportunity to speak so the 'outsiders' became included and were able to tell their story, sometimes a grim story of deprivation and abuse. In one important sense, although it was not a religious organisation, *Family Links* grew out of the University Church, because we raised seed funding for it, provided meeting space in the Old Library, and many of the initial volunteer trainers came from our congregation.

In her role as Parson's Wife she showed the same generosity of spirit. Perhaps the biggest laugh in my farewell speech when I left the University Church came when I said, 'She was always extremely nice to people – to make up for my failings in that department.'

At Southgate she ran the May Day Fair and started a group for young mothers known affectionately as the 'Wednesday Wobblers', a soubriquet I had rather rudely coined. It was one of these women, earning a bit of extra money by arranging accommodation for foreign language students, who badgered Annette into taking a couple to stay in the vicarage. Although working full time at Chase Farm Hospital, she gave in on condition she had the teachers and not the kids. Leandro and Teresa Marcucci from Falconara Marittima on the Adriatic coast of Italy turned up with their suitcases, bottles of wine and homemade *grappa* sealed in milk bottles. Leandro always referred to me as 'Reverendissimo Mr Brian' and claimed to be enraptured when I played Beethoven piano sonatas before supper. He insisted we visit them in Italy where we would barbecue the fish we had caught that day in the Adriatic and drink Verdicchio such as I had never tasted before. Being of mean spirit, I told Annette that in Italy all schoolteachers titled themselves *Professore* and they probably live in cramped quarters. Two summers later Annette had pushed me into it. We flew to Rome and took the train across Italy to Falconara where at the end of a very hot journey the Marcucci clan was waiting for us on the station with chilled white wine from the hills of Cupramontana. 'Here is the key to your car and this is the key to your house,' said Leandro. Over the nightly feasts prepared by Nona and unmarried cousin Alfonso I began to deduce that, while not a conventionally religious man, Leandro sought some sort of atonement through his act of hospitality and generosity to the 'very reverend' English priest. It was an example of religionless Christianity: raw, unchurched, yet sacramental. And I only tell the following story because Annette claims it is her defining memory of Italy and an experience that altered her take on family life.

One evening a great *al fresco* supper was arranged at the vineyard of Leandro's cousin, Nadino, in the hills near Cupramontana. Leandro took fish and meat, we brought bread, and Nadino provided the wine from his *cantina*, a disused chapel half buried and cool as a catacomb where in place of the altar stood a wine press and five antique oak vats. The best wine was buried in bottles around the circumference of the chapel and Nadino scratched away the dust with his hands to retrieve it. Outside they had erected a rough table with benches where we sat to eat, Nadino, Maria, Leandro, Teresa, Annette and me, Alfonso, cousin Lucia and her husband Cesare, and cousin Angelo, who, in the car driving over with Leandro, Alfonso and me (Annette travelled separately with Teresa) had seemed uncomfortable about the presence of the foreign priest and decided to confront me with a filthy story about a prostitute having her leather underwear eaten by a dog – Leandro translating. How would I respond? Fortunately, it was not unamusing.

On the table were bowls of salad prepared by Maria with tomatoes and lettuce from her garden, strewn with herbs and purple mallow flowers. As soon as supper was served Angelo took the bread in his dirt-cracked hands, broke it over the edge of the table and handed a great chunk to everyone present. It was an unexpected act, but recognisable as an *attentive* one.

After supper, banging on the table, Leandro rose to propose a toast. 'How do you say? Bottoms up! Here's mud in the eye!' He made the toast to 'Bread, Oil and Wine: the elements of our Mediterranean way.' First the bread which feeds us and gives us – *con pane* – good company. Second the Verdicchio of Nadino, which gladdens the heart. And finally the oil, the most difficult word in the English language for an Italian student to get – oil, ill, I'll, eel, hill, heel, heal, whole. How do you tell the difference? He pronounces oil with a slight aspiration so it sounds like h'oil.

The symbolism of these sacramental words was not lost on Annette and me, even if they were unintended. In a sense, Leandro's religion was what he called 'The Italian Way' – tradition – from the grasped thumbs of the Roman handshake to the hospitality of their intergenerational household living together *in famiglia*. We were so impressed with this that when Annette's parents, aged 92 and 84, could no longer manage to live independently in Cornwall, we agreed to look after them in the vicarage in Oxford. When her mother was on her death bed two years later, her father pleaded with her to live two years longer because then they could die together. Annette believed, as a 'true countryman', he knew his time and would shuffle off his mortal coil according to plan, but he lived five years more, to within one month of his hundredth birthday. As *Family Links* expanded, Annette had to work long hours and I often prepared his supper and took it in to his room on a tray. My speciality was Oxford Covered Market sausages and vegetables from my allotment, which he always approved as a 'good feed'.

Genesis

I stepped upon life's stage at the end of World War Two, between the German surrender and the bombing of Hiroshima and Nagasaki, and first became aware of the mystery of my own existence in our home in Loughton, twelve miles north-east of London. Detached, 1890, ochre brick with a high gabled front, the house was too narrow for its height. The ground floor was on two levels, kitchen at the back at garden level and front room higher by four stairs which rose from the side passageway. On the first floor were three bedrooms, but no bathroom. We washed at the stone sink in the kitchen and went to the toilet in the basement cellar. The garden was wild and unkempt, but what intrigued me most was the range of buildings on the south side consisting of a stable with a metal manger fixed in one corner and a triangulated floor sloping into a central drain. Adjoining that was a small barn with open front supported by heavy oak posts, littered with junk and old machinery, where I once (accidentally) cut open the head of my friend Edward Lloyd with a metal-bladed seaside spade. Even at five-years-old I felt the instinctive guilt of Cain and knew, although unintentional, this was an act of ancient violence that must be punished, and while Edward ran home with blood pouring from his head I hid in the barn in the hope the truth would never come to light, which of course it did that afternoon when his mother came round and asked accusingly, 'What have you done to my little Edward?'

At the bottom of the garden, beside a broken fence, I discovered an abundance of small, black berries, which I ate with the instinctive pleasure of the hunter-gatherer. To obtain food independently as a small child is a kind of miracle, a taste of self-reliance. I was so pleased with the discovery I took some currants to show my mother.

'You've eaten these?' she asked.

'Yes, blackcurrants.'

'They're deadly nightshade,' she exclaimed. 'My God, what do I do?'

The doctor advised an emetic and I was made to stand on a chair with my head over the stone sink and to drink a solution of salt and mustard water until I was sick.

'It's for your own good,' my mother insisted. 'You've got to get the poison out of your stomach.'

I was forced to swallow more and more of the foul mixture, but the spasm of sickness wouldn't come. I shouted and pleaded I hadn't meant to do anything wrong. There seemed no logic to this assault.

'You've got to get more down you. The doctor says you must be sick.'

When at last I spewed up, the vomit was yellow and black. The slime poured into the sink and down my front. My stomach felt like it had been ripped apart. I was cleaned up and put into fresh clothes but not cuddled or reassured.

'That'll teach you not to go eating what you shouldn't,' scolded my mother. 'I hope you've learned your lesson.'

She believed in being cruel to be kind. That was her motto. Years later I discovered what I had eaten wasn't deadly nightshade at all, but woody nightshade – far less poisonous – but I never said anything.

Dad was away at this time, at somewhere called 'coal', and only came home once a fortnight for the weekend. I remember sitting on the swing he had fixed from the frame of the back door waiting for his return and the excitement when he arrived. But his visits were short and I didn't understand why he must be away so much, despite the reassurance there was nothing to worry about. The truth was, in post-war Britain there was a serious dearth of schoolteachers, so the government introduced a shortened teacher-training course of one year. My father applied and was selected to train as a music teacher. It meant going to 'coal' in Worcester. He showed us photographs of him striding across Wenlock Edge with other thirty-somethings, men in Oxford bags and flat caps, the women in pleated skirts.

'Who's she?' asked my mother, pointing, 'and what's her name?'

In later years when there was something my mother didn't understand, he'd say cockily, 'But, of course, you never went to "coal", did you.' This infuriated her and she'd parry, 'You don't need to have been to "coal" to know the price of butter.' It took me a time to work out that 'coal' was in fact 'coll', short for college – Worcester Teacher Training College. I don't know whether this mispronunciation was modish or characteristic of what later became known as Estuary English.

Good old Dick

What kind of man did I discover my father to be? He was always warmly greeted in the street, thought to be amusing, and often referred to as 'good old Dick'. It was a time when first names were shortened whenever they could be, when Bobs, Daves, Rons, Berts, Bills, Teds, Lens, Geoffs, Franks, Sids, and Dicks inherited the earth. Dad was popular because he bore no malice, was fair-minded and even-tempered, virtues that sealed good relations with even the most difficult kids he taught at the local secondary modern school and for most of whom he had a nickname, a ploy by which they understood he was fundamentally on their side. In return they called him Jazz, not, as I'd thought, because he purported to hate the devil's music; quite the contrary, because he sometimes gave lessons on jazz and enthused about Dave Brubeck and his quartet, playing *Take Five*.

One afternoon, when I was about six and just beginning piano lessons, I was being looked after by Dad in his classroom while he supervised a class detention; one of those pathetically vacuous times when a group of resentful children must serve a corporate punishment for the sins of a small group of their classmates. It was a tense stand-off and he repeatedly checked his watch, obviously desperate for the whole thing to be over. Then a bright idea occurred to him, 'How would you like to hear an up-and-coming pianist play Lucy Locket?'

'Ooh, yes please, Sir.'

I was perched on the piano stool and, using both hands, punched out the single line melody of the nursery rhyme:

'Lucy Locket lost (right hand) her pocket (with the left and so on),

Kitty Fisher found it;

Not a penny was there in it,

Only ribbon round it.'

This was greeted with rapturous applause and with it all resentments seemed to evaporate, and mediation between the downtrodden citizenry and repressive authority had been successfully negotiated and defused.

Not everyone found Dick's mild-mannered way to their taste. It was impossible to think him capable of treachery, yet there was a question somewhere in the background only met by silence and sideways glances. There's a grainy black and white photo of my parents' wedding reception in 1942 in which my father, moustached and hair brylcreemed against his scalp, wears a stylish double-breasted, pre-war suit. The other men on his side of the family are in military uniform. And there's the clue: my father didn't wear uniform because he never had one. He was a 'conchie', a conscientious objector; in the minds of many including some of those present a coward and a traitor, hoping for peace in our time but unwilling to fight for it.

When the government imposed the full conscription of men in September 1939, Dick was 22 years old, physically fit, and in his prime for soldiering. To defend his refusal to join up he had to appear before a tribunal. He never spoke of it, but his case was religious objection. I imagine it ran along these lines: he believed in a Saviour who was the Prince of Peace, who, in the Sermon on the Mount, had taught us to turn the other cheek, love our enemies, and pray for those who persecute us. Then, the board members, who had heard it all before, would ask if he would stand by and watch his wife being raped or his children killed by an invading German. How sophisticated would the discussion have been? Would the tribunal have invited him to comment on the theory of Just War, on the grounds it was a mainstream Christian ethical doctrine, rooted in St Augustine, and a counter argument to his Christian pacifist views? Would he have replied that Just War is a theory which applies to states and not to individuals, or more subtly that modern war has stripped away the illusions of a *just* war anyway – too much devastation and very little justice?

Whatever happened, his arguments were accepted and he was ordered to undertake non-combatant work. Thus my parents began their married life in the Quaker village of Jordans in Buckinghamshire, built only a hundred years ago by Quakers who wished for a Christian Utopia where artisans could ply their trades and hone their skills in a rural setting. But the village's Quaker roots go back over three hundred years when the region was so remote it was safe for dissenters from the Church of England to live there. Hidden in woods nearby the modern village is the 1688 Quaker Meeting House, built in three months immediately after James II issued his *Declaration of Indulgence* in 1687, allowing Quakers and other non-conformist groups to worship lawfully for the first time – a simple square room with wooden panelling on the lower part of the walls and free-standing benches on all four sides facing a central table, the floor laid with seventeenth-century red fired bricks.

In Jordans he learnt to drive an ambulance with the Friends Ambulance Unit and to plough a field, typical civilian work regarded by tribunals as most useful in wartime. Although he never claimed it himself, his friends pointed out that driving an ambulance into London during an air raid required as much courage as fighting in the frontline of battle. I was never totally convinced, and felt they wanted to bolster my good opinion of him.

Dick had been supported in the process of making his stand and accepting its consequences, both official and personal, by the *Fellowship of Reconciliation*, a Christian organisation committed to peace. When I was about six or seven, the Fellowship brought a group of German soldiers to London as a gesture of friendship and building new relationships. Each one was lodged with a member. Our guest was Herr Werner Decker, now a school teacher, who had lost an arm in conflict, he never explained how and we were instructed under no circumstances to enquire, but, with one sleeve of his jacket permanently pinned across his front, the question was naggingly ever-present. By then we had moved to a tiny semi-detached house, so tiny my sister had to move out of her bedroom and sleep on a camp bed in in my parents' room to accommodate him, a sacrifice she was too young to resent. Having an extra person in the house meant being more tactical and self-giving than usual in the use of the toilet, an issue of etiquette that got me into serious trouble when I hammered on the door one day telling Herr Decker to 'hurry up'. His embrace of the English idiom was gallant: besides, this was an exercise in reconciliation and mutual understanding. But he was puzzled by the fact my mother served the meals he admired so much, and complimented her upon so readily, through the hatch between the kitchen and dining room. 'What is that called,' he asked, 'the *hatchet*?' Good old Dick assured him we had come together to bury the hatchet, not to use it, and Herr Decker took to that idiomatic phrase with vigour.

Walking to the bus with our guest, going to church, or out shopping, we drew hostile looks. What were people saying? Have you seen Dick's one-armed German? What a nerve! A conchie befriending a man who wanted to kill our children and parading him before us. It's double betrayal. When they met him they discovered Herr Decker was an English teacher who spoke good English, was the father of two boys himself, and had suffered a life-changing injury. Perhaps, after all, he bled as we bleed.

As I reflect now, many years on, stories like this say something morally crucial about how we see war. From a distance, the broad brush, large-scale view can seem banal, ordinary, beyond us, and too big to cope with. Whereas the close-up picture is at our level, in your face, and therefore emotionally unavoidable. For example, the image that did most to end the Vietnam War was the picture of a naked Vietnamese girl, burned by napalm, running down the centre of a road, arms stretched out in agony, face contorted with pain and incomprehension. In one shocking frame it shows the obscenity of war with a power rarely captured by films or newsreels of air raids, guerrilla skirmishes, or armadas. It has a galvanising moral effect through its economy of scale, forcing the viewer to be moved and therefore, subconsciously, to take the quantum leap of recognising within the long-shot of war how many such atrocities must have been brushed out. It's a bit like looking at Google Maps in satellite mode and zooming in: from a distance you see the reticulation of grey roofs and as you zoom in signs of human activity, with all its joys and sorrows, begins to appear – like taking a spade, digging a spit of turf and seeing the complexity of life beneath it. Herr Decker was the zoomed-in version of the aftermath of the Second World War and his visit witnessed to the possibility of healing even my grandmother's prejudice. Just as bigots discover Muslims, women priests, and dentists, when you get to know them, can turn out to be very nice people, so Werner Decker proved to be 'pretty good for a Kraut', and through that the Fellowship of Reconciliation had succeeded in living up to its name.

In 1982, after the Falkland's War, there was a service of thanksgiving in St Paul's Cathedral. The then Dean of Paul's, Alan Webster, told me Mrs Thatcher was against having prayers for the Argentinians and their dead soldiers included in the service. What the Government really wanted was a victory parade and a big propaganda statement of how we had stood for democratic liberty against the fascist dictator Galtieri. Eventually Cardinal Basil Hume, the Archbishop of Westminster, told Mrs T that if these prayers were not included, he would hold a service in Westminster Cathedral at the same time as the St Paul's service in which he would pray for the Argentinians. That did the trick. Canon Paul Oestreicher, who was working for the British Council of Churches at the time, unpacked the theology of it in what seemed to me a splendidly succinct way. He wrote that the task of church leaders is not to reflect public opinion or to bless political decisions, but to reflect the mind of Christ. A prophetic stance, he suggested, is to be in a state of *critical solidarity* with the nation.

*

Prior to this coda on war and peace, there I was sitting on the swing in the doorway looking forward to Dad's return. For a few weeks Mum had been feeling unwell during the day and I learned there was soon to be another arrival. My sister was born in Clapton General Hospital, run by the Salvation Army, where Mum had once been a nursing assistant. I would have been born there too had it not been for war time evacuation. Instead I took my first breath in Willersley Castle in Matlock, near Derby, which had been taken over by the Clapton maternity unit. A multitude of mothers from East London gave birth there, in the rhododendroned lushness of the domestic Peak District, giving a multitude of post-war kids delusions of grandeur.

'Where were you born?'

'In a castle.'

'What, you? Getaway, you're kidding.'

Dad was now in permanent residence and on Sunday mornings I was allowed into their bed. He made a cup of tea, and the baby suckled at my mother's enormous nipples, a phenomenon I noted with a very private curiosity.

I now had more freedom to play on my own, but there was one forbidden game: cowboys and Indians. Despite repeated requests, I was not allowed a toy gun, so I used a stick instead and my belt as the holster. One day my mother asked accusingly what I thought I was doing. I explained I was 'a boy who kept cows', but the subtlety was lost on her and she clipped me round the ear. I did eventually have a toy pistol that fired caps which exploded with a very satisfying crack, and an intoxicating smell of sulphur smoke. I think my mother relented on the grounds that forbidden fruit is much more enticing than what is freely permitted. She had been to an evening class on psychology and learnt about Freud and Jung. She theorised about love and said she was a Jungian because his ideas were more sympathetic to Christianity. When I was at grammar school I had a precocious familiarity with the idea of the collective subconscious, which, when I referred to it in class, prompted the master to ask if I knew how to spell Jung and when I answered 'J-U-N-G' he seemed surprised, almost disappointed.

By pretending to be a cowboy, far from nurturing my inner gangster, I was simply exploring how to be. It was a phase; I grew out of it. It was no different when, a few years older, I went to the Century Cinema and saw films like *Bridge over the River Kwai* and *Ice cold in Alex* and being so absorbed that when I came out I walked home with a bouncing step, either as an invincible hero or in love with Sylvia Syms. I didn't actually think I was a soldier in the Burmese Jungle or a soldier struggling across the Western Desert in a crippled lorry, but I had for a short time been in the shoes of those men, and suffered as they did, and faced the almost impossible moral dilemmas that confronted them: do I speak up for my men and face two days in a corrugated iron 'oven' prison? Do I hand over for execution the enemy officer who has helped us get through the desert?

Philip Pullman argues this much better than me in his essay *Imaginary Friends* in *Daemon Voices* where he describes his own experience of pretending to be Davy Crockett. He gets his trademark literary device – that everyone has a personal animal 'daemon' – from this experience of imaginative identification with a character in a story, or role-playing in a game: you want to continue being yourself, but you enjoy identifying with other lives and other roles, and you learn a great deal, often subconsciously, from the experience. That is the state of mind, Pullman suggests, in which you hear your daemon speak.

Discovering how to be, it seems to me, is a religious idea: you learn how to be by imagining what it would be like to be someone else, which is an aspect, among other things, of what it means to love your neighbour as yourself.

The walks of childhood

In his 1987 work of narrative nonfiction, *The Songlines*, Bruce Chatwin writes:

'Proust, more perspicaciously than any other writer, reminds us that the "walks" of childhood form the raw material of our intelligence.'

I like the image of walks as a metaphor for all the ingrained memories of childhood, from the topography of a bedroom, to a much-travelled route to school, to the sensation of being small and powerless in a gigantic world. Experience moves fast like a fairground ride, and through to your late teens your body chemistry is so volatile the way you see and imagine things is magnified, sometimes out of all proportion. For most people this is the only time in their life when they see as an artist – an enlarged, impressionistic, fantastic, and often deeply symbolical vision. At the time, childhood seems unendingly long, so awesomely all-consuming and world-shaping, you have no idea that seen from the outside it looks to others like a series of small and inconsequential events – the lost pen, the frightening picture on the wall, the misinterpreted word or action.

One of my 'walks' is the London Transport 38A bus route between Loughton and Walthamstow, where my paternal grandmother lived in Beulah Road, and my maternal grandparents in Wood Street, above their barber's shop. We didn't have a car until I was seventeen, so relied on buses and bicycles. To me, 38A was never a number, more a picture – a red Routemaster bus, with 'Victoria' in bold letters on its rolling destination blind displayed on the front. We used to wait for it to appear out of the distance, radiator and front windows like the face of a strong and reliable uncle. When it came to a halt, the big diesel engine turned over with slow deliberate strokes like the purring of a gigantic, oily cat. I liked best to sit at the front on the lower deck where I could peek into the driver's cabin and rub my shoes on the tooth-edged steel cover over the transmission, making a skiffle noise like strumming on a washboard.

The house in Wood Street, where my grandad stood all day behind one of the three swivel chairs in his barber's shop cutting hair and nattering about the Arsenal or the Korean war with men who sat there gazing preeningly into the mirror, has haunted me throughout my life. I used to watch from the benches at the back of the shop where men, waiting their turn, read the *Daily Mirror* or the *Racing Times*. After the customer had seen his hair from every angle in the hand-held mirror and nodded his satisfaction, Grandad would select a cut-throat razor from the console, sharpen it with a rapid flip-flap against the leather strop and shave away the wispy hairs with deft strokes of the deadly instrument, before finally blowing on talcum powder from a rubber puffer, removing the towel and brushing out the prickly cuttings from beneath the customer's collar.

As soon as there was a lull in trade, Grandad placed a wooden booster-seat across the arms of the chair and called me over, lifted me up onto the seat, tucked a clean towel into my collar, and, with the flourish of a matador enticing a bull, wrapped me round with a Bengal blue and white striped cape.

'How would you like it, Sonny?'

'Short back and sides, please, Sir,' I had learned to say. Then the haircut proceeded with many interruptions while Grandad sipped his tea or made butterflies from his cigarette papers which he blew into the air and I watched them flutter down like winged seeds into the litter of hair cuttings on the cracked brown lino. Most intriguing to me were the instruments on the console: the neat row of cut-throats, scissors with teeth, hand clippers of different sizes, tapers for singeing, unlabelled bottles of sweet-smelling coloured liquids, shaving brushes and lather bowls, and the styptic pencil. I knew what the styptic pencil was for, and that it stung, but couldn't understand how it worked.

'Have you ever cut anyone, Grandad?' I asked.

'Little nicks sometimes, but nothing to worry about.'

My Grandmother Rose died in this early period, just before I was old enough to go to school. She'd been ill for a long time with pains in her tummy and I used to visit her in the front bedroom. From that higher window on the third floor, I could watch the trains leaving Wood Street Station and the engines hissing and steaming.

'Come here and sit on the bed,' she'd say, and reluctantly, I'd leave the window and perch on the bottom edge of it, sickened by her smell. Moulded in the bedclothes I saw the shape of a shrinking human form.

'Come on, your grandmother's not a wolf,' she said, and I shifted closer, shyly smiling at her, but her eyes were distracted by pain.

'Shall I get out the musical box?' I'd ask. She'd nod and I

scrambled under the bed to pull out the heavy mahogany box. I opened the lid, wound up the handle, and pulled the starter lever. The brass cylinder began to revolve, and its spikes plucked at the metal tines producing a Viennese waltz. Grandma closed her eyes and briefly the tense lines of her face relaxed and she was twenty years younger. 'In the old days your grandad and I used to dance to this down at the Palais.'

I loved the journey home on winter evenings on the 38A in the warm cabin of the lower deck with the driver protected from the lights by a leather pull-down blind, and the damp gaberdine smell of people coming home from work on a wet night all flustered and pulling their belongings together to make room for someone else to sit beside them. At the front on the yellow paintwork was a sign which read NO SMOKING. Grandad told me there was a jazz musician, Nosmo King, who had taken his name from it, and I thought how clever to get a name out of a sign on a bus. Beneath the sign was an advert for orange squash in which a West Indian man is saying: I like IDRIS when I'S DRI. Perhaps Nosmo King invented it – the slogan.

Early one morning my parents stood solemnly at the foot of my bed.

'We have something to tell you,' said my father. 'Your grandmother, Rose, has gone to live with Jesus.'

I understood immediately what he meant. I wondered what living with Jesus would be like. She would be joining the budgerigar and the goldfish who had also been said to have disappeared to that happy place. I knew they were trying to soften the blow of death. A few days later, I heard Mum telling our neighbours they couldn't get the rings off Grandma's fingers, and Alf had decided to leave her wedding ring on but have the diamond rings cut off!

Mum and I continued to pay our weekly visits: she cleaned and prepared meals in advance for Grandad. But the house began to spook me. 'Just go upstairs and fetch the towels from

Grandma's room,' she said.

'Only if you come with me,' I pleaded.

'Don't be so silly. You're not afraid to go by yourself, are you?'

I was petrified. I didn't know what they had done with Grandma. I was scared she might be under the bed with the musical box, withered and skeletal and grimacing, with bloody marks where her rings had been, but I daren't own up because I could tell Mum would be annoyed and was determined I should go up there. Repeatedly, she found excuses: 'You know you like to watch the trains from the top window.' Or, 'I need someone to put these flowers on the washstand in Grandma's room.' Then I braced myself to clamber up the stairs into that nightmare world, where I was terrified I might stumble upon gruesome remains. I tried to keep the bed out of my line of vision, but it was impossible not to glimpse it, un-made-up, blankets folded into small heaps and covered with the counterpane, suggesting shapes which sent me wild with fear. I arrived back downstairs in a cold sweat, my heart jumping. That damned psychology class again.

Moving house

By then my mother had found insuperable problems with our house in Church Hill: a) it was rented and b) had no 'mod cons'. Wouldn't I like to live in a nice new house with a bath and toilet upstairs? I wasn't sure I would.

In 1951 her dream came true and we moved to a brand-new semi in Marjorams Avenue. You entered the glass-paned front door into a small entrance hall, with the stairs immediately in front of you and the kitchen beyond. To the right was a single long living room. They'd been given the choice of that or two small reception rooms and had sensibly chosen the former, which was fine until it came to doing homework and there was no private place to work other than a freezing bedroom with no table to write on. The house had no extension at the back; one of Paul McCartney's little boxes. By the front door was a black Bakelite telephone. No conversation could be private. When Dad answered the phone, he put on his half-crown voice. 'R J W Mountford speaking,' he would say, all la-de-dah, and if it was the minister phoning with the hymns for Sunday – Dad was the choirmaster – he'd continue in that manner.

'Do you have to use that half-crown voice?' my mother screamed from the kitchen.

My parents never moved again. Forty years later, when Dad died, I had to clear the house and sell it. What had seemed throughout childhood like permanence, was suddenly revealed as ephemeral stage scenery in which we had acted our play. The piano, the dining table and chairs, the gramophone, the framed print of *The Avenue at Middelharnis* by Meindert Hobbema, the only picture in the house, my mother having no time for pictures; these were things that had always been there, but now disposable items of little worth to anyone else. As I look at my own home now I try to imagine how my daughter sees it: the same illusion of permanence, the way the furniture is placed, the way the house is organised, all marks of our individuality, all ways of describing what we are and, when we are dead, she will deconstruct our symbols and behold the fleeting nature of our lives.

Good old Dick had been diagnosed with spinal cancer. He never even suggested he might need residential care. He wanted to continue living at home and didn't want to be any trouble to anyone. He was of a generation that had learnt self-sufficiency through austerity, reluctant to trouble the doctor unless an illness was really serious and consequently finding it hard to know when that point had arrived. Stoically he lived on at home sleeping in the living room with a portable toilet beside his bed to save his having to go upstairs and although carers visited the house each day, he never had a bath. One day, after much hesitation, he asked if I would bathe him. I was pleased and, if it doesn't seem mawkishly clichéd, honoured to be able do this for the man who had always been so gentle towards me. I could see this role reversal, in the same bathroom where as a child I had been washed, was emotionally costly, an admission of impotence, a kind of submission. First, we had to get up the stairs, me straining and shouldering him like a soldier supporting an injured comrade from the battlefield. Then he had to undress and I felt ashamed I had to see his naked body, fragile and bent, skin pale and spotted with brown moles that had grown large, wispy grey hairs soft and feeble around his nipples, and I embraced my ancient progenitor and lowered him carefully into the water. With evident delight he took the soap and massaged his head and hair into a lather before scooping up water with his hands to rinse it clean, but, unable to reach for himself, he asked me to scrub his back and as I did so sighed with pleasure, 'Ah! Lovely. How nice to feel clean.'

The morning he died he pressed his emergency button, but when the ambulance came he was already dead. I went to identify his body at the morgue where he had been laid out by one of his old pupils. 'Your father was a very kind man,' he said as he pulled back the sheet.

Coronation

In 1950, the average UK annual salary was just over £100. In 1952 my grandfather gave Dad £200 in one-pound notes to buy four televisions, one for us and one for each of Mum's siblings. It was a lot of money, a tenth of the value of our house, and my father was very edgy with it. On the bus home he held the wad of notes firmly in his trouser pocket, not daring to let go, and when we got in, he repeatedly counted them for fear one might have gone missing. In 1953 there were three million TVs in British homes and on the 2nd June that year 27 million people gathered round those screens to watch the coronation of Queen

Elizabeth II. Mum had invited our neighbours from both sides and kept up a running buffet of cups of tea, sandwiches and cakes. Mr and Mrs Traveller, the old couple from number 21 were quiet and grateful, which was more than could be said for the Bennetts from number 25. Jack Bennett repeatedly made loud-mouthed comments, even in the solemn moments.

It began with rain, Queen Salote of Tonga at six foot three, Richard Dimbleby, then our young Queen, happy and glorious, waving from the Coronation Coach, drawn by eight Windsor Greys, the archetype for Cinderella's pumpkin coach. Once in the Abbey the solemnities began. Mr Bennett never went to church and seemed to find it amusing. 'So that's what you get up to on a Sunday is it, Dick?' I wished he'd be quiet because the pageantry was affecting even to a boy of eight, and my emotions stirred at the sound of the trumpets and organ. The anthem, 'May the King live, may the King live, for ever, for ever' seemed odd for a Queen, but I understood (I think) a notion of kingship shared by whoever reigned. The climactic moment of the service was the anointing. Dimbleby announced in a whisper, 'And now – the anointing'. This was to be performed by the Archbishop of Canterbury beneath a great canopy where the camera would not be allowed in. 'I wouldn't mind seeing that,' said Mr Bennett. The adults smiled politely. The monarch was to be anointed not only upon the head, but upon the breast. 'Lucky old Archbishop. I bet he'll enjoy that bit,' leered Mr Bennett. My father chortled, with laddish obligation; the women glanced nervously at one another.

Since wartime rationing in Britain didn't finally end until 1954, my mother gave me enough coupons each week to buy two ounces of sweets. Sixteen ounces to the pound, fourteen pounds to the stone, eight stones to one hundredweight and twenty hundredweight to the ton. Sweets were purchased from Mr Cook the Grocer. On the counter stood a row of candy jars containing aniseed whirls, humbugs, liquorice sticks, lengths of toffee flapjack, sherbet lemons and sherbet dabs, twisted barley sugar and coloured chews. There was a jar of penny gobstoppers and another of bubble gum in pink wraps, both of which were forbidden to me on the grounds of their being common and only consumed by gutter snipes; my fear of my mother was such I never bought either. Mrs Cook, or sometimes her daughter, June, would measure the loose sweets in the metal pan of the scales and tip them into a white paper bag. As an alternative to sweets I sometimes bought a penny bun from Lewin's the Baker. These were soft and delicious but didn't last any longer than the short distance from Lewin's to School, whereas two ounces of sweets would at least last the day and usually two.

But there was a third shop with a deeper lure, 'Ernie's Bar', exquisitely sordid and risky. Ernie's was a few doors up Church Hill from the King's Head pub and the stinky outside toilets where we used to smoke drinking straws. Every classroom had boxes of these paper and wax straws through which we sucked the daily third-of-a-pint of bone-building milk the government had decreed every child should drink. It was easy to take an extra one. After school we assembled in the toilets, one person keeping watch while the others lit up. The straw would flame and we sucked in the disgusting smoke and coughed it out with much discussion whether straws contained nicotine. The only reason to suspect that they might was that the burning wax produced a foul brown grease in the tube of the straw. It seemed as daring to go into Ernie's, where stubbly men sat smoking and drinking tea. It wasn't a place for the fainthearted. The floor was covered in fag ends and biscuit wrappers and the men teased us: 'sure you can see over the bar, sonny?' 'Have some *Tizer* – that'll put hairs on yer chest'. The bar was famous for its fizzy drinks poured from 'Corona' bottles with snap-on porcelain caps. 'Corona' was another evil I was not allowed. On the first occasion I mustered the courage to enter Ernie's, my heart fluttered so much that when the great man asked, 'What do you want, sonny?' I replied, 'How much is a penny drink, Ernie?' At which everyone in the café, smoking men and scruffy kids alike, laughed and pointed at me and asked how much did I think, and wouldn't let the matter drop until I replied, 'A penny?' I wanted to appear tough in this cowboy saloon but ended up humiliated.

It was between the King's Head toilets and Ernie's that Terry Rattee asked me if I wanted to know the rudest word in the English language. To think I might be in possession of such dangerous information worried me and I said I wasn't sure, but he was determined to tell me anyway, or knock my bloody block off. The word of course was 'fuck', but no one could explain exactly what it meant, just that it was extremely rude and only to be mentioned amongst ourselves and never to be used at home or in public.

Terry Rattee's female *alter ego* was Carol Boyton, physically spare with the face of an urchin and a knowing huskiness in her cockney voice. Carol's older sister also had that East End rough diamond temperament, like a kid version of Barbara Windsor. When we were about seven or eight a rumour went round that Carol was in possession of a startling revelation vouchsafed to her by this same sister, and during playtime Carol held court to explain that to make a baby a man must push his ship into a lady's harbour, which actually meant putting his willy into her willy. This extraordinary claim seemed to us totally unbelievable, quite beyond the realms of credibility, or even likelihood. It was both disgusting and impossible to imagine. Had my parents done such a thing in the process of getting me? I hardly think so. I was far too clean a specimen to have started out through such a sordid act. Little did I know I was thinking through the raw theology of the Fall and original sin, a theology I would come to reject very early on.

Eleven Plus

The most life-changing event in our pre-pubescent lives was known by parents and children alike as 'The Scholarship'. The teachers at Staples Road told us it was about selection and what was best for us and not a scholarship at all. But everyone knew that a grammar school education was incomparably superior to a secondary modern one and we spoke of it as something to be passed or failed.

They had to lay on extra buses to get us all to Buckhurst Hill County High School for the exam. Although our junior school was mixed, for this purpose we were separated, the boys going to Buckhurst Hill and the girls to Loughton High School. Buckhurst Hill was the school I would go to if I were to pass. The building (1938 neo-Georgian, central green copper lantern above the main hall) had a kind of beauty, not evident to me then. That day in February 1956 it felt soullessly modern, the tarmac playground surrounded by cycle sheds and concrete air raid shelters. The playground howled with screaming kids from junior schools around the district until someone blew a whistle and told us to line up. There were two papers: arithmetic, including long division and pounds shillings and pence (if Jill's mother bought a cardigan for £1 3s 11d and three pairs of socks for 11d each, how much change would she have from a five pound note?) and English, which included writing a story.

We had to wait three weeks for the results and on the morning appointed, mothers up and down our road waited in their front gardens for the postman to arrive. He was like the angel of death, except in this case if he passed by your house you were doomed rather than the other way round. To my relief and my mother's joy, the postman stopped at our house.

In our class of forty, three boys and one girl had been awarded grammar school places. Sandra Moore hadn't received a letter and was slumped over her desk sobbing, with her head in her arms, while other girls gathered round as if at the scene of a road accident, but she was inconsolable, her life was ended and her hopes dashed. I had never seen such desolation. Her plight drew attention to the momentous divide thrust upon us that day, the rift between success and failure, but most children seemed to take the results in their stride, not having expected to pass in the first place. At 11.30am Sandra's mother came into the school: a letter had arrived in the second post and Sandra's desolation was turned into hysterical joy. She had always been such a quiet girl.

Flippin Ada

My Mum's name was Ada. By the time I was at the grammar school, in the borderlands of cockney London, I'd often hear the playground oaths, 'flippin Ada', 'bleedin Ada', or even 'fuckin Ada', none of which did anything to enhance my confidence in my roots. I knew no other Adas, young or old, until in 2018 the Norwegian international footballer, Ada Hegerberg, swerved and shimmied on the field of play. Yet the name had pedigree: the second woman named in the Bible, the wife of Lamech, was Adah. 'Adah bore Jabal; he was the ancestor of those who live in tents and have livestock. His brother's name was Jubal; he was the ancestor of all those who play the lyre and pipe' (Genesis 4.20).

10 words to describe my mother

Cross – without warning or apparent reason. When her 'cross face' threatened, we children knew to take cover.

Religious – that is to say, an ardent churchgoer, if not always obviously Christian.

Shy – lacking self-esteem.

Repressed – how painful it must have been for her to have all her love locked up inside her, unable to let it out or exult in it, and thus be loved in return.

Chubby – my father's term of affection for her.

Violent – ferocious temper with a bamboo cane in her hand and that in a pacifist household.

Bespectacled – National Health. Could seem bookish.

Dexterous – nifty with practical things, handy with a needle, or a brush, or a hammer.

Awkward – ungainly in society; rarely went to anything other than a church social.

Disappointed – felt she could have done better in life, but instead of blaming it on herself, laid the burden at my father's feet. It wasn't his fault she was jilted by the minister's son, or that the war happened when it did, or having won five prizes for matriculation she left school at sixteen because her father wouldn't/couldn't pay for her any longer.

Were the everyday words of diminishment, cemented into our vocabulary from an early age, expressions of the anger she felt? Twerp, clot, bugaboo, silly oaf, spiv, guttersnipe, juvenile delinquent, yobbo, and nincompoop. Her vocabulary was splattered with bloodies, bloody fool the most common, but no sexual swear words. She was puritan at heart.

She was the third of four children and her younger brother, Reginald, was a late addition to the fold, born when Rose was forty-nine years old. He studied piano at the Guildhall School of Music. This was the nearest any of that generation of my family came to going to university. On one of his rare visits to our house – I suppose I was about ten years old – he asked me what I was learning on the piano. I told him Bach's Prelude in D major (BWV 936).

'This is one of the most beautiful melodies Bach ever wrote,' he said and, with his hands over my shoulders, played the piece with such delicacy and phrasing that it seemed to me quite new.

Like me he developed his musical interest through church, in his case at St Peter's in the Forest, Walthamstow, an Italianate theatre of the divine, where he also served as an altar boy and discovered a vocation to become a priest. But his parents objected on the grounds that his father was a Jew. It wasn't until Grandad died, springing across the bed in a final death spasm, as Ada described the event to her friends, and Reg was nearly forty, that he was free to go to Wells Theological College to train for the priesthood prior to spending twenty-five years as a kindly, humorous, impoverished, and, truth to tell, bumbling parson.

During his time at Wells, we took a family holiday near Porlock and the Doone Valley. There was a bus trip from there to Wells and Ada decided it would be nice to make a visit. Three things I remember about that outing: the wonderful fourteenth-century Vicars Close, where Reg, Hazel and their kids were living; the visit to the organ loft where he played Bach's *St Anne Prelude and Fugue*; and when we took his guided tour of the cathedral, as we passed in front of the high altar, he suddenly and unexpectedly genuflected, down on one knee, and we tumbled over him creating a ludicrous scene. I assumed this catastrophic showing-of-ourselves-up would result in a later tirade of maternal wrath and scorn, but rather than tear us off a strip for being such clumsy imbeciles, she complained that Reg ought to have warned us he'd gone all high church and that'd teach him for trying to be clever. When, years later, in St Mary the Virgin, Oxford, I did exactly the same thing over Rowan Williams, the Archbishop of Canterbury, in front of my own high altar, I scarcely thought it wise to tell him not to be so High Church.

We never saw much of Stanley, my father's younger brother, because Ada was not his number one fan. She referred to him as 'your Uncle Shtanley' because he had a lisp and, as a child, had called my father 'Lishley', being incapable of getting his tongue round the word Richard.

In those days divorce in the family was a scandal and an embarrassment. If your marriage was on the rocks, you were expected to make the best of it. In the Church of England women could be excommunicated and drummed out of the Mothers' Union for it.

On her Thursday visits, Grandma Mountford had assailed us with stories of how well Stanley was doing at work, and how much he was earning. 'He's a thousand-a-year man, you know.'

'What nonsense. Stanley's never on a thousand a year, is he, Dick?'

Dad didn't know, or if he did wasn't going to say. Stanley often received small pay rises and was sent away on important assignments around the country on behalf of his company by a boss who clearly recognised his potential. 'Stanley? Potential? My foot.' What neither mother nor son recognised was that while Stanley was away transforming the commercial face of Britain, his boss was shagging my Auntie Iris, no glamour girl, but clearly more to her than met the eye.

When the divorce papers were filed, Ada told us not to breathe a word of it to anyone. She asked me whether I thought divorce was right. Being in my third year of Latin at school, I immediately recognised this as a *num* question, expecting the answer no. 'There you are,' she cried triumphantly to Grandma, 'Brian says it's wrong.'

For all that, I am indebted to Stan for one thing. He invited me to the great 'cathedral' of Congregationalism, the City Temple, to hear Dr Leslie Weatherhead preach. To get a decent seat you had to arrive early, queuing as if for a football match right across Holborn Viaduct, but without the shoving, or purveyors of replica team kit. I still remember that sermon preached on a text, surprising for a non-conformist, from Cranmer's prayer of 'Humble Access' in the Anglican Book of Common Prayer: 'and so to eat the flesh of thy dear Son'. It was about the sacramental meaning of Holy Communion and eating as a metaphor for loving. In the gallery people sat spellbound and when Dr Weatherhead observed in his grandfatherly way that a mother will sometimes look at her baby in its pram and think, he's so lovely I could eat him, there was an audible exhalation of breath from the many women in the congregation, who exchanged knowing glances of empathic self-identification with this commonplace expression now rendered theological. Having roused the emotions, he illustrated the same point with a slightly risqué joke about a husband biting his wife's ear. This man and wife were in bed together and the wife, about to turn out the light, said to her husband, 'Darling, once upon a time you used to kiss me good night.' So, he gave her a kiss. A little while later she said, 'Darling, once upon a time you used to put your arm around me.' Dutifully he put his arm around her. A little while later she said, 'Darling, once upon a time you used to bite my ear.' On hearing this, the husband very suddenly got out of bed and headed for the door. 'Where are you going, darling?' she whispered.

'To the bathroom to fetch my teeth.'

Laughter filled the Temple, women wept, possibly even thinking he's so lovely I could eat him, men guffawed, and above all everyone was on Dr Weatherhead's side, waiting for what he would say next, which was heavy and substantial: when you eat something it becomes a part of you and therefore it is essential for the Christian to take in Christ as a part of him or herself with that same loving desire, and in the process to be transformed by Christ. This is what the sacrament can do: 'and so to eat the flesh of thy dear Son'.

I had expected that when he prayed he would do so with similar oratorical flourish, but he spoke so quietly that at first I could scarcely hear him, and the congregation fell hushed into an extraordinarily concentrated silence. I was fifteen and moved by the message, but I also felt a thrill in my bones at his charismatic presence and wanted to have such charisma myself to be able to create this experience for others.

Gay

One day my mother came home from the Women's Meeting in a state of unusual agitation and ill-disguised excitement. 'Never go near that girl, Gay Shingleton,' she barked.

'Why not?' I asked.

'I'm not sure I ought to tell you.' She paused. 'She's not a good girl. She could get you into trouble'.

'With the police?'

'It could even come to that.'

I was genuinely puzzled.

'I don't want this getting around, so you'd better not mention to anyone. Last week her mother came home early from work and found her in bed with a man.'

Had Mrs Shingleton told the whole Women's Meeting and Mrs Shingleton didn't want it getting around?

'Seriously, you're to be very careful.'

Did my mother honestly think I might be next in line for such exquisite pleasure? She was the schoolgirl 'Brigitte Bardot' of our town, angel-faced, buxom, and provocative. When one saw a flash of her legs above the knee, there were holes in her black stockings through which pressed goujons of white flesh causing male hearts to miss a beat.

To my amazement, the next Friday night Gay turned up at choir practice. She had never been to church before, and now she was in the choir. At my mother's behest, Good old Dick had admitted her as a soprano as part of a campaign, co-ordinated by various parents, to divert her from the bedroom to the straight and narrow. What did the puritanical Sunday congregation make of this radiantly nubile presence in the front row of the choirstalls, tempting as Eve in Eden? I could see the men thought she was manna from heaven during those dull sermons. Instead of looking at the preacher in the pulpit on the opposite side of the church, they gazed straight ahead at the Lord's Table so, with an imperceptible shift of the eyes to the right, they could glimpse the young Jezebel. Yes, her story was out. Women studiously failed to notice her, but afterwards gathered round to shield her from their menfolk.

Oh, the complicated, inscrutable girl. In her presence I tried to hide my spots with my hand and waited for her to speak first.

'Don't be frightened. I won't eat you,' she said glad to talk to someone her own age. She seemed surprisingly innocent and ordinary. The choir experiment was short lived because in a matter of weeks she became a small-time celebrity, getting a job as a dancer on TV's Saturday evening *Top of the Pops*.

Gay was lucky she wasn't my mother's daughter. After I left home for university Ada had the most fearsome confrontations with my sister about boyfriends and curfews. There was a silly joke doing the rounds at the College of Further Education my sister attended: 'Mum,' (with two syllables – mu-um) 'I am going to have a baby,' (long pause) 'in ten years' time.' My sister didn't get past the first half of the joke before pandemonium broke out, involving the cane and a carving knife – no knife wounds, I might add – but today the police and social services would be called in.

On top of the kitchen cabinet she kept three bamboo canes. *Thrash* was her word, and it was apt because she would flail manically and indiscriminately, leaving weals on legs and arms. This biblical lady believed if she spared the rod, she would spoil the child. Despite those evening classes in psychology, she seemed to have no idea that while violence might force a kind of moral conformity, it might also drive a wedge of alienation between us for ever, but, having come from working-class East London, she was determined to claw her family up the social ladder into a world of wider opportunity. It was for our own good. 'Keep your shoulders back or you'll look like your father,' she'd scold as we walked down the road. 'Learn to say your vowels properly.'

Buckhurst Hill County High School

When reminded in recent years by a persistent Editor that I hadn't renewed my subscription to the Old Boys School Magazine, I explained to him my reluctance stems from the fact the school no longer exists. It was closed in 1989. News, therefore, can only be of those receding into the past towards extinction until no one is left. There is no longer an institution to belong to, no meaning to be found in raising funds for the future or supporting and mentoring a present generation of children.

From my first day I cycled the three miles from home to school and back again in the afternoon. On arrival, each of us was issued with a red school hymn book with the school song pasted in the back and every morning with military precision six hundred boys moved in silence from classroom to hall for assembly. Opened, as I say, in 1938 it was almost new and the type of school to have had instant tradition thrust upon it. The song summed it up:

'Firm set above the Roding stream

By calm and grassy leas

Our house stands fairly to the winds

'Twixt Essex lanes and trees.

And we within its walls are found

Like loyal sons we rest

Contriving how our varied gifts

May serve the school the best.'

When, five years ago, I parked my car by the perimeter fence, around which our cross-country runs always began, I snooped in and saw the building looking drab, the metal window frames rusty, the swimming pool green and neglected. And now the M11 runs through what was then a cornfield from which it was a punishable offence to retrieve a ball. I once received a detention slip on which the master had written, 'for trampling a growing crop'. If any reality corresponded to the line, 'twixt Essex lanes and trees', it was this area now desecrated by the motorway.

Like most grammar schools of the day, ours was run on traditional lines: all boys, streaming according to academic ability, beatings, privileges accorded to seniority, prefects, ties reflecting a hierarchical structure, house matches, masters who wore academic gowns and had fought in the war, all university graduates. Nearly all pupils were lower to lower-middle class, most from semi-detached houses, including the local London County Council Debden housing estate, which had taken an overflow of people from London's East End immediately after the War.

When I was eleven, I also won a Junior Exhibition to the Guildhall School of Music and Drama, at that time in John Carpenter Street, off the Victoria Embankment between the old City of London School and Sion College. As you approached it, especially in summer when the windows were open, you were bombarded by a cacophony of sound: instruments being played in different keys, the whining of strings being tuned, and the flourish of arpeggios. It was like a great out of control musical box in a nightmarish children's story. The interior of the building was maze-like, reaching up seven floors, with corridors of rooms each with a glazed door through which you could see 'the piano lesson', or 'the violin lesson', like Edwardian prints – prodigious pupils in manic animation, languid teachers hearing out unpractised pieces. It meant a fifty-minute journey every Saturday on the Central Line, changing at Mile End, and then the grimy District Line to Blackfriars on trains that were almost empty at the weekends, except in the holiday season when families piled in with suitcases on their way to Victoria and the South Coast. My instrument was the piano, with a smattering of violin, until I studied the organ with Howard Fletcher.

For many of my contemporaries, like Sonia Davidoff, Christopher Gunning and Anthony Pleeth, the son of William Pleeth, Jaqueline Dupree's teacher, this music opportunity was their chief pursuit. For me it was just one of many. At fourteen

I was in the school athletics team and when I excused myself from training because I had to attend an orchestral rehearsal, the PE master told me my trouble was I was a jack of all trades and master of none. He was right. And this religion business didn't help, either, because belonging to an active church family meant I had to attend scout meetings, choir practice, youth club, and three services on a Sunday.

Paper Round

Despite all that, after much cajoling I persuaded my mother to allow me to take on a paper round as well. Her fears had been that early mornings and socialising with other paper boys from the Debden Council Estate would inhibit my academic progress. On the first point she was right. Duffle-coated and gloved, in the depth of winter, I arrived at the newsagent's at 7.00am, eased my pile of papers into a newsprint-blackened canvas sack, and cycled off on my round. First the alms-houses, then the new four-bedroomed villas, and thence to the houses along the edge of Epping Forest on Baldwin's Hill, including one that had belonged to Jacob Epstein, with some of his sculptures still in the garden. The road ran along a ridge. At one point there were no houses and the grassy hill, a popular site for tobogganing in winter, fell steeply away into the widest part of the Forest. This was the prettiest part of our town. On the far side of the valley was a massive bank of dense woodland, which in April and May resounded with a dawn chorus that rang with sustained, climactic music, including the voices of many birds now rare or disappeared from the forest: fieldfare, yellow hammer, tree sparrow, tree pipit, chiff chaff, marsh tit, and corncrake. Above their accompaniment the cuckoo soloists threw insistent major thirds at one another.

Birds in spring, spiders in autumn: I had no choice but to observe the changes of the passing seasons. On September mornings tiny droplets of water glistened on the gossamer across garden paths, but on the dry mornings of those cobwebby days I had to proceed with a folded newspaper held erect in front of my face, like a cavalry officer's sword at the Trooping of the Colour, to break the webs before they wrapped round my face.

The boy selected to mentor me in the art of newspaper delivery arrived in the shop at 6.30am because he was a marker-upper who sorted the papers and scribbled the house numbers on them for an extra ten bob a week. Alan Robinson was strong and handsome in the manner of Alan Bates, with a smooth, muscular body, a snappy dresser, but not the sharpest knife in the box, a secondary modern boy who attended Roding Road School where my father taught music. Two years my senior, he brought to our friendship tales of Saturday night and Sunday morning as yet unknown to me. At the church youth club he had had the good fortune to dance with Lucy, the most beautiful girl in the club, long auburn hair, brown eyes, sweet nose, and shapely legs. She allowed him to feel her bra and touch her breast and hopefully she would let him go further if he could make her 'his bird'. What was the name of the dance... moonlight something? 'Must be Moonlight Sonata,' I said with utter confidence. He swore that wasn't right, but I insisted and he deferred to my superior musical knowledge.

On Sundays I finished my round before Alan started his second and, in return for a couple of fags, I'd help him with his to get round in double quick time. That was when we reviewed his love life. Lucy was a tease.

'Probably playing hard-to-get,' I suggested.

'But definitely worth it. Such a tasty bit of crumpet, I'd really like her to be my steady.'

'Perhaps you shouldn't go too fast; take your time, smooth it.'

I didn't have a clue what I meant by 'smooth it', but in an odd way I thought it profound advice.

Mum enjoyed a dance, so I quizzed her about dances

beginning with moonlight. 'Oh, Moonlight Serenade,' she replied immediately. 'Why? What do you need to know that for?'

'Oh, nothing.'

Alan and I played cricket for Loughton Union Church Cricket Club on the Council playing fields in the flood plain of the River Roding, changing in wartime Nissen huts with no running water, some distance from the field of play and rough-cut wicket which we had to roll ourselves. This is what the posh boys called 'agricultural'. We shared common kit: bats, gloves, pads, and protective box, which we shoved into tight swimming trunks to keep it in place, batsmen returning to the boundary after their innings, reaching into their trousers to pass the scrofulous item to the next man, who gratefully accepted it presumably because he valued the intactness of his private parts more than hygiene.

I tried to play the shots my father had taught me in the field behind our house, the cut, the glance, the drive and pull, but batters mainly slogged the ball, if they could connect with it, to 'cow corner' and bowlers aimed at raw speed, each imagining himself a Frank Tyson or Fred Truman. If you hit the ball into the river it was 'six and out'. Unsophisticated though our techniques were, in winter we took the tube to Leytonstone to practise in the indoor nets and to be coached by well-meaning older players. Alan smoked *Senior Service* cigarettes and with his extra jobs had more money than me. On the Central Line there was usually a 'non-smoking' compartment near the front and another near the back, so we boarded in the middle where yellow-fingered men breathed smoke across the carriage air. The atmosphere of the tube made my mouth dry and the motion of the train could make me nauseous.

'Are you taking it down?' asked Alan. 'I'm not giving you fags if you don't take the smoke down. That's just a waste of money.' I hadn't been inhaling and when I tried to, felt sick.

I have often reflected how addiction takes root in unpleasant initiation ceremonies spurred on by bravado. Once you've lived through the pain, the habit becomes somehow heroic.

'It's the Moonlight Serenade, isn't it,' I said to Alan.

'Yeah, that's it. How did you guess?'

'On the wireless,' I lied.

Holding his fag between his teeth, he held out his arms as if dancing and started to gyrate his hips, sliding down the carriage seat.

'Does Lucy like to smoke?'

'No, she likes to snog. Snooooog. Very tasty. You should try it.'

*

In my first two years at grammar school I came either top or second in the class, but as I reached puberty that performance tailed off to a mid-table performance, exacerbated by a growing teenage crisis, brought on by a battle with my mother which resulted in depression and sometimes being sent to Coventry by her for a week at a time. Also, I was on my own academically because neither of my parents seemed to have any idea how to help with the subjects I found most taxing like languages and history.

In order to shine at school I came to rely on public speaking. Fortunately, the school held speaking-well in high esteem and awarded an annual prize for it – 'The finest speaking of the year'.

I won verse speaking competitions and 'spoke' (the headmaster thought it a preferable term to 'recited') Betjeman's poem, 'Essex', at Speech Day:

'And as I turn the colour-plates
Edwardian Essex opens wide,
Mirrored in ponds and seen through gates,

Sweet uneventful countryside.'

As a result I was cast in the title role in *Henry the Fourth Part 1*, a static role, I thought, much upstaged by the Prince and Harry Hotspur. The next year, I moved up a grade to play Thomas Becket in T S Eliot's *Murder in the Cathedral*. This is a much bigger part and at the pivotal point of the play, Becket preaches a Christmas Day sermon in Canterbury Cathedral. As I delivered the words of the sermon I was conscious of holding the audience in my grasp because, apart from the power of Eliot's words, I knew the text so well I was able to look the audience in the eye and speak them as if they were my own. Eliot assumes the Archbishop could foresee his impending martyrdom, had felt it in his bones, and had time to reflect on what it meant, which adds a shudder to the moment. Writing to the headmaster afterwards, the Chairman of the Governors, Dr Pippard, enquired, 'Does Mountford intend to be a priest, because if so he has already established himself as an accomplished preacher.' This comment influenced me significantly in my decision to be ordained.

By coincidence, the next Sunday I was to give the sermon at our own non-conformist church on the text 'By the grace of God I am what I am', an engagement my mother had been instrumental in organising. It embarrasses me now to think of the spiritual presumption that motivated me to agree to do this and how, taken in by the ritual flummery surrounding the business of preaching in our tradition, I fell to my knees in prayer during the hymn before the sermon, seeking the guidance of the Holy Spirit when I had written down every word I was about to say. The verdict was encouraging but not ecstatic. I was not the new Messiah after all. However, I was invited to join the local lay-preaching circuit, resulting in one of the freakier manifestations of seventeen-year-old recklessness. The assignment was another addition to my already overcrowded timetable. It meant preaching in dying Congregationalist churches around East

London – my first experience of the demise of a Church – Church Going. I spoke in places like Hackney, Stratford, Wanstead, Old Ford, and Walthamstow. Looking back at those embryonic sermons they reveal little of what I actually believed – indeed, what did I believe? – and drew heavily on ideas taken from published sermons by Leslie Weatherhead and Leslie Tizard. These were old men whose writings were based on a lifetime of reflection and experience, their illustrations taken from the Second World War, China, extensive reading, and ministries in different churches around Britain. They were showmen and entertainers as well as expounders of Christian doctrine. I picked up their stories of prisoners of war who had been converted, and Durham miners who spoke in an incomprehensible dialect, but prayed in BBC English, and talked of people I had either never read or understood, such as Nietzsche, Freud, Feuerbach and Gandhi, and cobbled them together into orations which had few light touches, but seemed to engage the congregations I addressed. I now see it was not what I said that held people's attention, but the fact that I said it at all. Here in the sixties social revolution, in the 'death of God' decade, in crumbling and empty buildings that once pulsed with vigorous communal life and worship, was a seventeen-year-old boy enthusing about old religious values, and offering an unreconstructed theology which affirmed their old beliefs. I was my own best illustration, and I didn't know it. I was a youthful phoenix rising from the embers of a dying church.

My duties also included presiding at the communion service. The first time I did so was in Chigwell and I was so nervous I got the bread and the wine the wrong way round and gave out the wine before the bread. Afterwards, I just wanted to get out of there as quickly as possible, but one of the elders told me I hadn't done anything wrong or unbiblical because in St Luke's account of the Last Supper, Jesus takes a cup, then the bread, then another cup after supper. That kind of graciousness and consideration was typical. I was treated much better than I deserved on all occasions, including the payment of generous expenses anywhere between one pound ten shillings and five pounds. Add this to the ten shillings I received for a service as Assistant Organist at Chingford Parish Church and I was doing well.

Mansfield College, Oxford

My parents had two heroes of whom they spoke in reverential tones: both Congregationalist ministers and both named Norman. Norman Goodall had been Minister at Trinity Congregationalist Church, Walthamstow, when they were young adults and Norman Hyde, Minister of Loughton Union Church, in their marital heyday when they had my sister and me. They had studied at Mansfield College, Oxford, the intellectual centre of Congregationalism and my parents wished me to attend.

Mansfield wouldn't accept eighteen year olds as ministerial students or to read theology as a first degree, claiming the subject required maturity, although the real reason was that an early theological qualification would leave you kicking your heels waiting to be old enough for ordination. But they would accept suitable candidates to read other subjects at eighteen. The Principal, John Marsh, wrote me a letter explaining how he himself had spent seven years, a suitably biblical length of time, he said, preparing for the ministry, and therefore six years wouldn't be too long for me. But at eighteen that prospect seemed like a life sentence, and I thought of Jacob serving Laban seven years for the hand of… well, Leah, and then having to do another seven for Rachel, the woman he really wanted. The plan was I should read music first, which Marsh thought always handy in church life. So, I sat the entrance examination and remember most clearly writing a three-hour essay on 'Art for Art's sake', having little idea of art history or philosophy or the context of that title. I didn't really get any of the other essay titles and this was the nearest to being intelligible to me. I grasped the obvious meaning that art has a self-authenticating value independent of what people might want from it – meaning, moralising, instruction, pleasure – but I certainly was unable to place it as an idea at the end of the nineteenth century and see it in relation to modernism. I recall writing something about Plato's theory of tragedy as catharsis and being asked at a subsequent interview to explain Plato's theory and remembering in that scary moment that it was of course Aristotle!

A week later he wrote to tell me Mansfield would accept me to read music in eighteen months' time, but first I should spend a year studying for an organ diploma at the Guildhall School of Music. I hadn't found the Mansfield experience entirely satisfactory; it didn't feel like a proper college and in the neo-gothic chapel the pulpit stood where the altar should be, Word trumping Sacrament. Little did I realise then I would spend thirteen years living in the shadow of that building in the University Church vicarage, before it was demolished to make way for the new chemistry lab.

First Love

1963 was an *annus mirabilis*, not just because of the Lady Chatterley trial and the Beatles' first LP. It was in January of that cold winter, after a rehearsal for Handel's Messiah, involving the choirs of several local schools, that I met a chatty girl at the bus stop who suggested we might meet again. For a first date we went to the Odeon, Leicester Square, to see *West Side Story*. Marjorie had the same nimble figure as Natalie Wood and we began at once our own enactment of Romeo and Juliet. Had I ever asked myself what would it be like to be in love? I think I hadn't, nor did I now. I simply knew it. Like Romeo and Juliet, we came from different houses: mine the puritan, impoverished house of non-conformist religion, hers a house of scepticism, affluence and step-parenthood. One of the first things Marjorie told me was that her step-father, an industrial scientist, became very fed up if anyone failed to address him as Dr Groves. I liked him and admired his success, but we saw each other as a challenge.

They lived in a pebble-dashed Edwardian house in one of the smartest roads in Woodford Green. On a Saturday night Dr Groves liked to go out for dinner, sometimes with his wife *a deux*, occasionally taking Marjorie and me as well in his chromium-rich Humber Hawk. In a French restaurant in Soho, he told me to order anything I liked. On an income of £3000 a year, money was no object. The menu was in French and he decided we must choose without benefit of translation. 'Escargots? You want to try escargots? You know how to eat them?' I quickly worked out how to skewer the garlicky snails, but left each empty shell neatly in place on the compartmentalised metal plate instead of putting them to one side. 'Chablis or Sancerre? You choose.' Well, at Christmas Mum liked a sweet Sauterne from Sainsbury's, so, guessing, I nominated Sancerre and Dr Groves approved. Decently, he'd given me a no-lose option. He could have said Claret or Sancerre, leaving me more exposed.

Marjorie was a twin, not identical, but close. Her sister was dating a guy who had just graduated in maths at Cambridge, who seemed immorally old, but harmless. Their natural father was an American airman, with whom her mother had a fling at the end of the war, and no doubt a very different sort of cove from the formidable Dr Groves, who for all his bravado suffered the vulnerability of step-parenthood, sensitive that the twins were not his own flesh and blood. He liked to be in control. Marjorie told me that at the weekend, when her parents read the Sunday papers in bed, she and her sister had to parade in the parental bedroom in their underwear. Maybe she didn't use the word parade, but that's how I heard it, and visualising the scene filled me with rage. I regarded it as mental rape and my admiration for him dropped like a brick.

One weekend, as part of my mother's own attempt at control, Marjorie was invited to Sunday high tea, the apogee of her social repertoire. Marjorie arrived in a sleeveless dress and a flared, knee length skirt. Ada eyed her as if she were Gay Shingleton, flaunting forbidden fruit before the innocence of her first-born son. She could probably smell the pheromones in the air. Conversation was stilted and uncomfortable, Marjorie endlessly polite, as we tackled ham and salad with Heinz salad cream, followed by jam puffs.

Marjorie and I walked to church on an evening when the horse chestnuts were luminously green, their flowers bursting into creamy, pink-throated clusters. It wasn't that she herself was religious, but had we not attended I would have had to cope with my mother's derangement. That evening there was an adult baptism service. What I hadn't reckoned on was the emotional effect of the ceremony. Amongst those being baptised was a girl of our own age. Dressed in a white robe, she stepped down into the baptism pool, and, supported on the minister's arm, was immersed backwards beneath the water, being 'buried with Christ'. Immediately after the very audible splash the choir sang, 'Be thou faithful unto death and I will give you a crown of life'. Then the neophyte emerged drenched, robe clinging to her body, rubbing the water from her eyes, immediately to be enfolded in a towel by an attendant matron to save her modesty. It was moving, emotional, profound, and sexual. I could tell Marjorie was affected and afterwards she was unusually standoffish and uncommunicative. When I asked her what the matter was, she couldn't say. I hadn't seen her distracted like this before. I wanted to embrace her but she pushed me away, begging me just to let her go home, but I was confused and bewildered and wanted some explanation, some resolution before we parted. This damned religion had backfired horribly and suddenly threatened our blossoming relationship.

Just recently, when a student asked me for what she

called spiritual advice, she told me she was concerned about the meaning of certain religious experiences. She had been attending choral evensong services in Oxford and as she listened to the music, and saw the expression on the faces of the choristers, she felt a sense of divine well-being moving through her body, filling her heart until it expanded to a point where she found breathing difficult. After such an experience she would want to be left alone, actually finding it physically difficult to talk, so she remained in her seat at the end of the service until everyone else had left the building, such was her need not to communicate. Overwhelmed, she had no desire to speak, no desire to be assisted, simply to rest in a kind of post-climactic well-being. She asked what I made of this. It just reminded me of Marjorie forty-two years previously.

It was my last term at school and my mother decided to take my blazer to the cleaners, just when she might have thought it had done its duty and, even if a tad dirty, would very soon be consigned to dust for ever. Perhaps she imagined ceremonies and closing convocations when for a last time she might take pride in a dapper model student, her son. 'What was this doing in your pocket?' she asked, holding up a dog-eared packet of French letters. Caught red-handed I resorted to the drug smugglers' defence that they must have been planted and it was a common, if banal, joke amongst schoolboys of a certain age to do this to one another in the hope perhaps of creating an embarrassing situation just like this. Then to my complete surprise, the matter was dropped and the conversation ended. Surely she could not be that gullible. Years later I learned she had sought advice from one of her matronly friends. She'd had coffee with Betty Ranson and said, 'Betty, you'll never guess, I was taking Brian's blazer to the cleaners and found a packet of rubber johnnies in the pocket. I knew that bloody girl was no good for him. What should I do?'

And Betty roared with laughter, delighted to see my mother's strait-laced puritanism ripped open at the bodice. 'Well, you should be delighted, Ade: at least he's not a homo,' she said, her great Jewish breast heaving, 'and now you know that if he can't be good, he's careful.' And, wiping the tears from her eyes, 'the best you can do is put them back in the pocket and say nothing.' But my mother always had to have the last word.

This reverie couldn't last and a crisis was looming. The term was ending and Dr Groves, the Lord Capulet of our drama, clearly considered the relationship had become too intense ('How now, my headstrong! Where have you been gadding?') so he arranged for Marjorie to be banished for the summer to her uncle's farm in Northamptonshire. The decision was sudden and absolute and was to take effect on the first day of the holidays. Marjorie said her uncle and aunt were quite relaxed and felt sorry for her and would let me stay there too, but not for the whole time, and in return I would be expected to help with the harvest. The wily farmer had seized his chance to get cheap casual labour and unwittingly taken to himself the role of priest to the star-crossed lovers, giving us the blessing our parents were not pleased to grant.

Marjorie and I decided to get married as soon as our courses were over, her teacher training and my degree. But the Mansfield plan stood in the way; it would be a marathon and the start would be delayed for another year. My solution was to apply at the very last moment through the universities central clearing house to Leeds, Birmingham, and Durham. I took no advice and sought no second opinion; I was simply intent on clearing the path for love. Durham was my first choice, but I had to decide which college, and with a stroke of naïve foolishness chose King's College linking the idea in my mind with King's College, Cambridge. But King's, Durham, was in Newcastle and destined in four months' time to become Newcastle University. When I went for my interview and the train steamed out of Durham Station, leaving the magnificent mound of the cathedral behind,

I counted the miles to Newcastle, kidding myself it was within striking distance after all, but of course it wasn't.

I had second thoughts there and then, but it was already July and the only alternative was to remain at home and be dragged back into that repressive regime. Blindly I marched on into a situation certain to stymie my future. Closing my eyes and hoping for the best is a character weakness I must own up to: I did it when accepting the living of Christ Church, Southgate, and when buying a development property in Scotland with a large sum of borrowed money. I know I am doing it but am unable to stop myself.

My acceptance at Newcastle being such a last-minute affair, all the student accommodation had gone. I wrote to the warden of Eustace Percy Hall, but he had no vacancies. I wrote to the accommodations officer who had nothing to offer in Newcastle itself, but there was a room in an unused clergy house belonging to St George's, Gateshead, and, since I was to read theology, he thought it might suit. Number 5, Patterdale Terrace was a red brick back to back 'Coronation Street' style house looking out over the barren Team Valley, where now the A1 motorway snakes through. I was isolated in one of the country's most depressed towns, half an hour from the campus, in probably the worst student digs in Britain.

The first day I walked into the junior common room of the theology department I discovered all the undergraduate theologians were women except for two men who had been bumped off the honours course to the general degree. Many of the women were from the North East, like third-year Brenda from Sunderland, red haired and bosomy, who might have come straight from the set of a Northern soap opera. I amused Brenda because she thought me a bit of a Southern toff and wanted to mother me. We smoked and drank instant coffee in this characterless, plasterboard room fitted into the Victorian *Armstrong Building*, across Queen Victoria Road from the

Royal Victoria Infirmary, which loomed black and soot-stained through the window. This was another country and a very far cry from the Oxford I had been accepted by just a few months before and I felt a sickness in the pit of my stomach at what I had done.

In our eager bid to sustain the drum beat of passion, Marjorie and I write to each other every day – the pre-cell phone version of manic texting. Twice that term she travels from Canterbury to Newcastle, taking on the immense journey because she had more money than me, and I consider my academic discipline more important than hers. The second time her visit falls on the day of Kennedy's assassination. When, on a news stand, I read the momentous news. I am on Newcastle Central Station. Fearful of being detected by eagle-eyed parishioners, we enter the spartan clergy house through the back door with groceries and flowers in a vain effort to make the place feel like home, but nothing can magic up carpets onto the bare floorboards or transform the two filthy gas rings into something fit to cook on. This is love in a cold climate. Everything militates against it, social prejudice, poverty, winter, an alien land. By December I can tell her letters are cooling, but she continues to make the effort. As soon as we return home, it is clear our *amour de jeunesse* is over. When the telephone by the front door rings, it is picked up by mother: 'It's Marjorie for you.' The living room door is closed. We agree to meet one last time, to wind up our affair. I wear my green check suit because I think, mistakenly, it lends me a kind of dignity.

To anyone more decisive, or on the receiving end of experienced advice, that would have been the moment to cut one's losses and quit Newcastle; to admit to having been hoodwinked by the irrepressible chemistry of puppy love, and not to wince when told you are young and foolish. But I stuck it out in that wind-chilled city, on one occasion, on Tyne Tees Television, arguing, without being lynched, that Newcastle was twenty-five years behind the times, on the grounds that you should be proud of who you are and not to assume the London new-fangled *avant garde* is always better.

As for theology, was this the worst department in England? It was run by George Boobyer, known not altogether affectionately as 'Boob'. His theology department was a small wilderness where the emphasis was on biblical studies. I don't recall any of my teachers asking me a theological question. They were concerned with dictionaries and definitions and the minutiae of biblical commentary. The eight students in my year sat round the table in Boobyer's study translating Luke's Gospel verse by verse with the help of Creed's commentary. Boob never saw the big picture, just the verses, like looking at the brush strokes of a painting at far too close a range. It was a kind of textual archaeology, an approach that rested on an implicit assumption that the questions and problems of Christian faith raised by the biblical text could only be elucidated by discovering the *real* meaning of Greek or Hebrew words. It was as if the Bible were a conundrum, a palimpsest of English over Greek over Aramaic over Hebrew, written perversely to obfuscate meanings that, if only they could be deciphered, would make the world see the light. I regarded it as a form of biblical fundamentalism, a scholarly respect for text in one dimension, in which the other two dimensions, the really interesting matter of response to divine mystery and the questions raised by that experience, are overlooked. In Boob's defence one might adduce the *sitz im leben* argument – a German term used in biblical criticism to denote the social setting of a text – that we were at the back end of the mighty influence of the German School of biblical criticism – Strauss, Bultmann, Wellhausen, and Weiss – and predated narrative theology or deconstruction and the analysis of the dynamic relation between reader and text.

One of my teachers, Bernard Reardon, was of a different cut. He taught church history and therefore had to address the history of ideas as well as events. On one occasion he reflected on the Thirty-Nine Articles of Religion, and he and I debated whether works undertaken before the reception of grace had the nature of sin. It was a momentary excitement. I admired Bernard for his eccentric, donnish style. I even grew long sideburns like his. He was an archetypal high churchman, educated at Keble, sensitive, effete, and as he often told me, only able to get through the ordeal of his finals with round the clock pastoral care from Harry Carpenter, then Warden of Keble. (Harry's son, Humphrey, the biographer and broadcaster, became a good friend of mine when I lived in Oxford and I presided at his funeral when he died prematurely and unexpectedly, aged 58, of Parkinson's Disease.)

While studying in Newcastle I continued to be a peripatetic preacher, joining the North East Congregationalist circuit, visiting such places as Amble and Warkworth (mentioned in *Henry IV part I*) and industrial Blyth. I also went South once or twice. On a snowy night in 1964 I drove to Consett in County Durham, the mining and steel town. It was remote and raw, and the chapel was all wrought iron and high Victorian chestnut whirls, with a large coke furnace, and gas lighting. It must have been in such a place that Leslie Weatherhead heard the Durham miners at prayer inexplicably forsaking their dialect to speak to God in 'tongues' of plain English.

This coming-of-age story has proved painful for me to write, churning up a past I have long repressed. In the North East I felt like a stranger in a strange land. I had gone there in haste to solve a problem and when that problem just as quickly disappeared, I was derailed and disoriented. But I did learn about resilience and survival and spent much of that time coming to terms with my years spent in the maternal concentration camp.

There's a paradoxical need deep within the human experience, and reflected in Christian theology, to be both accepted and other at the same time. God is on the one hand external, transcendent and beyond, and on the other one of us, incarnate, experiencing what we undergo. In my last term at the University Church (February 2016) I invited the philosopher, Amia Srinivasan to give a University Sermon and in it she explored this theme, developing the idea that relationship and separation is central to the drama of human consciousness: 'Each of us starts life lost in an other,' she writes, 'or rather, at the beginning of life there is no other, and no self, just the undifferentiated union of parent and child. The self is born through a traumatic act of separation, by coming to see itself as distinct from someone else. And yet that separation is never truly complete. For the self depends on the other in order to be itself. This is a desperate, unbearable situation. It is why we all, at some level, have the urge to destroy those we love, to assimilate the beloved into ourselves, to annihilate him or her completely. What's needed is a way through the paradox, a way of being at once familiar and strange, in communion but unassimilated. Christians, of course, will look to the figure of Christ, that paradoxical instantiation of both man and God. Perhaps in Christ God's ambivalence is finally contained and expressed; perhaps by being born a man, God not only answers humanity's longing, but also His own.'

This insight provides me with a far more sophisticated methodology for understanding the trauma of breaking free from the tyranny of childhood. My first act of defiance was scarcely a shaking of the foundations: I decided to leave Congregationalism behind to become an Anglican, the religion I had learned while playing the organ at Chingford Parish Church. I defended my decision before sixty people at a meeting at St James Congregational Church in Newcastle. Having been so hospitable and tolerant they deserved an explanation. I was confirmed by the Bishop of Barking at a church in Gidea Park in nondescript East London, a place I had no connection with at all, with four family members present. It was bleak, but I was one of nature's Anglicans and was coming home. The only problem was my new Church was itself in terminal decline. I could have read the signs, because in his sermon the Bishop said he often heard people say that the Church is dead. Then he told a story of a vicar who, frustrated by his congregation's relentless negativity about this, told them to come along next Sunday and he would hold the funeral. When they arrived, there was an open coffin standing in the chancel and in the middle of the service he invited them to come forward to view the body. They filed up, looking pious like they did for Holy Communion, and when they looked into the coffin it was lined with a mirror and they saw themselves.

In Newman's Pulpit – Oxford

I was on the cricket field at Tring Park, playing for the Diocese of London against the Diocese of St Albans, when the chap at second slip told me Peter Cornwell, the Vicar of the University Church in Oxford, had resigned to become a Catholic priest, following the steps of John Henry Newman on the path to Rome. I knew at once I wanted his job. I wasn't alone. When I arrived for interview there were seven of us on the shortlist, including several who went on to hold high office in the Church. It was the first time the job had ever been advertised.

My first Sunday was a freezing February day and it turned out the heating oil had been totally consumed the previous Thursday at my institution service. At 10.15am Professor Maurice Wiles delivered one of his Bampton Lecture Series on 'God's action in the world' – for which, by the way, he didn't see a great deal of evidence. He was a kind and polite man, but afterwards berated me as if I were the caretaker. At 11.15am sixty people arrived for the Parish Eucharist: I felt a deflating sense of defeat. In Southgate I'd been used to three very well-attended services each Sunday and at least three times as many at the Parish Eucharist. In the clear light of day, the church itself looked shabby and down-at-heel, the nave altar platform like a section of grubby primary school staging and the desultory flower arrangement, a reed broken in the wind, against the soaring perpendicular pillar where Thomas Cranmer had been tried for his life and lost. I wondered what I had come to and why ever the job had seemed so enticing. There were few, if any, students present, which seemed odd for a 'university' church. I shouldn't have been completely surprised because during the previous week Bishop John V Taylor had led a University Mission in the Sheldonian Theatre and each night Anthony Phillips, the Chaplain of St John's, had announced that the 'new Vicar would be available afterwards' in the Old Library of the University Church to discuss questions raised by the evening's talk. No students turned up, but the sessions were used by parishioners to get a sneak preview of the new man. One evening, the distinguished medieval historian and expert on Joachim of Fiore, Dr Marjorie Reeves, brought a young man in my direction and eagerly declared, 'Let me introduce you to our student.' He was a shy, tongue-tied mathematician from Brasenose and the hope of the Kingdom of God rested upon his shoulders.

When I came to Oxford, my vision for St Mary's (the 'University Church' is technically a soubriquet) was modelled on my experience of Great St Mary's, Cambridge, of which I had wanted to be vicar ever since Westcott House days when hundreds of students piled into the church at 8.30 on a Sunday night to listen to archbishops and cabinet ministers and professors and film makers thinking out loud about the teasing questions between the sacred and secular, between theology and science and the arts – the bread and butter, at least it seemed so to me, of what university churches should be doing, challenging faith while trying to build it up.

That was 1966. By 1986 we were a more secular, multi-faith society and, under Margaret Thatcher, a more managerial one. The internet was about to take off. The deregulation of Sunday was just eight years away and already on the political agenda. Mrs Thatcher attempted to get it through in 1986 but failed. College life in Oxford and Cambridge was now, with very few exceptions, co-residential, creating a new dynamic of self-sufficiency in colleges; no longer did students have to venture outside the walls to meet members of the opposite sex. College choirs improved and chaplains lured the great and the good to preach on Sunday nights with the promise of a high-table dinner.

Despite these adverse signs, I still believed in showbiz

Christianity and thought I could re-ignite St Mary's with it. In the Trinity term, I held a series of talks at 8.30pm on Politics and Religion. George Thomas, a Welsh preacher and the popular Speaker of the House of Commons, drew a crowd of two hundred, Bishop Trevor Huddleston spoke about South Africa and apartheid, Monsignor Bruce Kent about nuclear disarmament, but the week Donald Trelford, the Editor of the *Observer*, came there were only forty-five people and we decided to sit in the chancel. He was furious to have given up his precious Sunday evening to speak to so few and I realised there wasn't much future in this special-event ministry. You were only ever as good as your last show, and a fickle public would pick and choose on the basis of celebrity rather than commitment. Years later the BBC Presenter Samira Ahmed told me she had been present at Trelford's talk and it had been a key moment in her decision to become a journalist. When you go to bed thinking an event has been a flop and a waste of time, you never know if for one person present it has been a moment of epiphany. A hard and humbling lesson for the entrepreneur to embrace.

But I didn't give up showbiz completely. Donald Reeves, the then Rector of St James', Piccadilly, invited David Conner, the Vicar of Great St Mary's, and me to meet in London. He recognised we were responsible for similar churches with similar aims and that we might usefully be able to combine resources. Being located in the great intellectual centres of England was itself an attraction to many leading commentators and opinion formers. If we were to offer a combined invitation to lecture in the three churches, our pulling power would be so much more effective. With typical braggadocio, Donald suggested we begin by inviting the Pope. In the end, I persuaded Penelope Lively, who had recently published her immensely popular novel *Moon Tiger* to talk about her faith and life as a writer, which she did magnificently. But my *coup de théâtre* was to get the cellist Paul Tortelier to conduct a master class in all three venues. I'd seen him do it on television ten years before and had been captivated both by his playing and his philosophical reflection, talking as he played. I recorded some of his *bon mots* in my book *Postcards of the Road to Heaven* including this example:

'I do not play like the baroque players, da da da da da da. They play like that because they cannot play the cello! Do not try to be a purist. Jesus Christ was not a purist – he was pure – but he was not a *puriste*. He would play with freedom, (Tortelier plays some Bach) but not too free; (he plays with extravagant rubato) this is sentimental. In all things not too much, but just enough.'

That night he played to a packed house and it remains one of the most memorable events at St Mary's during the twentieth century. What was achieved by such occasions? They avoid introspective churchiness – that pervasive Christian sin, the Pharisaism Jesus so detested. They have no doctrinal or proselytising purpose. They speak about deep matters in a language comprehensible to a secular society. They have the courage to ask questions, not to be bullied by the Church or by tradition into some holier-than-thou, formulaic presentation that leaves people bewildered or champing at the bit to get to the pub. We had made space for questioning faith, for those on the exciting edge of faith and doubt.

One wag commented that there were 'signs of new life at St Mary's as Brian Mountford brought the church roaring into the sixties.' The barb struck home because I wanted to be seen above all things as up-to-date, but today I look back at the 1960s as an opportunity missed by the Church of England as it subsequently retreated into conservatism in the face of the ebbing tide of faith.

Like many of my contemporaries, educated in theology in the sixties, I had been an admirer of Harry Williams, who was Dean of Trinity College, Cambridge, during that decade, and particularly his book *The True Wilderness*. He was a clever academic theologian who had come to think that theology could only be made real through experience. In the Anglican mind, articulated by the sixteenth-century theologian Richard Hooker, authority rested in scripture, tradition, and reason, but what was the value of these if they remained purely conceptual and separated from the person you are. In *The True Wilderness*, Williams had written:

'In the middle of the 20th Century the Redeemer meets our needs as they are felt and understood by us. If the ministers of His Church preach a fourth century or a sixteenth-century, or a nineteenth-century Christ, then when people ask for bread they are given a stone.'

In another context – that of explaining the effects of a mental breakdown he had had to work his way through – he said,

'I realised that the Christian truth I tried to proclaim would speak to those who listened only to the degree in which it was an expression of my own identity. Previously it seemed to me I had often been like a man who, while perhaps he enjoyed a good tune, was essentially unmusical and who attempted from the books he had read to describe the quality of Beethoven's quartets. And I wondered how much I had thereby contributed to the emptying of the churches by making the Christian gospel appear unreal and irrelevant to people's lives.'

In Southgate I had been uninhibitedly myself, but in Oxford I felt like a rabbit in the headlights of other people's brilliance, and I froze. Besides, you never knew who would turn up in the congregation: the Professor of New Testament, the University's Public Orator, the Presiding Bishop of the American Episcopal Church, Melvyn Bragg, or, for a term while on sabbatical leave in All Souls, the Archbishop of Canterbury himself. I began to think of my job as having to make a stage for other, wiser people. I found Oxford a very daunting place to speak. To tell the truth, I felt a bit of an idiot. I knew there was always someone present who knew a great deal more than me about whatever I was speaking about. Kindly and learned North Oxford ladies would approach me after a sermon and ask, 'Have you ever thought of reading X? I could lend it to you if you like.'

I should have taken the advice of Michael Green, then Rector of St Aldate's, who told me he had invited bishops and luminaries, but had found that the home team usually did better. On the whole that is a view I now take myself. It is, for example, much easier to speak to your home congregation than to 'preach away', where you don't know the audience. While preaching might appear to be a one-way communication and something of a show, in fact it's a dialogue of sorts with people you know, whose needs and interests you are familiar with, and whose joys and sorrows you have lived through with them. Gradually I realised that the visiting experts weren't illuminating the gospel message in proportion to their status and qualifications, which caused me to grow increasingly frustrated. The penny finally dropped when the Revd Anthony Freeman was kicked out of the Diocese of Chichester by his bishop for not believing in the external reality of God. I debated with him in St Mary's, me arguing for a traditional God. The place was full. Afterwards, the great Professor Henry Chadwick complimented me, and someone else said I ought to speak more often, and I resolved that that is what I would do.

When you take a new job, you face a basic decision: do you come in as a reformer and make changes straightaway, or do you bide your time, listening to everyone's point of view and then hope to move with consensus after a year or so? The danger with the latter is that you become so much part of the *status quo* it's hard to break away and the problem with the former that you upset people and make many enemies. I brought to Oxford the no nonsense wide-boy attitude which had served me so well in North London and decided on a 'Night of the Long Knives' policy. Just as, in the scale of things, the assassination of Archduke Franz Ferdinand in Sarajevo was a small factor in the cause of World War I, so it was a small thing that sparked my war. The congregation disliked having to wait until 11.15am on a Sunday morning for the parish eucharist to begin. Their lunch was necessarily later than they would like. And the cause was the archaic and liturgically clunky University Sermon. A woman on the Parish Church Council, who worked in the University Offices, advised me to write to the Vice-Chancellor. 'Address him as Dear Mr Vice Chancellor,' she instructed.

You don't always recognise when someone's advice is more of an ego-trip for them than well-considered counsel for you. It was disastrous advice. I sent a letter to the very princely Sir Patrick Neill informing him that I had decided to reschedule the university and parish services to 10.00am and 11.00am respectively. The North London approach would have been slowly, slowly, catch your monkey, but I ignored it. The fall out was immediate. That night, at dinner in Oriel College, Ben Brown, the chemistry tutor, who had been on the panel that appointed me, told me the V-C was not amused, furious in fact.

'They're saying you're gauche,' Ben said.

Towards the end of my first year, the Earl of Stockton, better known as Harold MacMillan, and Chancellor of the University, died. I received a phone call from the University Offices wanting to fix a date for a memorial service in St Mary's and asking if I would conduct it. This was agreed and I assumed all was now well with my relationship with the ancient institution. But not so easy. The member of staff who had made the phone call had perhaps been over-zealous, and when the powers that be learned about the arrangement they called upon the Dean of Christ Church, Eric Heaton, to have a word. Eric phoned to say he would conduct the service. I replied that I had already agreed to do it, so Eric invited me to the deanery for a chat.

The waters of the Isis were already perturbed when I put on what my wife called my 'Newmarket' suit, a check of blue and grey, as a kind of protective layer, a bit like St Paul and his whole armour of God. With a dog collar it created a kind of visual oxymoron, with me looking more like a bookie than the successor of Cardinal Newman. When we sat down in the deanery, the Dean said to me, all matey like, 'Don't you worry about the University. You look after the parish and we'll look after the University.' He didn't explain who *we* were, but I was learning. I hadn't taken this job just to be a glorified curate and, as the temperature of the conversation rose, I said bluntly, 'If you want to conduct the service yourself you will have to hold it in the cathedral.' That was game set and match, but to mix a sporting metaphor, he wouldn't let go of the ball and we argued on through a period of extra time during which Mrs Heaton thrice poked her head round the door to tell the Dean his lunch was ready.

I did conduct the service, and through the kind intervention of the Archbishop of Canterbury, even attended the lunch in All Souls with the family beforehand. Archbishop Runcie was to be present to give the blessing. On my appointment, a year before, he had sent me a hand-written letter saying how pleased he was and that as an Honorary Fellow of Brasenose and the Visitor of All Souls he 'surrounded me on every side' and would want to support my ministry. At that moment, I had assumed I had *arrived* in the Church of England.

All this was a catch 22. On the one hand, I was having to establish myself as the Vicar of the University Church in an environment that wasn't particularly welcoming; on the other, the University was to celebrate the life of its Chancellor, a famous national figure whom I had never met, and it was natural that those who had known him in the university should preside at his obsequies. To them I was an imposter. After I retired, the same tension cropped up repeatedly when people I had known well for a long time died and had wanted me to conduct their funeral. In many cases I had sat down with them in their home or at their hospital bedside and we had prepared their funeral service together. It put my successor in exactly the same position as I had been with the Dean and I was grateful to be allowed to lead the prayers or, on one or two occasions, to give the eulogy. This was always by invitation of the vicar.

*

Just as news of discontentment with the new vicar seeped through the defensive walls of the University Offices, via Ben Brown and the Dean, so the chill of unwelcome was exacerbated by the slow leak of poison from another clandestine network. I discovered that a group of bachelor clergymen met for lunch every Saturday. They were part of an influential, if institutionally marginalised, largely gay, misogynous, subculture within High Church Anglicanism, once described by Fr Kenneth Leech as 'gin, lace and backbiting'. Leading figures included Gary Bennett at New College, Geoffrey Rowell at Keble, and David Brown at Oriel. David was the conduit for what little information I received, usually after dinner in the Senior Common Room of Oriel, the very room in which the Oxford Movement had been fashioned by Newman, Keble and Pusey. I never found anything malign in David's attitude; he was but the messenger bearing an unpalatable and profoundly undermining message. Gary Bennett made no secret, apparently, of his disdain for the new vicar, whom he regarded as an outsider and a lightweight, a poor appointment, for which David Brown, as a senior member of the patronage committee, had been partly responsible.

But it wasn't a matter merely of disinterested judgement. It turned out that Gary Bennett felt he had been overlooked for promotion in the Church of England despite having been encouraged by senior clerics that he was 'on the list'. I was just forty years old. Even before I was interviewed, I was told that whoever was appointed Vicar of St Mary's would soon be made a bishop. This was a widespread view through the early years of my appointment, and I got fed up hearing it. Gary would have felt such prophesies as a splinter beneath the fingernail. Theological Liberalism, he considered, compromised the spirit of the age and diluted the Christian faith, his great dread that the liberals were going to ordain women as soon as possible.

As for me and preferment, who knows? Like the Parousia, so earnestly expected in the early Church, it never came. I was never a yes man or a flatterer; and never able to utter the church-speak that litters the discourse of our ever-shrinking club, 'discerning the will of the Spirit' as code for making decisions in your own interests or signing one's letters with that singular and most unctuous word, 'Blessings'. Then, as my time came, George Carey was appointed Archbishop, more by luck than judgement, and the Church of England changed in an instant. Literally. He is said to have accepted the offer from the Queen by return of post, whereas Bob Runcie, when he received the plain envelope from Downing Street, took a week or more to make his decision, and was even filmed by the BBC at prayer in his episcopal chapel in St Alban's discerning the will of God. Carey had been appointed by Mrs Thatcher, almost as her last act in power, because she so disliked the other candidate, the clever Etonian John Habgood Archbishop of York. With Carey, the Church became an evangelical stronghold and liberalism was marginalised.

I was interviewed three times by the Prime Minister's Appointments Secretary in 10 Downing Street for what was known as a 'dignitary' post. The first time by Hector MacLean and subsequently by William Chapman. One nervously greets the policeman on sentry duty at the famous black painted door, and is met inside by an engaging junior staff member who leads you across the hall and up the famous staircase on which one has seen successive ministers of state ascending and descending like angels on Jacob's Ladder. Within the scale of things, Hector MacLean's room, like his name, was a little bit grand, a sort of early twentieth-century London study cum drawing room. By the time I met William Chapman, the Appointments Secretary was stuck in an attic at a remote end of the domestic labyrinth in which all the apparatus of our *de facto* head of state is crammed.

Hector's style was totally non-committal, which made for dull conversation and the niggling worry that there might be no actual purpose in one's being there at all. He explained that he was taking *soundings*. When, a couple of weeks later, the Bishop of Oxford told me, 'Well, I'm afraid Hector Maclean didn't like you,' I realised those three cigarettes afterwards, chain-smoked between Downing Street and Buckingham Palace, via St James' Park, had been pointless. I felt anger that my future seemed to lie in the hands of one man, whereas previously in my career I had been appointed on merit by a representative group of people from the institution I had applied to serve.

In the 1990s the whole process of appointments in the Church of England was medieval. Senior posts weren't advertised, you couldn't apply, and no one ever told you whether you were being considered seriously, perhaps they didn't know themselves – there was no freedom of information. Decisions were taken under a cloak of secrecy and it was unclear who had the real power, except to say, surprisingly, it was not the Archbishop of Canterbury. Things had not really changed since Henry VIII promoted clergy according to their capacity to do his bidding. The Prime Minister had a say, although Tony Blair and Gordon Brown didn't seem particularly bothered and perhaps thought, ideologically, they ought no longer to influence a church they didn't belong to. In any case, the only appointments that really had significance for them were those of bishops who would sit in the House of Lords and thus have a vote in national political life. During his administration, Gordon Brown abandoned the role of Appointments Secretary (it turned out, on a temporary basis) for the reasons given, but this had the effect of diverting power into another undemocratic lap, Lambeth Palace, where there was now an archbishop's appointments secretary, Caroline Boddington, married to a diocesan bishop, a relationship which some thought created a conflict of interests. She keeps the 'Pool', a highly secret list of those clergy deemed to be ready to be made a bishop. It is true there is a Crown Nominations Commission of twelve people, plus the two archbishops which meets to select the bishop, but they can only work from the shortlist provided by the Secretary. Of Caroline Boddington, Ysenda Maxwell Graham wrote in the *Spectator*, 'She has become more and more influential during her 11 years in the role. Because she works at Lambeth Palace and hangs out with the Archbishop of Canterbury all the time, the sense is that "if your face doesn't fit" with those two at Lambeth, you've got no hope of getting on to the list.'

A few years after my Downing Street interviews, William Chapman visited Bob Reiss' house in Little Cloister, Westminster Abbey, to speak to a clergy group I belong to about his nine years at Number 10 as PM's Appointments Secretary. This is an extract from my diary at the time:

Pin-striped with pink spotted tie on pastel blue ground, his gaunt figure seems not quite to fill the clothes he sits it. He jokes that he is unlike Queen Victoria 'in nearly every respect', an aside which draws a guffaw from some of those present. Amongst his successes he numbers the appointment of Rowan Williams and John Sentamu to the archbishoprics, and the fact that he opened up preferment to a significant number of *unmarried* clergy. I remember once the Dean of Salisbury asking me whether I was married and when I said I was, he replied, 'Well, that's your problem, Brian.' Now I see the truth of that remark: William Chapman appointed his own kind. He regretted the lack of attention in the C of E to theology, which I thought fair enough, and, presumably to let us know he moved in such circles, that he hadn't appointed at least one aristocrat to a bishopric.

But who is this man and where did he get his posh accent? 'My mother was a Jew, so I suppose technically I am Jewish,' says William. 'My great grandfather was Moses Moss the founder of Moss Bros.'

Extraordinary to think that this flawed character had so much power; power to appoint church dignitaries, Lords Lieutenant and to award honours. Okay, so no one's perfect but the real flaw is in the structure, especially in a democracy, which leaves power in the hands of one person.

On the third occasion I met him, it was clear he was tiring of my visits and made it clear I was past my sell-by-date. He offered me Tewkesbury Abbey, that watery, Romanesque gem in rural Gloucestershire, but why would I leave the vibrant, international ministry of the University Church for a sleepy backwater?

The University Sermon

As I have already mentioned, from my very first weeks as Vicar of the University Church I began to feel the weight of a millstone around my neck – the University Sermon, which took place in St Mary's most weeks in term. It imposed on the church the burden of what the evangelicals call 'dead religion'. No joy, no sense of Christianity as having the vitality to change lives; instead, a pompous, antique, bare bones of a liturgy (no biblical reading, for example), designed by Archbishop Laud in the seventeenth century, mirroring the extreme hierarchical nature of society at that time. The bidding prayer beseeched God for the 'Queen's Most Excellent Majesty', for 'Archbishops and Bishops, as other Pastors and Curates', 'the High Court of Parliament', and 'the whole Commons of the Realm'. As Mrs Alexander had said of God in 'All thing bright and beautiful', 'he made them high and lowly and ordered their estate.' What was worse, I had no control over it. Remember the Dean: 'You look after the parish and let us worry about the university.' I might be the incumbent, enjoying the freehold with all its rights and dignities, but by long tradition, the University controlled the 'Sermon' via its *Committee for Select Preachers*, which did exactly what it says on the tin at an annual hour of brainstorming, when names of possible preachers were thrown into the ring to be picked up by the 'Summoner of Preachers', a university civil servant, who subsequently sent out invitations to the lucky nominees. In the past it had been a prestigious invitation and speakers, in due course, would record their honour for posterity in Crockford's Clerical Directory with the entry, 'Select Preacher before the University of Oxford 1989' (or whatever the year happened to be). Only trouble: the university wasn't there to hear it. Dead religion has never been popular, and the Sermon was poorly attended, despite the high profile of some of the preachers. For the Bishop of Armagh, Robin Eames, I think there were fewer than twenty in the congregation. It seemed to me an insult. During my time, fifty per cent of the Diocesan Bishops must have preached at that service and naturally they assumed it was my job to make it flourish. Judging by what some of them said to me afterwards, many thought I had cancelled the drinks party because the brewery was fully booked.

At first, I attended the Select Preachers Committee as an observer, until, after some lobbying, I was made an *ex-officio* member. In those days the Vice-Chancellor himself presided and the meetings were held in his office in Wellington Square. Gowns were obligatory and getting past the entrance lobby like airport security. Once beyond the initial identity checks, you were led past frosty offices, between the desks of secretaries, who peered at you over half-moon spectacles, until at last you approached the antechamber of the V-C's suite.

Repeatedly I tried for reform. Should we not adopt the Cambridge model of just two Sermons a term, putting all efforts into making these well-supported and satisfying occasions? Shouldn't we use the allure of the Vice Chancellor's invitation to persuade world class religious thinkers to visit us? Hans Kung or Gary Habermas? Several times I came close to change. When Sir Peter North was V-C I thought we had crossed the line. And then, during the long vacation, diehards emerged from the woodwork putting their objections. There is an old joke which asks how many university dons it takes to change a lightbulb?

Answer (in an incredulous tone of voice): 'Chaaange?'

The Sermon was never high on anyone's agenda, and the prospect of political warfare in Congregation, the university's parliament, on what seemed to the movers and shakers so small a matter never appealed. It was the equivalent difficulty to an MP succeeding with a private member's bill.

The university seemed to me trapped in a romantically medieval and even, dare I say it, smug view of itself as a kind of self-governing Athenian academy, immune to what was happening in the world outside. Around that time the university was also conflicted about whether to have a business school and whether to take on the Methodist teacher training establishment, Westminster College, on Harcourt Hill at the edge of the city, as part of the Department of Education. The misgiving was whether business studies and teacher training respectively were truly academically proper subjects. I couldn't talk. When at Sidney Sussex, I'm ashamed to say, I had voted against the admission of Homerton College into the University of Cambridge. I was on the losing side, but that doesn't mitigate the sin. Moving into the future can be unsettling. Society was hurtling into secularism with the deregulation of Sunday, and Oxford was admitting more and more international students into what was quickly becoming a multi-cultural and multi-faith society, yet men (and it was then largely men) like Dennis Nineham, who had been radical in their day, couldn't let go of this esoteric university religion.

Then in 2004 Sir John Hood became the first full-time professional vice-chancellor – a businessman rather than an academic, which ruffled the feathers of many old school dons. The Sheldonian Theatre was out of commission for refurbishment, scaffolded out for the cleaning of Robert Streater's paintings on Wren's ceiling, which meant the installation ceremony had to be moved elsewhere. The natural default venue was the University Church, where all university ceremonial events, sacred and secular, had been held before the Sheldonian had been built. I think this established a bond between Sir John and the church and, in his early days, he presided at some of the University Sermons, commenting afterwards on the poor attendance. He wanted all university events to aspire to the highest standard of excellence and for the sermons this would include actually getting more people to listen to them. On Boxing Day that year we woke up to the news of a tsunami in the Indian Ocean that claimed the lives of 230,000 people and did catastrophic damage to property amongst some of the poorest people in the world. Apart from the fact of the humanitarian disaster itself, we had students from around the world whose families were affected and within days John got on to me to suggest a multi-faith service of prayer and memorial in the University Church. The significance of this was enormous. In my time the university itself had not thought of promoting services in St Mary's other than its antique sermon. And this was to be multifaith. At one of the Select Preachers meetings, I had proposed we invite Sir Claus Moser, the Warden of Wadham, to give the endowed sermon on 'The Sin of Pride' only to be told we 'couldn't have a Jew' giving the sermon in a Christian Church. I wish I'd been quick enough to enquire whether in that case Jesus himself would have been eligible.

Thanks to the practicality of John Hood, who saw the university without tradition weighing on him like a pile of dusty books, the number of University Sermons was reduced to two per term in St Mary's. Needless to say, Oxford's innate conservatism prevented a clean break and forced the retention of the endowed sermons, which were allocated to college chapels – not a bad thing for any college wanting to make an occasion of it, with a dinner, special music, and a procession of begowned bedels carrying antique silver sticks in the crook of their arms.

These reforms liberated St Mary's and I was given a great deal of autonomy over the selection of speakers, which immediately I used to drive the events in a different direction, away from the all too predictable Anglican bishop route, propping up the lacklustre piety of the current establishment, towards the questions people were really asking. Amongst those who fitted this category were Philip Pullman, Andrew Motion (the Poet Laureate), Booker Prize winner Howard Jacobson, Andrew Nairne (Director of the National Portrait Gallery), Jon Snow, Tony Benn, and Savitri Greer, a young virtuoso violinist. The Point about Savitri was that I had emphasised how important music was as a way of accessing a sense of the transcendent, so I thought a sermon without words was called for. I provided a short commentary on what we were trying to achieve, but the music was the thing. Of course, there was a showbiz element, but then beautiful liturgy in a great church is intrinsically dramatic and the more effective for being so. Several of these guests were agnostic about Christian faith and one was a non-practising Jew, but that was the part of the intention. Christianity was to dialogue with the world, not just with itself. When a religion speaks only to itself, it is bound to become more introspective and its judgement more clouded. And the university officials who were obliged to attend, *ex officio*, loved it, because most of them were coming from an agnostic and often reluctant position. Nobody wanted holier-than-thou. No one wanted saccharin certainties. And a trust built up with the consequence that the church began to be used more by the university, for example, every Christmas after that I co-hosted, with the V-C or

Pro-Vice-Chancellor, a reception and carol concert in the church for an invited audience of major donors.

We also worked with the University's chamber choir, *Schola Cantorum*, on two broadcasts for the BBC, a Jazz Evensong in the Radio 3 Choral Evensong slot, which won a BBC award, and a Jazz Mass, both composed by Roderick Williams and directed by Jamie Burton.

In 2011, with our own choir and a script that I wrote, we provided the Radio 4 Morning Service entitled 'Protesting Faith' in which I explored the problem of doubt. The response was positive and enormous, with the church receiving over a hundred emails and messages from the public. As much of this book has observed, and tried to illustrate, doubt is a theological theme greatly under-emphasised in the mission of the Church, yet one the public wish to discuss. I have included the substance of what I said in that service at the end of this chapter, because to include it here would create a hiatus.

*

It may be true this was a breakthrough in terms of central university religion, but Oxford and Cambridge universities have a particularly baffling array of autocracies. Each constituent college is self-governing, chooses its own undergraduates, and in most cases has its own chapel and chaplain. The central university is responsible for academic faculties and their buildings, labs, examinations, and the award of degrees. When you combine college chapels and city churches you find there are more priests in Oxford than might normally be considered useful. And, although we vigorously deny it, we are as competitive for disciples as fishermen in the North Sea for cod.

In North London my church was the only Anglican church in a population of twenty thousand people. As I went to church in Oxford on a Sunday morning, I could hear the bells of multiple towers clashing with one another and was acutely aware that being a clergyman in Oxford was a matter of the survival of the fittest. In 1986 Richard Holloway charmed them in Mary Mag's, Michael Green at St Aldate's, where he once preached a Freshers' Sermon under the title, 'God is dead, Marx is dead, and I'm not feeling very well myself', Caryl Micklem at St Columba's, and Mac Ramm at St Michael's at the North Gate. Week in week out they provided worship which was a model of what their tradition had to offer. Then there was Anglo-Catholic Pusey House, Conservative Evangelical St Ebbe's, the Dominican Blackfriars, Wesley Memorial Church, New College, Magdalen College, and Christ Church Cathedral, with their choral foundations and, today, Exeter, Merton, Queen's, and St Peter's with excellent mixed voice choirs. The competitive spirit could be shameless. On one occasion a very cocky student whom I met at the church door told me he was 'shopping around' and showed me a piece of paper on which he had given different churches marks out of ten. This was enough to fuel my paranoia at the beginning of the Michaelmas Term when the marketing techniques of some churches included not only singing their own praises but maligning their rivals. 'St Mary's,' I have heard it said, 'is not a student church. You have to wear a gown there and the services are in Latin.' Unfortunately, this was partly true: you were supposed to wear a gown for university services and each term there was a celebration of Holy Communion in Latin. In thirty years, I never once attended this elitist travesty of the Reformation. Cranmer's matchless English prose had been translated back into Latin, because it was 'the common tongue of the university', which was stretching a point a bit since from the 1960s Oxford hadn't even required O Level Latin for matriculation.

Giles and Jane

The Associate Priest at St Mary's doubled up as Chaplain of

Wadham College. Although this meant being pulled in two directions, with understandably conflicting loyalties, the role provided a bridge between the church and the student population. I had a succession of very talented colleagues: Christopher Foster, Ian Paton, Michael Roden, Rebecca Watts, Giles Fraser, and Harriet Harris. Two have become bishops, one a Canon of Bristol, one a well-known broadcaster and polemicist, and another Chaplain to Edinburgh University.

(In 2006 the post of Associate Priest was separated from Wadham College and became a full-time post at St Mary's, a role that was splendidly filled successively by Craig D'Alton, Rachel Greene and David Neaum, and finally by Alan Ramsey.)

When Giles Fraser was in post, Jane Shaw, now Principal of Harris Manchester College, was also on the staff, 'serving her title' – a Church of England term for doing her apprenticeship as a priest. Her main job was to teach history and theology at Regent's Park College. In response to student demand, she and Giles dreamt up the idea of an evening course which they called 'In search of God'. We advertised the series in large letters on the High Street. Some asked mockingly what kind of church had to admit it had not yet found God. Others got the subtlety of the message and recognised we were being honest about faith by acknowledging it as an elusive commodity and therefore something to be approached from a wide variety of angles. We didn't claim to be breaking new ground and, in any case, had no agenda to distance ourselves from the historic continuity of the Church. That is why we took for a motto Anselm's eleventh-century maxim, 'faith seeking understanding'. The meetings used the Alpha Course format: a meal together followed by a talk and discussion. But the presentation was a joint effort between Jane and Giles: one would set out an orthodox Christian idea and the other would critique it, noting possible objections and setting out other ways of approaching the question. The idea was for those present to see two theologians creatively disagreeing with one another and, in turn, to feel comfortable about disagreement and debate themselves, whereas the more conservative 'Alpha' approach is to provide answers and look for certainties. Giles used to call his talks, and sometimes his sermons, 'provocations'.

It was a creative time. Jane, Giles, and I were each markedly different kinds of person – Jane a serious bespectacled academic, Giles a bolshy philosopher with a young family, me, by then, a seasoned vicar becoming more and more critical of the Church I had adopted with such a sense of liberation at the age of nineteen. We sparked ideas off one another and didn't pull our punches.

Giles didn't restrict his provocations to 'In Search of God'; he brought them to the pulpit with an oratorical style that, although occasionally wild, was thoroughly compelling. At first, I felt threatened by this: he had people on the edge of their seats in a way I knew I didn't. On Mothering Sunday he began with Larkin's poem, 'This be the verse', the one with the F-word, which he changed, seemingly at the last minute, to 'mess' – 'They mess you up, your mum and dad' ... 'They fill you with the faults they had.' It was a master stroke and the parents loved it because, despite Larkin's hopeless negativity about life ('get out early as you can/and don't have any kids yourself') he had cut through the sentimentality of the day when we pretend all mothers are perfect. If I felt any envy, I soon began to learn that fundamental lesson of leadership that ego damages corporate effort, and the gifts of those around you have the capacity to reflect back on you. As is often said, always try to appoint junior staff who are better than you.

Then, one Sunday just as the choir was to make the long procession from the high altar to the nave for mass, Giles casually asked, 'Brian, do you mind if I use the word "shit" in my sermon today?' I suppose even he was worried this might be a step too far. But he went ahead and it was the beginning of his unpacking of a major theme developed in his doctoral research on Nietzsche, contrasting kitsch and shit. The idea was that the German concept of kitsch, referring to garish and sentimental art, is the denial, or sweeping under the carpet, of all things vile, corrupting, cruel, criminal, dark, cancerous etc., summed up in the word shit, which could be employed both literally and figuratively. Milan Kundera had used the distinction to great effect in his 1984 novel *The Unbearable Lightness of Being* where kitsch *is* that eponymous 'lightness of being' – superficial sex and the conning banality of the totalitarian state in communist Prague, where politics, like its art, pretends life under its rule is happy, uncomplicated, and evident in the naïve reductionism of its posters. Reviewing the book in 1984, John Bayley wrote: 'This Kundera suggests is the vilest outcome of the totalitarian kitsch of our time: that it negates any natural and individual pattern of responsibility and weight in private life ... Kitsch has no answer to death ('kitsch is a folding screen set up to curtain off death'), just as it has no relation to the true necessities of power and love.'

You can see how easily this critique can be applied to religion: there's a parallel between political totalitarianism and the imposition of doctrinal conformity; and a parallel between sentimental, lying art and a dumbed down religion, which pretends, in a facile way, that all shall be well for those who believe in Jesus. Thus, 'All things bright and beautiful' is kitsch. Chatty, colloquial prayers can easily become kitsch. The irony is that kitsch misses the truth of Philip Larkin's greatest insight into the nature of religion, that 'someone will forever be surprising/A hunger in himself to be more serious.'

Giles' exposition of this idea culminated in the addresses he gave one Good Friday during the traditional 'Meditation on the Cross'. (The whole topic is covered in his *Redeeming Nietzsche: On the Piety of Unbelief*.) Fidgetily pacing up and down the aisle and eyeballing the congregation, he explained why Christianity must not sanitise the crucifixion but face up to the harsh reality of human cruelty and greed – namely, 'shit'. Only that way is redemption feasible. The kitsch of Good Friday isn't just the hot cross buns and the chocolate Easter bunnies waiting in the drawer for presentation in 48 hours' time, it's the whole liturgical romanticisation of the cross represented, for instance, by veiling crucifixes, processional crosses, and altar reredoses in purple or sackcloth during Passiontide so that on Easter day, when they are removed, worshippers will feel the joy of having them revealed again. The 'suffering' of their being hidden is a complete dumbing down and blasphemy against suffering itself. And why hide them anyway? Isn't the crucifix exactly what we need to contemplate on Good Friday? Maybe. But so many of these graven images make Christ look strangely comfortable on the cross and in some cases as, *Christus Rex*, the figure stands up strong and seemingly above it all. How kitsch is that? It reminds me of the assistant in the St Mary's church shop selling crosses and crucifixes who asked a customer whether she wanted 'a plain one, or one with a little man on it'. So often Good Friday misses altogether the horror of crucifixion and, while I have no desire for people to indulge themselves masochistically in shocking violence, the absolute 'shit' of it needs to be faced, a fact brought home to me when watching recently (as it happens for the first time) the 1950's film *A Town like Alice*, set in Malaya, in which an Australian soldier, is to be crucified by the Japanese for stealing chickens. The anticipation of the event, which is not shown, made my guts tremble with fear.

Archbishop Tutu

Someone else who in a very different way illustrated the interesting paradox of being orthodox and radical at the same time is Desmond Tutu. I first met Archbishop Tutu in 1994, when he received an honorary degree from Oxford. He'd already agreed to return the following year to spend a week in the city to lead the Oxford University Chaplains' Mission. To begin planning the event he asked me along to the Old Parsonage Hotel to find out what we wanted of him. When I arrived in his room, he was laying out an altar on the bedside table where, for the next half hour, he would celebrate the mass, with me and his secretary, John Allen, as the congregation. The hotel had provided a very nice bottle of chilled *Saint Véran*, the first time I had ever had an *intentionally* chilled wine at the Eucharist. At the offertory, the Archbishop poured a generous glassful which, after we had each taken a sip at communion, he drank up with relish. When nine months later he arrived again in Oxford, I had arranged for him to stay in All Souls College where they gave him Lord Hailsham's rooms. The bursar came to see everything had been provided and offered the Archbishop a selection of anything he wanted from their famous wine cellar. He could have had the *Chateaux d'Yquem '45*, or the *Pomerol '64*. Laughing impishly, he asked whether they had any rum and coke, which of course they hadn't, and the bursar had to trudge up the High Street to *Oddbins* to buy some.

Tutu spoke for four successive nights to a Sheldonian Theatre crammed with students, dons and townspeople. Being backstage with him all that week, what impressed me especially was the meticulous planning he and John Allen undertook beforehand and their careful debriefing afterwards. Did the message get across? Did the jokes work? How could he have done better? And this from one who was already a master communicator. My own estimate was that his theology was straight down the line, what you would expect from a clergyman, even one trained at King's College, London, but it was his social record that was radical. This man had fought apartheid and suffered for it, was a prophet of social justice on the international stage, was inclusive on sexual matters, and had changed South Africa for the better. As I walked with him around Oxford, people crossed the road to greet him, wanting to shake his hand and thank him for what he had done. He was a superstar.

I had also arranged a number of ancillary events. When we visited Oxford Prison, still a penitentiary in those days, he stood before the prisoners and told them Jesus loved them. One shouted out, 'What are you on, Guv?' But he was totally unfazed, kept to his theme of God's acceptance and won them over. In Headington Girls School, he spoke at school assembly and asked them if they could imagine having two universities, one for students with big noses and one for students with small noses. They roared with laughter. 'Then why should you have one university for students with white skin and another for students with black skin?' And the point was made so effectively it induced a reverent silence. As he left the school pupils ran after his car, touching it and screaming as if he were a pop star.

We had lunch one day in Rhodes House, built from Cecil Rhodes' bequest, which also set up the Rhodes Scholarships, always including scholars from South Africa. But Cecil Rhodes was a white supremacist and an architect of apartheid. Tutu did not hesitate to let people know he was uncomfortable being entertained in that building.

On the Saturday night, in celebration of his visit, All Souls put on a grand dinner, beginning with a reception in the magnificent Lodgings of the Warden, at that time, Sir Patrick Neil. Sir Patrick repeatedly advised the Archbishop that it was their custom not to have speeches at their dinners, yet I could see Tutu had no intention of respecting the tradition. Halfway through dinner, he tapped the table, stood up and said he knew they didn't like to have speeches, but he was 'tickled pink' to be there and was going to thank them whether they liked it or not. He seemed very fond of this idiomatic English phrase which played on the irony of it being difficult for a black man to be pink, subtly reminding people that he crossed the barrier of racial difference in his very person, this man who was a creedal Christian, yet radically challenged co-religionists to re-think what it meant to love your neighbour as yourself. To coin an old cliché, actions speak louder than words and, in this case, they led to a new movement – 'Truth and Reconciliation'.

Spiritual?

Here I must break off to ask more a biographer's than auto-biographer's question: am I a spiritual man? The question awakens my inner paranoia, because I suspect, although I have little evidence, most would say I am not. I know. I know. What do I mean by spiritual?

For me it has to do with prayer. My more 'spiritual' colleagues seem to pray a lot – in small groups in church, on retreats, online, before meetings, and they usually add a written prayer at the end of any parish bulletin. It is never clear to me to what extent this is a reflective exercise that might be paralleled by mindfulness or secular meditation, and how much it is a combination of telling God what to do and seeking God's instructions for the days and weeks ahead as if God were a kind of prime minister somewhere out there running things, the kind of God who ought to be interrogated by the *Today Programme*. We had better ask God to sort out the COVID-19 problem or discern God's latest plan for Church re-generation. I don't buy it.

Maybe 'religious' would be a more telling word. Am I a religious man? In a kind of way, I am. I've been a minister of religion for fifty years, so I suppose I must be, and I do find in many ways that Christianity, or my interpretation of it, captures the seriousness, the joy, and the meaning of things.

When my successor, The Revd William Lamb, for whom I have a very genuine respect, arrived at St Mary's he immediately introduced much more prayer; more services, prayers in the weekly online bulletin and a prayer after reading the banns for those to be married. Will is different from me, but I still felt judged, not intentionally of course. I began to think I had simply not been holy enough. Had I let people down? Had my ministry been too secular? There are no answers and I still live with that doubt. Of course, I had my followers, those who liked the way I did things and the priorities I had, and no doubt there were those who thought I missed the length and breadth and height of whatever 'spiritual' is.

Then, one day, I'm taken aback when my daughter, Charlotte, asks over Sunday lunch, 'Do you ever pray, Dad?' I'm very uncomfortable when faced with what I see as an intrusively intimate question, and immediately become evasive, as if being asked if I've ever watched porn or shop-lifted from the supermarket.

'Sort of,' I reply.

'I pray,' she declares, quite matter-of-fact, 'as part of my meetings.'

It hadn't occurred to me before that there was anything spiritual about *Narcotics Anonymous*, although Annette and I had often joked, when she had hurried back to London from a weekend at home to 'do the coffee' for her group meeting, how much like church that sounded. Since the age of thirteen, Charlotte had always asserted her agnosticism, but now embraces the NA teaching on the importance of spirituality in its therapy. Participants are asked to connect with a higher being or higher force. In a traditional way, some call it God, others think of it as a chi or life-force. But whatever nomenclature you use, the important thing is to recognise a power greater than yourself and to have a sense there is a good in the universe, a supportive energy. Although usually happy to cast all this in traditional Christian language, that is how I see prayer myself, as some sort of engagement with a creative life-force. As part of my professional duty I'm used to praying publicly, both *ex tempore* and using established written prayers which have withstood the test of time. When alone, however, in the wakeful hours of the night, it's different: I wrestle with my failure to 'get through', to achieve any sense that I'm communicating with anything other than my loneliness. I imagine being imprisoned in a dark cell and wonder if I could possibly cope and try to pass the time by remembering hymns from my past and not getting all the verses right or in the correct order. In prison I'd have time to sort this out. I've mastered 'Dear Lord and Father of mankind', but still get muddled with 'O God, our help in ages past' and 'O worship the King all glorious above'. If I'm facing an issue about which I'm deeply troubled, I turn the palms of my hands upwards, outwards into space, a movement that, when you do it, you find is physically unusual, and imagine my hands are kind of satellite dishes receiving and emitting rays between me and the source of all being, the divine other. And sometimes I have a tingling sensation which feels like getting through. It's rare and hard-earned. I know this makes me sound a fruitcake and that's why I find any question about it intrusive. Philosophically, I want to say prayer is auto-suggestion, a religious way of expressing communal social concern or corporate seriousness. I'm familiar with the idea that prayer can only be greeted with divine silence, or that prayer ought to be praise or meditation or self-confession, or silent reflection – all non-acquisitive, non-asking modes. But even though I'm a sceptic, a pragmatist, and unromantic about it, I still have an intuitive sense that one can be in tune with the ground of all being, the rhythm of the universe, the values and virtues present in the stuff of the Big Bang, written into the DNA of the stars. Speaking of hymns, I am equally happy to express those ideas in Charles Wesley's words: 'O Thou who camest from above/the fire celestial to impart.' Just as you can believe and disbelieve at the same time, so you can be naïve and philosophically critical at the same time. Perhaps I am more spiritual than I think.

Three ground-breaking appointments

Claire

Claire was an undergraduate at St Hughes when she began attending St Mary's. Studious, half-French, with a cascade of black hair, but not, I suspected, much drawn by the usual excesses of student life. As she sat in the second pew from the front, there welled in her a sense she might like to become a priest, and one long vac she worked on the Jellicoe Project at the *Centre for Theology and Community* in the East End of London. That made up her mind. When she graduated with her biology degree, we had a vacancy for a Ministerial Assistant, a post usually with a tenure of one year. Biology isn't far from theology – perhaps nothing is. Anecdotally one recalls what a row it caused when Darwin published *On the Origin of Species* and his theory of evolution seemed to undermine the Genesis story, and how the Bishop of Oxford, Samuel Wilberforce, and biologist Thomas Huxley slugged it out in Oxford's Museum of Natural History, at one point 'Soapy Sam' Wilberforce asking rhetorically whether Huxley thought himself descended from a monkey on his grandmother's or his grandfather's side. But on a more nuanced note one thinks of how biology is interested in the study of living things, including us, through cellular and molecular biology, raising questions about the mechanics of mind and consciousness and ultimately who we are. Ah, solving that question would bring the priests running over the fields.

But the beauty of this appointment was that, whereas ordained clergy have to be licensed and approved by the Bishop, when it comes to offering internships to young lay people we can choose who we like, free from the dull hand of diocesan bureaucracy, thus introducing fresh genes to the gene pool of ministry. For a long time I had feared open-minded young ordinands were brainwashed at theological colleges, partly by the pressure to conform to the sort of spirituality I have just described. If they hadn't got it already, they tended to catch the virus of partisanship and the party prejudices of church politics. They became clericalized and 'churchy' and might easily lose the freshness of their own opinions. Besides, was being a clergyman or woman such a complicated business? Did you need theological college? Didn't you learn to be a priest by doing it?

Some will think this sounds like the petulance of student politics. Clearly, the Church needs regulation, core teaching, universal standards, and that is what episcopal authority and seminary training ensures. In my book *Christian Atheist* I asked what is the essential core of Christianity; at what point, as you question belief and practice, do you have to admit you are no longer a Christian and cannot reasonably claim to be one. Answering that question is an important and creative exercise, but not the point here. I'm not diminishing historical tradition or belief, just saying there is so much more to Christianity than that, a breadth and freshness to religious experience that expands the Church if only it is allowed to. Introspection in religion is a sure way of failing to see the wood for the trees. It's true, I'm not an admirer of diocesan structures, which seem to me remote from the day to day business of the parish life they try to bureaucratise, and there are many aspects of my childhood Congregationalism that appeal much more. COVID-19, they say, will force a restructuring of the Church, particularly in regard to buildings, which would be a start.

Even before she took the job of Ministerial Assistant, Claire had fallen in love with scholarly Tim. Tim had yet to complete his D.Phil on volcanoes and when he did, decided to do another doctorate, in theology. I had once told Claire's father, who writes about sport for the *Daily Mirror*, that after her year at St Mary's she'd get a proper job and earn some money, but she stayed three years, a fact he reminded me of with an ironical grin at her wedding. Claire had no arcane theological agenda, no desire to be dressed up in fine vestments, didn't look in the mirror in the morning and ask who is the holiest of them all. She was a thorough administrator, a reliable colleague, and a far, far better exponent of the Christian faith than she believed, whether it was in *All Bar One* or the pulpit. May the lay ministerial assistants flourish.

Penny

My penultimate years at the University Church were taken up with a vast refurbishment project financed largely by the *Heritage Lottery Fund*. In return they required us to establish an education programme as a way of 'paying back' to the whole community, the people who had bought the tickets in the first place. The Fund would pay for a three-year 'Education Officer' post and the HLF officials would play a key part in making the appointment and would then maintain a supervisory role with the appointee. They didn't entirely trust us. After three years the educational work would have developed in such a way as to be self-financing. Their conditions also required us to display 'Funded by the National Lottery' signs, with the fingers-crossed logo, outside the church. Talk about kitsch. I was pretty sure the naff symbol originated from betting on the cross of Christ and protested it was unsuitable outside a church. In a secular age few people put two and two together and the HLF officers couldn't see why I was so agitated, but in the end allowed us to use more sober artwork. Equally, the officers were unconcerned whether the appointee was Christian or not. They were supporting 'heritage', not religious faith. In truth, they were very nervous about Christianity because they knew it was identified with the indigenous culture and a potential offence to people of other faiths. This politically self-confident, anti-religious agenda was annoying and insulting. But remember who had bought the tickets. People of many different religions and none. Presumably not Muslims, though, because when the local Imam asked me how he might raise money for the Mosque, I suggested he apply to the Heritage Lottery Fund and he cooled with immediate awkwardness saying they couldn't possibly accept money raised from the proceeds of gambling.

Penny wouldn't describe herself as a Christian, maybe not even religious, but she was sympathetic and would be pleased occasionally to sing in the choir. I should make it clear it was I who chose her rather than the HLF. Perhaps my irritation at their anti-religious stance was more injured pride that my authority could be so easily undermined. She had read English at UEA, excelled both as an undergraduate and on the post-graduate creative writing course there, and came to us as a published poet. This seemed ideal to me – an artist in residence – and completely congruous with my conviction that religion is more about poetry than prose. In the Republic of St Mary's we needed open minds and ability. Who wants a staff of yes-persons all toeing the party line? True, you probably wouldn't want Richard Dawkins, or anyone determined to undermine your project. In the Democracy of the Kingdom of God, for the church to be a healthy and creative institution it must be inclusive and artistic as well as worshipful and loving. To be the Body of Christ it needs to incorporate people of ability and diversity regardless of credal conformity. As Jesus might have said, those who are not against me are with me.

Besides, most church musicians fall into that category anyway and nobody seems bothered whether they believe the creed so long as they make a joyful noise to the Lord. If not the choirmaster, then why not the Education Officer. Penny 'reached out' more than the most ardent evangelist.

Charlotte

My third outside-the-box appointment was of the Revd Charlotte Bannister-Parker as part-time, self-supporting (i.e. unpaid), Associate Priest. She had told me years before on one of the weekends she visited her parents, Sir Roger and Lady Bannister, she was thinking of being ordained. Eventually she trained for the ministry on the part-time North Thames Ministerial Training Course, married a well-to-do American and had four children, all boys. When they moved to Oxford she needed a parish to be ordained to. The Oxford diocesan authorities were sceptical as usual about the suitability of the University Church for training a new deacon, on the grounds it was an atypical parish – loads of visiting preachers, just one church building, and scarcely a funeral to be had. How do you get to practise the basics? But Charlotte was appointed and, raising all those kids, had to pick and choose what she could and couldn't do to contribute to the team. My mind went back to the *Episcopus Vagans* at Westcott House, the wandering bishop. There was a role for a minister without portfolio, someone who would concentrate on special events, adding a sort of extra-curricular value. It certainly helped to have a famous father. Charlotte was very well connected. She attracted a new clientele to St Mary's from North Oxford and further afield, including a number of evangelicals looking for a less prescriptive, but nevertheless enthusiastic, religion. Having trained on an evangelical course, with weekends away in the virtually Calvinist Oakhill Theological College, Charlotte had a foot in that camp.

An early priority was to try to bring people of different faiths together, socially, if not theologically. To love your neighbour as yourself might be an aspiration common to all religions, and the bloodlines of religion might have evolved from a narrow gene base of common human needs and experience, but theological difference is jealously guarded. After the Islamic terrorist London bombings of July 2005, the Muslim community in Oxford invited the churches to join them in a public display of solidarity in South Park. They were worried about violent reprisals. But the groundwork had been laid the previous year when Charlotte initiated an 'Interfaith Friendship Walk' from the Jewish Synagogue, via the University Church, ending up at the Central Mosque, witnessing to a determination to improve relations between people of different religions. She managed to get hundreds to participate, carrying white balloons and banners through the streets on a bright summer night at the height of summer. The good will created was, and continues to be, huge and permeating.

Charlotte brought two other issues to her 'without portfolio' ministry: climate change, addressed by George Monbiot and Jonathan Porritt, and international social justice, especially her work for the South African 'Children's Radio Aid Foundation', culminating in a visit from Kofi Annan. It was a bonus to have a staff member, with a flair for the big public occasion and a filmic approach to Christian ethics, dedicated to leavening the lump of our everyday ministry. And Sir Roger, by then retired from the Mastership at Pembroke College, attended the majority of these events. The buzz of his presence made me aware of the charisma of celebrity and why organisations benefit from having famous patrons. In a fraction less than four minutes, back in 1954, he had endowed his whole life with magnetism. I often puzzled about this. He was the first man in the world to run a sub-four-minute mile. Given the cinder track at Iffley Road and the primitive spiked running shoes he wore, a massive physical achievement, but as importantly, but no doubt not obvious to him at the time, along with Hillary's conquest of Everest the previous year, it became an iconic moment in Britain's emergence from the privations of the Second World War. Visitors to St Mary's from all over the world, were excited to meet him.

Oxford Is a Hub

Only a small one, but a hub nevertheless, around which many luminaries rotate. I remember when Roy Jenkins died boasting to the Dean of Westminster about the memorial service we were going to hold, only for him to smirk smugly and tell me they were going to hold a bigger one.

There were famous people who worshipped at St Mary's and other shining ones who passed through. When Archbishop Runcie dedicated the new Metzler organ, he took his text from I Corinthians 12.14 'For the body does not consist of one limb or organ but of many.' At lunch afterwards in the vicarage, the phone rang and it was for him: his special envoy, Terry Waite, had been captured by Hezbollah in Beirut where the poor guy was to be held in solitary for more than four years.

Prunella Scales agrees to read poems by T S Eliot in church and beforehand we have a drink in the KA (King's Arms) with her son Sam West who was then a student at Wadham. Why we were there is a curious tale. Down the Abingdon Road there lived a butcher by the name of Stanley Revell. Stanley was a shy, introspective type; an only child who never married. In the Second World War he joined the army where he was bullied and came near to breakdown. When he sought advice, his commanding officer suggested he read the poems of T S Eliot. An unlikely therapy, you might think, but the young Stanley became so enthralled he resolved to buy everything the poet had ever written, if possible in a first edition, with the result that he now owned one of the finest bibliographic collections of Eliot in the world. A member of our congregation Anne Ridler, herself a distinguished poet, had been Eliot's secretary at *Faber and Faber*. She knew of the collection and also knew Stanley was suffering from the late stages of cancer, so she wanted to exhibit the collection in St Mary's before he died. Her husband, Vivian Ridler, who had been Printer to the University, published a limited edition of a short essay of Eliot, discovered by Stanley and not listed in Donald Gallup's standard bibliography of Eliot's work. Prunella was invited to launch the exhibition with a reading.

Several young people start attending the church in order to qualify to be married there. Natalie Cassidy was one of them.

Afterwards at coffee, people introduce themselves to her in a don't-I-know-you sort of way. Natalie explained she was an actress and these academic types became covered in confusion as they had to admit they watched East Enders.

Tom Hollander's sister Julia sings in the choir and she suggests Tom might read the lesson. He was totally convincing as the Revd Alan Smallbone in the BBC comedy *Rev*. As he and I fuss around the lectern finding the passage for him, he seems completely bewildered and I think, 'Oh, come off it. You're a bloody vicar, aren't you?'

At the Christmas Carol Service Rowan Atkinson is to read the Eighth Lesson, 'The Wise Men are led by a star to Jesus'. He sits in the front row next to his agent, Peter Bennett Jones. The church is packed. And when he gets up to read fifty others in the congregation, mainly Japanese, stand and let off their phone cameras in an explosion of flashlight. Undeterred, he reads with immense authority and no hint of *Four Weddings and a Funeral* whatever.

The *Mail on Sunday* columnist, Peter Hitchens, always attends the International Advent Carol Service because we use the King James Bible for that one and it's the only version he can abide. I don't mind that: I can be a reactionary old fart myself and I frequently ask him to read one of the lessons, in his deep English Gentleman voice.

And there's Joanna Trollope again, sitting next to her daughter Louise. I wonder if she might be studying me for her next novel. Then I read *The Rector's Wife* and find some very sexy bits and think I had better not be in it after all.

Her Majesty the Queen attended St Mary's just once in my time, on the occasion of the 750th Anniversary of the founding of University College. As custom dictated she was last to enter the church, accompanied to her seat by me in my capacity as incumbent. After the service she pointed out that the choir, placed behind the organ screen, had not been heard to full advantage and I thought, well, you are the Head of the Church of England. You're right to upbraid me even though it's not my choir and I had advised the University College Director of Music the organ would drown out the choir. I wanted to defend myself but deferred.

Her Majesty was represented on many other occasions, particularly at memorial services, often by Sir Isaiah Berlin, on the grounds that he held the Order of Merit. Isaiah would approach the Radcliffe Square door and announce deliciously, 'I am the Queen.' And I'd accompany him to the seat in the front pew on the right-hand side, where I would bow and he'd look amusedly imperious. I think he was the 'Queen' at Dorothy Hodgkin's memorial when the church had to be closed from 8.00am to all but sniffer dogs because Mrs Thatcher, Dr Hodgkin's former pupil, was to attend.

And what shall I more say? For time would fail me to tell of John Simpson, David Sheppard, Derek Worlock, Richard Dawkins, John Habgood, Mervyn Stockwood, Chris Patten, Thom Yorke and George Martin, the 'Fifth Beatle'.

Some will recognise here my allusion to the eleventh chapter of the Epistle to the Hebrews, where the question arises about whether those who came before Christ were saved: if people are justified by faith in Jesus Christ, what about those great figures of Jewish history who lived before Jesus? Are they excluded from salvation? Surely Abraham and Jacob and Moses couldn't be on the outside! It is not an obscure question. I was asked recently by a group of teenagers why, if people can only be saved by Jesus' sacrifice, he showed up at a time when his message couldn't possibly reach everyone on the planet such as Native Americans or Australian Aborigines? Fair point.

In Hebrews 11 the argument is that Abraham & Co were saved, or reckoned as righteous, 'by faith'. It couldn't have been faith in the saving work of Christ because that hadn't happened. It must have been a broader category of 'faith' than that. Its exemplars include Moses, Abraham, the Hebrew people who escaped from Egypt across the Red Sea, Gideon, Barak, Samson, Jephthah, David and Samuel, but also, surprisingly, a prostitute called Rahab. Who was Rahab? She was a Canaanite prostitute/innkeeper at the wall of Jericho. She gave cover to the Israelite spies before the Battle of Jericho on condition that she and her family were protected from rape and slaughter when the siege of Jericho ended. Some think it's a story to explain how Canaanites came to be part of the Jewish nation. You might think it extols a traitor and collaborator. But this was the 'Chosen People' she was helping, and nationalism must be rewarded.

Can you generalise this argument by saying all those, whatever their background, who have a sense of the divine other, and find in that a motivation for a good life, are embraced by Christ's salvation? If salvation worked by non-specific faith before Christ, surely it must work by non-specific faith after Christ! It is not just Christians who are saved, but many besides. And we begin to move more towards a view of universal salvation, of inclusivity. Therefore, the story of salvation becomes a metaphor, or parable, rather than a description of some sort of cosmic action. Traditional theologians would, of course, object. No, they would say, the theological idea behind Hebrews 11 is that in the time of the OT Christ was already promised by God: it was his saving grace that was valid for the heroes of the Hebrew Bible just as it is for those who have lived after Christ's sacrifice. In a sense, it doesn't matter when the act of salvation happened (i.e. one Friday at Passover in about the year 33CE). God's grace is valid for all time.

The people I have mentioned include some who were leaders of the Church and conventional in their views, but others who are agnostic, atheist, pugnacious, or simply desirous of a nice wedding. And they are all included in my St Mary's book of life. The more diverse they are, the more the kingdom of God is made present in our midst. We had a great thing going – we reached beyond the self-protective walls of the church. Reaching outside was easy because, as a major tourist attraction with 500,000 visitors a year, the world came to us. But would we welcome them? It is too easy to think the general public in large numbers detrimental to sacred space, as if we who worship week by week use it properly, while those who drop in on a day out sully it with their shallow disrespect. I understand entirely why some religions make you take off your shoes in a sacred space or cover your head or your bare arms. The place on which you stand is holy ground, where hopefully you might experience the awe of sacred mystery, what German theologian Rudolph Otto called the *mysterium tremendum*. Many more people than we imagine do experience a sense of awe, and ten minutes in the church can be the highlight of their day, the event they go home to tell their neighbours about, especially if there was some live music playing or the sunlight beamed through the stained glass windows at a certain angle. All of a sudden, they were surprised by a hunger to be more serious.

Would we welcome them? The question came home to me during the Easter holidays when we were always overwhelmed by tourists and, if it was sunny, the churchyard would be full of the clatter of coffee cups and chatter. But on Good Friday we used to close the church, only allowing in the devout few who wished to attend the Three-Hour Service. This was intended as a mark of respect, witnessing to 'the world', as we thought, the solemnity of this sacred day when Christian values of self-giving and unconditional love challenged the shallowness of consumerism.

Then I noticed how many people, especially from Catholic countries, were puzzled and angry, unable to understand why they were excluded. What began as a good intention ended up sending out entirely the wrong message. I decided to open the church all day and to put on a programme of events where people could drop in for as little or as much time as they liked.

I wanted to show that sacred and secular could exist side by side and hoped something of the Easter message might rub off. We enacted the Stations of the Cross (scenes from the Passion of Christ) in a procession that went into the surrounding streets; the choir gave a concert of Passiontide music; and for half an hour teenage members of the congregation read poems and prose passages related to the Passion, which they did with great intelligence and dignity. I didn't want an exclusive space for the holy, but tried to share a little seriousness with the holiday crowd. I published the poems they read, with a commentary, in my book *Friday's Child.*

Before leaving this theme of the hub, I want to mention two other examples of linking up with the wider world. Peter Bennett-Jones, the founder of the TV company *Tiger Aspect* and producer of *The Vicar of Dibley*, worked with Richard Curtis in the *Make Poverty History* campaign. Controversially they were going to launch it in an episode of 'Dibley' and Peter sent me Richard Curtis' script to get a vicar's eye view of it and to look out for ecclesiastical gaffes. I was flattered. To be honest the script seemed thin and marginally vulgar to me, but with no obvious gaffes. I had little sense of how extremely economical and clipped TV dialogue is. When realised on the screen, it comes across as much more natural, because your brain is filling in so much more with the visual imagery. You only have to turn on the subtitles on your television to see how this works. This reveals too the very annoying ploy of actors pausing half way through a sentence with 'erm', a cliché written in by many writers.

Not long after, Philip Pullman asked me to read a draft of his *The Good Jesus and the Scoundrel Christ* which arrives immaculately packaged in a blood orange folder with his self-designed cartouche, depicting a raven (his daemon – 'because it steals things'), pasted on the front, with the title written in his own hand. Again, I feel honoured but out of my depth. Who am I to critique such an established author? My first reaction is that he has lifted it straight out of Luke's Gospel. It is written, cleverly, in the manner of a gospel and he interfolds actual biblical story with his own conceit that Jesus has a brother called 'Christ' who exploits and corrupts the 'good news' to his own advantage. Nothing especially new here, except for the story-telling technique and Pullman's bright theological take.

Theology recognises a difference between the historical Jesus of Nazareth and the highly theologised interpretation of Jesus the Christ developed in the centuries immediately after his death. It is hard – nigh on impossible – to disentangle the Jesus of history from the Christ of theology even in the gospels, which are themselves highly interpretative. You only have to turn to St John's Gospel to find Jesus talking about himself in wholly unlikely literary speeches as the 'bread of life', the 'true vine', or 'the resurrection and the life'. In an interview for the Guardian in October 2017 Pullman said, 'So my attitude to the church is twofold. Firstly, it's where I belong – I'm a cultural Christian. Secondly, I have learned to have a grave suspicion of all religious power wielded politically.' I think he has become such an interesting theologian because he's free of all the baggage of what most Christians think they *ought* to believe, or might go to hell if they don't believe, so he is able to strip away that protective layer to talk about what lies underneath. He does this most effectively in his book of essays, *Daemon Voices*, where, for instance, in *'God and Dust'*, he argues against the idea that the silence of God proves his presence or, as R S Thomas puts it, 'It is this great absence that is like a presence.' This mystical tradition of what is sometimes called 'apophatic' theology has enjoyed a renaissance in contemporary spirituality, but Pullman suggests it is tantamount to saying the garden is full of fairies and the fact that you can't see them proves that they are there. He calls this 'cheek on a colossal scale'. Naturally theologians will protest he has mocked their ideas in a reductionist argument. But theologians need to hear the argument; they don't get enough of it.

In extremis

Walking across Magdalen Bridge with one of his pupils, C S Lewis was approached by a beggar who asked him if he could spare a quid. Extracting his wallet from the inside pocket of his jacket, Lewis gave the man a pound note.

'Why did you do that, Sir?' protested the undergraduate, 'He'll only spend it on drink.'

After a moment's thought, Lewis replied, 'Well, that's probably how I would have spent it myself.'

Oxford has long been a magnate for beggars and homeless people; the pickings from tourists, and undergraduates more compassionate than the one in question, comparatively are rich. When I was chair of *Oxford Churches Together*, back in the late eighties, we were accused by the Oxford City Council of salving our consciences about the social evils of homelessness by preaching about it but doing nothing to alleviate it. We enquired of the Council where the gaps in provision were, and they quickly replied that between 5 and 7.00pm, when the Night Shelter and other safe havens were being cleaned, there was nowhere for people to go. We decided to open a café to fill that gap each evening in the basement of the Northgate Hall, opposite the Union Society in St Michael's Street. Initially churches took it in turns to find eight volunteers to make sandwiches, talk to the guests, and do the washing up. From the safety point of view, the basement was about the worst possible place. You entered through a door at street level down a long narrow staircase. There was little chance of a quick escape if trouble boiled, and the demographic was volatile: men whose wives had kicked them out, those with mental health disorders, people high on drugs, paranoid, schizophrenic, threatened, testosterone heavy, grateful but ready to explode, like the evening one muscular extremist, wielding a baseball bat, sent everyone rushing for the staircase.

We raised funds too to provide proper financial help for those in genuine need. Most of us were fed up with the relentless hassle to spare some change and, when we refused, the angry shout intended for everyone around to hear, 'Call yourself a fucking Christian?' And visitors turn to stare at you as if you yourself were some sort of psycho: Yes, what kind of fucking Christian are you, you who trample the head of the poor into the dust of the earth, and push the afflicted out of the way? Our financial support of the homeless ought not to be so random. We felt guilty enough as it was, without having our consciences manipulated like that.

But like the single leper, a Samaritan (a foreigner), who, in Luke's story of Jesus cleansing ten lepers, is the only one to return to give thanks after showing themselves to the priests, there were other stories of hope and encouragement.

One Christmas Morning I opened the church doors and a guy staggered in all battered and bruised with a big puffy eye as if he'd just done eight rounds in a boxing ring. He said he was an alcoholic and would I give him some money. Well, I thought, it *is* Christmas and gave him a tenner. He sat in a pew for a while and then Corinna started to rehearse the Bach she was going to play on her violin during communion. He took a chair and sat very close to her, listening attentively. When she had finished, he said, 'That was wonderful,' (long pause) 'just like being on the Titanic.' Did he imagine the orchestra playing as the ship went down? Or, in his condition, was he going through an eschatological moment, an existential crisis? Whatever it was, he seemed transformed.

St Mary's is a major tourist attraction drawing pilgrims, history bibbers, music-lovers, families on a day out, and those simply herded in by tourist guides in vast numbers. There is also an extremely popular café, enjoying exclusive rights in

Radcliffe Square, surely one of the greatest squares of Europe. The management of this requires a large staff and occasionally you get a rotten apple. One Sunday morning I entered the chancel to celebrate the 8 o'clock Holy Communion for eight or nine old ladies to discover a fellow in full kitchen whites and chef's hat, looking not unlike an archimandrite in clothes whiter than 'no fuller on earth could bleach them', standing at the votive candle stand. At first, I thought what a change to have a devout *sous chef* until I noticed the money box was open and he had the key in his hand. He protested he was acting on behalf of the caretaker, emptying the box to prevent the money being stolen by tourists later in the day. The countenance of his pale, flaccid face said, I know this is implausible, but I'll give it a go.

A crew of students and sixth formers worked part time in the church gift shop. A young woman studying law at Oxford Brooke's University was a regular and when she had finished her course and moved away she said she loved it so much she'd like to continue working three days a week, even though she had to travel over an hour to get here. No one questioned this, although I did think that, by the time she had paid her travel expenses, the change from a basic living wage hourly rate would scarcely be worthwhile. After her shift, she often reported how few customers there had been that day. Then we noticed every time she worked the takings were unusually low, well below average. It turned out most of her fellow workers knew she was pocketing money without using the till, but no one was willing to testify. I changed her job spec to work in the office for the same remuneration, but she was having none of that. Then a South Korean girl on the staff said she would testify. I sacked Anna immediately. A week later I receive a solicitor's letter saying that if she were not reinstated we would be taken to an employment tribunal. I reply that I know she wants to become a solicitor herself and that since one of her colleagues is willing to give evidence against her at the court, she will be found guilty and never work in the law. We heard no more.

*

It was a bleak March morning, the icy wind so cutting few people were about. At 11.30am Helen from the Coffee Shop comes running to the vestry to say there has been an accident in the churchyard, so I dash out to see what has happened and find a man dead on the stone pavement at the foot of the tower, a small pool of blood discharged from his mouth. As shock gathers into realisation, there is panic amongst the staff, who at first think it is their fault. The wind has blown over one of the massive outdoor gas heaters on top of him and they will be accused of lack of care under health and safety. First, we have to disperse a party of forty foreign schoolgirls assembled in the adjacent shop waiting to climb the tower, some already having paid their entrance fee. They must be reimbursed. They want to know why they can't go up and can't understand our panic. It feels like there's no time to explain and that, in any case, the explanation is too grisly for them to bear. The police and ambulance have been called. The coffee shop staff believe there may be life in the perfectly still body and, under instruction from the emergency services, turn him over and pump his chest, but are only pushing at broken ribs. With touching gentleness they wrap their coats over his body to keep him warm, but when I return I see his glazed eyes staring upwards into the cold air of this particularly bitter day. Around the body are the remains of a wooden slatted café chair, hit with such force by the falling man that it is has been shattered into splinters, some of which are mingled with the now darkened, treacly blood.

The police arrive in six cars, screaming up the High Street. Bursting from the car doors, they rush into the church shouting and pushing people aside, including me, in what I consider an unnecessarily rough way, saying this is now 'a crime scene'.

Their alarm exacerbates the tension. Anyone who has been close to the body must make a statement, and several of the coffee shop staff are corralled off, like suspects, to be interrogated, their entirely justified protests that they were only trying to help rudely ignored. No one actually saw the man fall. When more senior officers from CID arrive, they are calmer and more respectful.

Very quickly the police cordon off the churchyard. After about two hours the inspector in charge tells me he is satisfied the death 'is not suspicious' and that an undertaker has been called to remove the body, now contained in a black body bag. He asks whether this is private or public land and when I say it is private, he looks apologetic and tells me I am therefore responsible for clearing up. He could give me the telephone number of a company often used by the police in circumstances such as these, but that, of course, there will be a charge. So I call them and discover there will be a five-hour delay before they can arrive. But we have now reached the point where the police's work is almost done and as soon as the body has been removed, they will lift their cordon and we will be left to our own devices. It seems to me therefore that I must start clearing up myself, because I would not ask any of my staff to help, given their obvious distress. A constable offers me rubber gloves, part of his basic policeman's kit, which I gratefully don as he watches me set about the task. To my surprise, I am not fazed by the experience and it crosses my mind that in Baghdad people are facing much more gore and horror every day without an ambulance, let alone rubber gloves. The worst part is dealing with the bloody splinters for fear they might penetrate the gloves. I have previously had a conversation with the police speculating how long infected blood remains dangerous; surely the HIV virus is passed on by the exchange of warm body fluids and after a short period outside the body, when cold and exposed, the viral organisms cannot survive. The police are interested but haven't a clue what the answer is. You would think it might be part of their basic training.

The man's name cannot be released for the time being, at least until his family has been informed, which of course is right, but it means that for days he remains in all our minds simply as 'the man'.

When his identity is released, we discover he was Dr David Brunton, a master at Magdalen College School, aged 39. His wife was pregnant with their first child. Pupils bring flowers to lay where he died. He was immensely popular with the boys as an unconventional and inspirational teacher, I imagined like Hector in *The History Boys* who stretched the minds of his pupils beyond the curriculum, forcing them to challenge the consensus views on the history they were studying and to think for themselves. Also, that he had contributed to the *Oxford Dictionary of the Christian Church*.

The flowers left me with a moral conundrum. I was moved by the affection of the boys, but to build a floral shrine outside on the York stone pavement I had so recently hosed clean of human tissue drew attention to a tragic and gory suicide of a man suffering from bipolar disorder. I felt guilty that I worried the City Council would close the tower to the public on grounds of safety, or rather lack of it. I decided the flowers must be brought into the church and laid at one of the altars, which, in a way, was a more dignified memorial anyway.

About nine months later, a young woman with a mental health disorder bought a ticket, climbed the 127 steps, scaled the parapet of the viewing gallery, and sat on the not very secure metal rim of the church clock. She was a talker. She talked to me. This time, when the police came, a woman officer did a brilliant job in persuading her to let them haul her back to safety. Had she jumped or slid off the clock she would have landed in the same spot as Dr Brunton.

*

After three decades in the same job, the years meld together. St Mary's became my life's work, when I didn't mean it to, and latterly I was embarrassed when people asked how long I had been there. It was bad enough after fifteen years, worse at twenty, and ridiculous after that. People didn't know what to say in response because they were thinking: what has he done to get stuck here all this time? He must be more incompetent or more offensive than meets the eye, and they'd try to change the subject. Until I was sixty, they sometimes said, I imagine by way of encouragement: well, you must still have one more job left in you.

The oldest part of the church was the tower, built in 1280. Taking that as a starting point, the church was 836 years old and I had been vicar for 30 years, one twenty-eighth of its history. I was becoming part of the fabric and by the end knew every stone of it. I never recovered from the ambivalence I felt on first being appointed and my relationship to the building and to the job was bittersweet. The question is whether it would have been any different elsewhere, or whether my feelings are just part of my nature.

My daughter, Charlotte, who has read this wants me to end on a high point. She says, you've spent all your life as a vicar and this is the high point. Was there a high point? What does it add up to? She wants me to go out with a bang, not a whimper and she is right, but my life isn't over yet and there are professional high points that have come in retirement. For now, I was proud of what I did at St Mary's: I made it a centre for liberal theology, I re-discovered the beauty of the building by cleaning it up and removing the decorative mistakes of the past century – ugly lighting and heating, crude paintwork, dreadful nave altar furnishing – I created a thriving tourist business and coffee shop, nurtured music and the arts, involved us in social commitment, developed a ministry to the fringe, the doubters, the sceptics and Christian atheists. 'Oh, Dad, and you were great with children,' insists Charlotte. If that *was* my talent, I had chosen just about the worst church in which to deploy it – a geographically tiny parish occupied almost entirely by university students in their colleges, no church school – but I had this inherited gift of speaking to children on a level they accepted and understood. My theory is I never grew up and that's why I never spoke down to them, but was nevertheless always ready to take them on and let them challenge me back. Thanks also to Mrs Mountford we had a flourishing Sunday School – which sounds dull, I know, but definitely wasn't – and I wrote plays which they performed throughout the year but especially at Christmas. A definite high point in my career is that in 2020 I stood in for a term as Chaplain of Wellington College, a distinguished co-educational public school in Berkshire, and found I hadn't lost my knack. There were seven hundred students in chapel each Sunday. The moment I told these 13–18-year-old young people that I understood most of them were not religious was the moment I won their confidence, and this enabled me to explored some of the basic religious ideas that most people will engage with once the questions are set out before them.

Protesting Faith

This chapter provides the core text of the BBC4 *Morning Service*. I include it because it sums up the philosophy of what I tried to achieve theologically at the University Church. Although I wrote the script, I shared the presentation with Charlotte Bannister Parker whose voice, the producer told me, was ideal for radio. I have edited out some of the liturgical sections because I thought they would be of less interest to most readers.

Charlotte Bannister-Parker:

Welcome to the University Church of St Mary the Virgin, Oxford. This is where Archbishop Thomas Cranmer was tried for heresy in 1556 and where, as Vicar, John Henry Newman led the nineteenth-century Catholic revival in the Church of England, known as the *Oxford Movement*.

Standing in the centre of the city and visited by many thousands of people each year from all over the world, St Mary's provides a natural interface between the sacred and the secular.

Part of our work at St Mary's is to be a place where this interface is explored. We are trying to build bridges between the sacred and the secular so that we can interpret the Church and its beliefs to the world, and, as importantly, interpret the world's beliefs to the Church.

Brian Mountford:

I often meet people who are drawn to Christianity, and the life of the Church, but who find themselves uncomfortable with the Church's basic teachings, especially the idea of a metaphysical God. I'm not just talking about those who never darken the church door, but people who are actively involved in the life of the Church – singing in choirs, engaged with social activities, or sitting unobtrusively in the pews.

I'm really interested in whether today's church is open to this kind of questioning and doubt? Could it be that the Church is failing to make space for those who struggle with faith in these ways?

But why should anyone be interested in Christianity if they question its basic beliefs?

Here are three typical reasons why.

The first is that they are committed to the Christian community – part of the Big Society, if you like – often for their children's sake – and because, in an age of individualism, they value the opportunity to do things together. Second, they admire Jesus' moral teaching, especially his insight into the nature of self-giving love. And third, they value the great aesthetic heritage of the Church in music, liturgy and art, where they find a sense of otherness, of being drawn out of selfish concerns to reflect on a wider meaning.

I'm talking about people who belong to the Church and yet question its teaching and its orthodoxy. To many Christians this can be a very provocative position to take. Besides, Christian worship emphasises what Christians do believe, rather than what they don't. It affirms rather than denies.

So, it might seem as if the church is only for those who have signed on the dotted line. And what is that dotted line? A good question.

In worship, I suppose, it would be the creed – I believe in God.

Whatever you think, whether you're a convinced Christian believer or rather agnostic about it all, I think it's helpful to set contemporary faith alongside the great statements of faith from the past. There needs to be a starting point, a baseline from which to begin a religious search.

Charlotte:

This short creed, based on St Paul's letter to the Philippians, speaks of how Christ reveals the glory and the love of God by emptying himself of godliness to accept suffering and death.

> Though he was divine,
> he did not cling to equality with God,
> but made himself nothing.
> Taking the form of a slave,
> he was born in human likeness.
> He humbled himself
> and was obedient to death,
> even the death of the cross.
> Therefore God has raised him on high,
> and given him the name above every name:
> that at the name of Jesus
> every knee should bow,
> and every voice proclaim that Jesus Christ is Lord,
> to the glory of God the Father. (cf Philippians 2.6–11)

Brian Mountford:

Recently I asked an American Baptist minister if he ever doubted his faith. 'Absolutely never,' he replied. I wanted to say, 'You can't be serious. Do you really mean that?'

Faith inevitably runs into challenges and paradoxes. Quite apart from the intellectual challenge of science and philosophy, there's the emotional challenge of bitter experience: illness, bereavement, disablement in war, bankruptcy, the death of a child: each can make a person doubt God's benevolence. These experiences can raise questions that undermine faith and bring a person to rail against God.

In theology, it's called the Problem of Evil: how can a loving God allow suffering in the world? William Blake asks this question in his poem 'The Tyger'.

Reading:

Tyger, Tyger, burning bright

In the forests of the night,
What immortal hand or eye
Could frame thy fearful symmetry?
When the stars threw down their spears
And water'd heaven with their tears,
Did he smile his work to see?
Did he who made the Lamb make thee?

Charlotte:

William Blake compares the sleek killing machine, the tiger, with a mild, defenceless lamb. Could a benevolent creator create both? We find some answer in the Christian image of a self-giving God, who embraces pain by suffering himself: the Lamb of God that takes away the sin of the world.

But there's a side to doubt that admits to a much more positive, creative interpretation and it's exemplified most clearly in the father of the epileptic boy who in Mark's Gospel says to Jesus, 'Lord I believe, help my unbelief.'

Reading Mark 9:16–23:

A father said, 'Teacher, I brought you my son; he has a spirit that makes him unable to speak; and whenever it seizes him, it dashes him down; and he foams and grinds his teeth and becomes rigid; and I asked your disciples to cast it out, but they could not do so.'

Jesus answered them, 'You faithless generation, how much longer must I be among you? Bring him to me.' When the spirit saw Jesus, immediately it threw the boy into convulsions, and he fell on the ground and rolled about, foaming at the mouth. Jesus asked the father, 'How long has this been happening to him?' And he said, 'From childhood. It has often cast him into the fire and into the water, to destroy him; but if you are able to do anything, have pity on us and help us.' Jesus said to him, 'If you are able! — All things can be done for the one who believes.' Immediately the father of the child cried out, 'I believe; help my unbelief!' Jesus rebuked the unclean spirit, 'I command you, come out of him, and never enter him again!' The boy was like a corpse, but Jesus took him by the hand and lifted him up, and he was able to stand.

Charlotte:

The experience of the boy's father, battling for faith, is echoed in John Bunyan's 'Who would true valour *see*', where in the colourful imagery of lions, giants, goblins and devils, he describes the challenges which beset the Christian pilgrim in search of God.

Who would true valour see,
let him come hither;
one here will constant be,
come wind, come weather;
there's no discouragement
shall make him once relent
his first avowed intent
to be a pilgrim.

Whoso beset him round
with dismal stories,
do but themselves confound;
his strength the more is.
No lion can him fright;
he'll with a giant fight,
but he will have the right
to be a pilgrim.

Hobgoblin nor foul fiend
can daunt his spirit;
he knows he at the end
shall life inherit.
Then, fancies, fly away;

    he'll not fear what men say;
    he'll labour night and day
    to be a pilgrim.

In the story of the Epileptic Boy, having been asked to heal the child, Jesus challenges the father's faith: 'If you are able! — All things can be done for the one who believes.' And he receives the reply: 'Lord I believe, help thou mine unbelief.' This is the real nature of belief and the Bible has many examples. In the famous passage about faith, hope, and love, St Paul speaks of seeing through a glass darkly. The light of faith is dimmed by human limitation. Even when Peter has the revelatory experience of seeing Jesus transfigured, he is puzzled and confused and suggests building shelters for Jesus, Moses and Elijah rather than proclaiming his utter conviction in the face of the glory of God. But the prime example must be the cry of Jesus from the cross, 'My God, my God, why hast thou forsaken me', echoing the Judaic spirituality of Psalm 22. Here doubt is placed at the centre of Christian theology, at the very point in the story where salvation is achieved in the death of Christ, acknowledging the underlying experience of the silence of God and how, in the deepest hour of need, however hard you pray, God might not answer.

From Psalm 22

My God, my God, look upon me; why hast thou forsaken me: and art so far from my health, and from the words of my complaint?

O my God, I cry in the day-time, but thou hearest not: and in the night-season also I take no rest...

All they that see me laugh me to scorn: they shoot out their lips, and shake their heads, saying,

He trusted in God, that he would deliver him: let him deliver him, if he will have him.

Brian Mountford:

In the Psalms I find many examples of what I've called 'protesting faith' – a challenging of God which you might think rude or disrespectful. Yet for all its robustness the questioning of God remains loyal. Other significant biblical examples of this robust challenge are when Jacob wrestles with God at the river Jabbok and when Job, plagued with boils and financial loss, argues the toss with God but remains faithful.

In English literature, too, we find evidence of religious doubt which is protesting but loyal. Philip Davis, Professor of English at Liverpool University, observes that in *The Pilgrim's Progress*, from which the hymn, 'Who would true valour see' is taken, when Evangelist points the Man, the potential Christian, to the way of salvation, he asks, 'Do you see yonder Wicket-gate?' Bunyan simply writes, 'The Man said, No.' But it is not an angry, anti-religion 'no'. He knows the right answer would be yes, but reluctantly he has to be truthful and say no. Then he is given a second chance by Evangelist who asks, 'Do you see yonder shining light?' Of course, a St Paul or a Billy Graham might say, 'Hallelujah, yes, I see the light,' but the Man manages a less than certain, 'I think I do.' However underwhelming that may feel, it's nevertheless a form of belief and perhaps the very essence of belief. It's positive and has the same ring as 'help thou mine unbelief.' Davis cites other examples, including the mighty Luther who declares, 'Here I stand. I can do no other. God help me.'

I ought to have added at this point (but there wasn't time in the programme) a quotation from the great scientist Richard P Feynman, writing in the 1950s: 'We absolutely must leave room for doubt or there is no progress and there is no learning. There is no learning without having to pose a question. And a question requires doubt. People search for certainty. But there is no certainty. People are terrified — how can you live and not know? It is not odd at all. You only think you know, as a matter of fact. And most of your actions are based on incomplete knowledge and you really don't know what it is all about, or what the purpose of the world is, or know a great deal of other things. It is possible to live and not know.' In other words, science is as agnostic as religion must be.

Prayers (led and written by David Neaum):

God of our beginning and of our end, we pray for your guidance along the way. We pray that you will guide our questioning and inquiring, that by them we may be led into a deeper knowledge of your truth and assurance of your love. We pray that you will unsettle our false securities and easy certainties, that you will lead us towards the depths of the love that gave up all earthly security on the cross. Teach us the way of the cross, that through our doubts and uncertainties we may come to your eternal life in Jesus Christ.

Lord, I believe: All: Help my unbelief.

Lord God, We pray for your church – giving thanks for those Christians who have, over two thousand years, held their faith for us. We give you thanks for the hope they have handed down to us. We pray that we may find ways of faithfully expressing that same hope for our own generation. We pray that this church may be a place of open inquiry, a place that strives to speak your truth for today's world.

Lord in your mercy. All: Hear our Prayer.

Spirit of Peace, we pray for reconciliation in places of conflict, for harmony that does not crush difference, for love that allows people to be themselves while sharing in your greater love. Bring peace and stability to the land of Libya after the turmoil of the past years. Bring your healing power to all troubled communities and broken families, bring love to the marginalised and lost.

Lord in your mercy. All: Hear our Prayer.

We commend to your care those whom we love, those troubled in body, mind or spirit, the recently departed and their bereaved.

Lord in your mercy. All: Hear our Prayer.

Brian Mountford:

What I've been saying in this service is that doubt is the flip side of faith – a natural, inevitable, and proper part of it.

It's a fact testified to in the Bible and doubt and faith, for the Christian, are held together in nothing less than the life of Jesus himself.

Some people criticise me for lack of Christian courage and for surrendering to the spirit of the age. But that is to miss the point. I am optimising faith, not minimising it.

In fact, I'm convinced the Church would be wise and honest to admit the difficulties of faith in the present secular age, and to give permission to its members to express their misgivings and to include all seekers, doubters, questioners, and confused persons who wish to be part of the Body of Christ. For it is in the person of Jesus that we find our unity and inspiration... There really can't be any point excluding people who are searching for God, and generally inclined to support the Church, however uncommittedly, just because they don't believe in exactly the same way as us.

What I Expected in 1968 and How Things Turned Out

Knowing I was writing this memoir, Andrew Allen, the lively Chaplain of Exeter College, emailed to say he thought it sad that my ministry 'has spanned such a large decline in the Church' and asking whether, when I was ordained, I could have imagined the Church would become 'so irrelevant', adding that, in his view, this irrelevancy is primarily attributable to a lack of 'vision and courage on the part of church leaders'.

I wondered whether I had actually asked myself that question at the time. I have said elsewhere that my upbringing was so steeped in church life that I fell into ordination, almost as a default position, without any dynamic sense of vocation, but I am sure I wouldn't have gone through with it had I really thought I was flogging a dead horse. Coming of age in the wake of JFK, Martin Luther King, the establishment-challenging sixties satire boom, and the nascent women's lib movement, I knew we were living through a time of accelerated change. The change was theological too: as a student I had read Paul Tillich's ideas of God as the 'Ground of Being' and the 'Eternal Now', and been particularly drawn to his idea of faith as concerned with 'ultimate questions'. I read Harvey Cox's *The Secular City*, Bonhoeffer's *Letters and papers from Prison*, with his vision of what he called 'religionless Christianity', and I engaged loosely with the 'death of God' controversy, rekindled by the American theologian Thomas Altizer and written up in *Radical Theology and the Death of God* (1966).

This theological agenda had already been brought to popular attention by Bishop John Robinson's best-selling 1963 book, *Honest to God*, which despite its theological vocabulary hit the headlines and caught the public mood in such a way you were likely to hear it discussed on buses and in pubs. After a decade it faded from view, but in its fiftieth year was published in an anniversary edition, containing an essay by Rowan Williams in which he accuses Robinson of reducing Christianity to little more than a feeling of 'intensity' or 'seriousness' about life, hardly mentioning God, failing to uphold the fundamental doctrine of the Trinity, and by default denying God's action in the world. The problem is: the idea of the Trinity is precisely one of the traditional doctrines the average Christian has never really understood or believed in, just as they have not been convinced that God acts in the world, however much they have prayed that he would. You can elaborate the mystery of the godhead as much as you like and as well as you can, but Joe Public still doesn't get it. Williams reads Robinson as an academic theologian when he's actually a populariser attempting to make Christian ideas accessible. In the end religion can only exist by consent: its truth lacks weight if most people think it's up a gum tree or too obscure to be grasped. Because, even if you believe doctrine is revealed – for example by God through the scriptures – it still must be experienced in order to take hold, and in that sense is human, rather than divine.

So, to answer the Chaplain of Exeter's question, whilst I smelt the whiff of change in the air, I was undaunted and excited because I thought this prospective change boded well for the future of the Church. People were engaged by the questions of belief in a secular age and I really thought, as I think now, they were far more likely to be convinced by a Christian theology which could adapt to contemporary intellectual critiques of religion and supernaturalism, than they would by conservative attempts to defend classic doctrines such as the Trinity. As soon as I began working as a priest, I found that was exactly the case: people wanted me to speak their language. They liked explanations of traditional theological ideas, but needed to be allowed to play with those ideas, to experiment with them, and shape them to their needs. That is how doctrine is received, it seems to me, as a living rather than a dead thing. Christianity isn't locked into a first-, or fourth-, or sixteenth-century view; the very fact that one can point to different theological moods in the New Testament, the Council of Nicaea, and the Reformation demonstrates the adaptability of Christian faith. Therefore I think a Christianity in which the word *God* functions as a poetic term for the *other*, or ultimate value, or intimations of transcendence, can just as easily and properly be received into the canon of belief as Trinitarianism. For years I refused to entertain Don Cupitt's view of God as a non-real entity. I stuck with realism (whatever that means), despite the intellectual challenges, because I thought it was my duty as an ordained priest. Now I accept both real and non-real interpretations at the same time. You might call it a *quantum* theology: from the idea of a quantum particle capable of being in two places at the same time. The Church refused to listen to Cupitt who was well ahead of his time because they thought his ideas threatened the security of the institution, but the institution was in decline anyway and might have found greater traction in society had it engaged with his ideas.

Arrogant as it may sound, I had no doubt the Christian message as interpreted by me would withstand social change, and the experience I have described in this book justified that, especially as secularisation advanced, I engaged in what was known as 'The God Debate' with those who wanted to challenge the Church. My take on the Christian faith went down well and church attendance bore it out. I realised reckless confidence was the only way forward, as with Bill Westwood's aim to convert the whole of North London to Christianity. It was like 'The Heavenly Host appearing over Queensway' on the Christmas Card at Lancaster Gate.

Amongst the clergy I detected what seemed to me a self-conscious conformity not only of arcane churchy vocabulary but of outward demeanour, as if not to appear somehow holy would mean exclusion from the club. I ought not to have been surprised: you only have to read about the Barchester of Anthony Trollope's novels to see it was nothing new. However, at theological college had they after all really meant all that earnest prayerful look, with their heads buried in their hands? I never really trusted it. In parish life I discovered the majority of people were not so taken with all that either. Pragmatic, with busy lives, they look to religion and the Church for a grounding in Christian values and occasional glimpses of transcendence. I was confident through the Thatcher years, as in city bars market traders began to order Dom Pérignon instead of beer and house prices went through the roof, that the gospel I proclaimed remained compelling.

How about Now?

No view of religion in contemporary Britain can ignore the recent data (2017) on religious affiliation, from NatCen's British Social Attitudes survey, that 53% of the people in Britain say they have 'no religion' and that of those, 70% of the 18–25 age-group claim to have no religion. When I was Acting Chaplain of Corpus Christi College, Oxford in 2018, my first encounter with the new intake of freshers was at the introductory Welfare meeting, where I faced an auditorium full of eighteen-year-olds looking down challengingly at me from seats tiered as steeply as the Colosseum. When I stood up to speak, I sensed intuitively that I must begin by acknowledging we live in a multi-faith society, an international society, a post-religious society, where 70% of their age group in the UK claim to have no religion. The sight of nodding heads made me more relaxed. Thus, I acknowledged the unwritten terms and conditions on which I was to act as Chaplain.

In St Hilda's College, where I was Chaplain until 2020, the room designated as the chapel has been demolished as part of a major re-development programme. The Governing

Body decided not to replace it, but to create a Multifaith Room instead. Why should Christianity, and Anglicanism in particular, be privileged in this contemporary, secular society, they argued? If you were building a college from scratch, would you include a chapel at all? Many of the objectors have never attended a chapel event and most have no religion themselves; they have a new dogma of inclusivity and equal opportunity in which they imagine every creed, philosophy, prejudice, cultural difference and gender issue harmonising into one equal music. But we know from long experience that ecumenism holds little attraction even within the same religion. Whether it is Sunni or Shia Islam, Orthodox or Reform Judaism, Conservative Evangelical or Liberal Christianity, people belong to these groups for a reason and don't want to be part of a mishmash religion with no distinctive identity. The universal can be rooted in the specific. For this 18–24-year-old generation it is *no religion* they are identifying with, not protesting against lack of provision for multifaith religion. In any case, this multifaith 'inclusion' automatically brings exclusion, because conservative religionists have no desire or motivation to compromise their beliefs.

Had St Hilda's had an historic chapel building and world class choir the argument wouldn't so easily progress: not only would the planners not allow it, but the aesthetic virtues of uplifting music would be seen as self-authenticating and as transcending the perceived small-mindedness of theology. It is clear Christianity as a default, as a norm, is gone, even in Oxford University where, until the late nineteenth century, you had to be an Anglican in order either to teach or study.

I have been struggling to understand in what ratio religion in Britain (and people like me who represent it) is faced with indifference, as opposed to antipathy, or untroubled ignorance. These are three very different things. Most seem to be happy to live and let live: if religion is your predilection, or your hobby, no one's going to mind too much so long as you don't thrust your beliefs down their throats. Antipathy is a minority view because few wish to waste their energy on campaigning against it.

As religion has become marginalised, this drip, drip of increasing indifference over the last three or four decades has naturally led to ignorance particularly of the Bible and its literature, but also of what a church actually looks like from the inside: what is the font, the pulpit, or the altar and what do they represent. And knowledge of, say, the Reformation, despite countless television programmes about the Tudors, is a mystery to most people – possibly because the programmes celebrate Henry VIII's sex life rather more than his theology. Such unfamiliarity with our religious past presents a barrier to understanding much of our literature, history and art which has taken for granted, as a social given, the gospels, the commandments, the parish church, the sagas of the Hebrew Bible, and the parish priest.

However, if people are untouched by religion, I haven't found them necessarily immune to what you might call spiritual values, and it's not uncommon to hear someone describe themselves as 'spiritual but not religious', by which they mean, I think, to go back to Larkin, they are occasionally surprised by a need to be serious in a trivialising culture and to look for transcendent values that endure. They have an interest in what Paul Tillich called 'ultimate questions': Who am I? What's life about? Does it mean anything? It is easy to confuse antipathy towards religious institutions, which have marred their reputations through the violence associated with Jihadism or the evil of clergy abuse of children, with indifference towards the spiritual.

On the other hand, theologian and psychotherapist Mark Vernon has argued ours is a 'flat' society in which people cannot (or rarely) see through 'spiritual eyes' – they have neither the intuition nor the vocabulary for it. I think I see what he is getting at, which I take to be connected to lack of imagination, consumerism and social malaise, but I still think the raw material of ultimacy pushes people, however spiritually inarticulate, towards a search or desire for the transcendent. Maybe my view is too influenced by the Oxford bubble that I live in.

If I am right, how to tap into people's curiosity about the ultimate, spiritual questions is the big challenge, especially without the help of a flourishing institution. Anecdotally, I can testify that nine times out of ten, when I go to a party, I end up in an absorbing conversation about religion. And when I was acting as Chaplain of Wellington College, seven hundred young people were obliged to be present and I was able to start those conversations in public. Frequently now, COVID-19 permitting, I preach in rural churches near Oxford and find congregations respond enthusiastically to sermons that include critical discussion of basic theological ideas and Biblical criticism. It isn't just the highbrows either – no one wants to be talked down to or treated like a primary school child. Indeed, primary school children particularly don't like being talked down to. I am not saying a more intellectual approach would fill these churches, but it would be a start. A senior Oxford academic recently wrote to me lamenting what he regarded as the Church of England's lack of interest in critical theology. To my mind he is right: critical theology is essentially creative, not a tropical storm threatening to sink the fragile ark of Christianity.

Richard Hooker, an influential sixteenth-century Anglican theologian, argued that the authority for Christian ideas rested in scripture, tradition, and reason. The trouble is reason sometimes struggles to get a look in. In his 2019 book, *A History of the Bible*, John Barton expresses some surprise that when it comes to preaching and teaching in the church, parish clergy tend to 'soft-pedal or even ignore' all they have learnt at theological college about the history of biblical criticism. It seems this has always been the case since the biblical scholar

Adolph von Harnack (1851–1930) noted the same thing with his students. It puzzles me too because I have found congregations fascinated when I have explained, for example, that the letters of Paul pre-date the Gospels and yet Paul provides scarcely any biographical detail about Jesus, or that Matthew, Mark and Luke draw on common material and that Luke wrote the Acts of the Apostles as well. The illumination is similar to listening to a piece of music with the score in front of you, so you can understand more about the structure and orchestration of a piece.

Former Bishop of Oxford Richard Harries has argued in the *Church Times* that 'the crisis facing the church in our time is the dismissal and disdain of a sceptical culture. It is no good talking about new forms of mission or different styles of church if this is not faced. People simply do not believe what is being put before them, for a mixture of reasons, many of them very understandable. This means that every Christian communicator, priest of lay person, must by a subtle apologist.'

The Church needs to listen to this criticism and to tease it out of its supporters, and critical friends, because churchgoers are usually too polite to come straight out with it. When preachers serve up a mushy diet of hastily prepared piety and feelgood spirituality, their hearers, while affecting a pose of thoughtful attentiveness, see right through it and think that's what the clergy would say, wouldn't they. And the counter argument you sometimes hear that the first Christians were uneducated fishermen and farm labourers and therefore it is good to be 'fools for Christ', is a very weak one. That route only pushes the church further and further towards the margins and into further disdain.

What I think the 18–25s fear most about religion is moral censure. They have some reason to suspect religion, and its representatives, will likely condemn or belittle the ethical paradigms they take for granted, such as the LBGT+ culture.

273

In an honourable second place is the perceived battle between science and religion. This age group have been students within the dominant intellectual paradigm of empirical science, demonstrable proofs and mathematical logic – what you might call Secular Reason. They are inclined to see religion as pre-modern, mythological, morally unreconstructed, and, to a degree, concerned with subscribing to absurd metaphysical claims, belief in God itself coming high on that list. This crude setting of religion and science at loggerheads with one another is escalated by fundamentalism within religion, which treats religious belief as a kind of science and makes believing in the impossible a badge of honour for faith and is so unsubtle it sets itself up as easy to dismiss.

For these reasons and others, such as the Church's perceived failure to campaign effectively for the environment and its innate antipathy to other religions, this age group has declared itself to have *no religion*.

These comments of course touch on the question of leadership raised by Andrew Allen. Given the seismic force of the secularisation process, it is scarcely fair to lay the demise of the Church of England entirely at the door of its leaders. Maybe even St Paul himself would have failed in twenty-first-century Britain. We have reached an institutional tipping point where so many of the things taken for granted when I was ordained in 1968, such as attendance at church at Christmas, Easter and Whitsun, the popularity of church weddings and baptisms, basic biblical knowledge resulting from compulsory religious education in schools, and a benign, if sometimes amused, affection for the *Dear Old Church of England*, have slipped over the edge never, I suspect, to be recovered.

Having said that, church leaders have done little to save the day. I'm thinking of all those clergy who daren't say what they really believe about redemption, or the incarnation, or the status of Holy Scripture, or sexual ethics, because they think it would set light to a Pandora's Box of theological fireworks, which, ironically, their congregations want to enjoy rather than be protected from.

This timidity is matched by the practice of episcopal cabinet solidarity – the idea that the House of Bishops must always speak with one voice and not to do so would imply division and weakness. One of the things that made the Church of England attractive when I was ordained was the number of Bishops, and parish priests, willing to give a confident lead independently of any prevailing party line. Trevor Huddleston, famous for his radical work against apartheid in South Africa, was Bishop of Stepney. Michael Ramsey, the Archbishop of Canterbury, was a liberal with a national political profile supporting what we now call gay rights and opposing both the Vietnam War and the right-wing politics of South Africa and Chile, under Pinochet. When Mervyn Stockwood became Bishop of Southwark in 1959, the then Archbishop of Canterbury, Geoffrey Fisher, told him he had been appointed to say, 'Yes, yes, yes,' when others were saying, 'No, no, no.' Not only did he encourage liberal theology in his diocese but appointed as suffragan bishops John Robinson and David Sheppard, one of whom, as we have seen, wrote a radical, best-selling book, while the other was a prominent evangelical and England cricketer. At that time, most of the bishops had been trained in the broad-church colleges of Westcott House and Cuddesdon, both of which had a reputation for intellectual rigour and an outward-looking social agenda.

In 2005 the Church of England decided to phase out the parson's freehold and replace it with what they called 'common tenure', which essentially transferred much more authority to the central bureaucracy. As a vicar, I always had the freehold, which meant I had ownership of my church and vicarage with the rights of independence that any freeholder enjoys. As a freeholder it was easier to be your own man and think aloud your thoughts without fear of censorship. Now the Church of

England is driven by process, form-filling, annual reviews, risk assessments, and reputational risk management. It isn't the only institution to have gone that way; universities are as bad. But in the Church's case, risk aversion seems incompatible with good theology and serious Christian action. When Jesus says to a would-be follower, 'Sell all you have, give the proceeds to the poor, and then come follow me,' surely he is demanding risk on a massive scale. The move to centralisation of management then requires more central administrators, archdeacons and even 'assistant' archdeacons, to manage the process. And the syntactical banality which betrays the true nature of this life-draining policy is the verb *to do Church*, as in the sentence: We must consider how to *do Church* in the countryside. It is followed closely by the verb *to be Church*, examples of which you can no doubt work out for yourself. But you note, the emphasis is entirely on *Church*, not on love, or hope, or faith, or what life means, but the fading institution that needs propping up.

When I was at Southgate, I was an active member of a movement called the *Open Synod Group*. Our aim was to focus liberal theological insight in the Church of England and to open up its General Synod to socially more inclusive attitudes, particularly the ordination of women. We decided to publish a book of essays, *Living the faith – a call to the Church*, addressing the issues we thought the Church should consider and I found myself in distinguished company alongside Alan Webster, the Dean of St Paul's, Cambridge Professor, Geoffrey Lampe, and Frank Field MP. My essay was titled 'Church or Sect?' a distinction first made by Max Weber and developed by Ernst Troeltsch. The basic sociological idea is that by definition a church is an organisation that is outward looking, relates to society, and is accepted by society. On the other hand, a sect is introspective, self-contained and its tenets not open to question. Writing the keynote chapter, back in 1980, Alan Webster said, 'The choice for the Church of England within this changed national setting [i.e. Britain in 1980] is either to grow into a Church for all people, or to become an Anglican sect.' The arguments he adduced to support this view are very similar to those I have referred to in this chapter. When I set out to answer Andrew Allen's question, whether, when I was ordained, I could have imagined the Church would become 'so irrelevant' by 2020, I thought the answer was clear: no I could not. The Church now is completely different, yet I discover in *Living the Faith* the seed for 2020 was germinating in 1980.

Art made tongue tied by authority

Since I retired from the University Church in April 2016, I have viewed the Church, with a capital C, in a different light. Now I am no longer responsible for services and making sure the weekly round of worship happens, I find myself increasingly uninhibited in my criticism of worship. Sitting in the pews (as I do now and then) I ask myself why people bother to go to church at all when it's so dull and out of touch and takes twice as long as necessary to say what it wants to say. Clergy tend to assume the congregation wants its pound of flesh when what they really want is a concise and pertinent ceremony followed by a social half hour. Perhaps the truth is I am so egocentric I only really enjoy services if I am conducting them myself.

Theologically, too, I feel released. Although I was known as a liberal in the Church of England, and in some quarters reviled for it, I still felt a responsibility to be a defender of the faith – more so than I thought. There is often a fine line to tread between shouting about your own intellectual honesty and not wishing to upset those people who have come to the church for an old-fashioned blessed assurance. Nevertheless, in my final years at the University Church I could tell people *wanted* to be shocked; they wanted more sauce on their dinner, more challenge, to dice with danger. They wanted someone who would lead the charge against the Church's refusal to come to terms with modernity and post-modernity.

In his novel *The Noise of Time* Julian Barnes writes about the Russian composer Dmitri Shostakovich, of his harassment under Stalin, the denouncement of his music as 'non-political and confusing', and his subsequent collusion with the State and how he despised himself for making that compromise. Shostakovich was accused of formalism and experimentation when he ought to have been producing tuneful soviet music for the people to sing along to. I hadn't realised he had been persecuted in this way and been subjected to corrective tutorials on the party line. I know there is no comparison between the last thirty years in Britain and the purges under Stalin, but I couldn't help seeing parallels between the dumbing down of the arts under the Soviets and the dumbing down of Christianity, and along with it the Church's renewed bid for doctrinal control, during the period of my ministry. Julian Barnes describes the culture of centralised doctrinaire control in 1930's Russia thus:

'[T]he political bureaucrats had soon arrived to take control of the project (art), to leech out of it the freedom and imagination and complication and nuance without which the arts grew stultified.'

Immediately I think, ah yes, theology needs freedom and imagination and complication and nuance too – if it is to survive or make any headway. But do we find that on Sundays? Then, later in the book, Barnes astonishes me with a line from Shakespeare I wasn't familiar with:

'When Pasternak read Shakespeare's sonnet 66 in public, the audience would wait keenly through the first eight lines, eager for the ninth:

And art made tongue tied by authority.'

Probably what Shakespeare understood by art was different from us – more *arts and crafts* than music, painting, literature, and theatre – but the force of it stands. Immediately I adapted it to: 'and theology made tongue tied by authority', which we have seen from time to time throughout the Christian centuries not only with creeds and articles of faith and inquisitions and burnings, but with the almost paranoid defence of scriptural literalism.

Two more quotes from *The Noise of Time*:

'But even more than poetry, tyrants hated and feared the theatre. Shakespeare held up a mirror to nature, and who could bear to see their own reflection? So Hamlet was banned for a long time; Stalin loathed the play almost as much as he loathed Macbeth.'

'They didn't want you to fake adherence to their banal taste and meaningless critical slogans – they wanted you actually to believe in them.'

These questions raised by Julian Barnes are of universal significance: the operation of power upon art, 'the limits of courage and endurance, the sometimes intolerable demands of personal integrity and conscience.' And, it seems to me, organised religions need to face up to those questions too. That is what I have been trying to argue.

Before the Throne of Grace

In Chapter 2, I mentioned how the General Ordination Exam (GOE) was affectionately known as God's Own Examination. Let us just imagine how I might respond if at the end of my life I had to face an actual GOE. How will I answer at the dreadful Day of Judgement?

There are plenty of jokes about it, usually involving St Peter quizzing people at the Pearly Gates. My favourite?

St Peter imposes a simple test on those entering heaven. He asks an easy biblical question, and if you get it right, then you can go in. On the day in question the first arrival was a woman. 'What is the name of the second Gospel, and how do you spell it?'

'Oh, that's easy,' she said. 'Mark. M-A-R-K.'

'Welcome!' said St Peter.

Next was a man. 'What is the name of the first woman in the Bible, and how do you spell it,' asked Peter. The man thought for a moment and replied, 'Eve. E-V-E.'

'Very good,' said Peter, 'and I wonder if you would do me a small favour. I promised my wife I would fetch some milk, so could you guard the gate until I get back? You've got the drill. It's very easy. Just ask a biblical question and then let them in.

No one came for a bit, then the man saw his vicar coming down the approach road. 'What are you doing here?' he asked.

'Well, on the way home from your funeral, the hearse took a corner too sharply... and here I am.'

'Okay,' said the man, 'this'll be a piece of cake for you. Name the Seven Churches of the Apocalypse, and how do you spell them?'

(In case you need to know, they are: Ephesus, Smyrna, Pergamum, Thyatira, Sardis, Philadelphia, and Laodicea.)

God: Question 1

Are you surprised to be here?

Answer

Is this one of those awkward *believing* questions? Do I believe in
life after death? I talked about this in the story Henry Crimond
in the chapter 'The edge of Metroland'. That was the case of
a dying man who wondered if life after death might be like
England in summer and whether he would be reunited with
his family in that pleasant land. More recently, when my friend
Richard Wilson died, his widow asked me this same question.
But Richard was an agnostic intellectual whose attempt at
faith had been shattered by the death, at thirty-nine, of their
talented eldest son from cancer. We agreed that Richard had
not altogether given up the religious quest and that he *kind of*
thought there was an underlying hope to life and that it had a
meaning beyond the period between our birth and death. We
wrote this prayer for his funeral, and it contains one version of
what I believe myself.

> *O mystery of divine Love, source of life and ground of being, we*
> *celebrate today the life of Richard Wilson. We give thanks for his*
> *capacity for friendship with people from all walks of life, for his*
> *intellectual curiosity and humour, his gift for story-telling, his*
> *passionate commitment to protecting our heritage and righting*
> *injustices, and above all for his devotion to his family and friends.*
> *We remember him as a man in search of faith and find comfort*
> *in Pascal's words concerning God that 'you would not seek me*
> *if you had not found me.' May Richard find peace in the eternal*
> *purpose which transcends time and the changes of the world.*
> *Amen.*

Yes, I am surprised to be here because I have always thought
there was something infinitely more subtle than pearly gates
in Jesus' words in Matthew's Gospel about life, death and

meaning: 'For whoever wants to save his life will lose it, but whoever loses his life for My sake will find it.'

God: Question 2

Do you believe in me?

Answer

I am tempted to reply with the philosophy student's famous answer that 'if that is a question, then this is an answer' – for which it is said she received top marks. My problem is I do not entirely understand the question. For example, I never think to myself: in order to have a relationship with my wife I must first establish whether I believe in her – relationship is more instinctive than that, less cerebral. Same with God: do I believe in you? I keep coming back to you and referring to you and that is the point. Knowing a person is interactive.

When in Chapter 4 I mentioned my granddaughter asking who made God, I didn't record my reply. My answer was that you are a *necessary* being and have always existed. Therefore, no one made God. I don't think she understood, and her mother was unable to explain. You might think I ought to do better than that. Besides, the first clause of the creed is 'I believe in God' and I have said it often enough.

However, it seems to me, we are not generally so precise about how we use language and we often use a phrase like 'I believe in God' as a shorthand for something more nuanced and widely allusive. For example, when I experience meaning, purpose, beauty, love, or hope, I have reason to think there is something deep and dynamic underlying life and this fills much of the space I call *God*. Given the culture gap between the first and twenty-first centuries, I think this is what St Paul is expressing in Romans 8 when he writes: 'We know that all things work together for good for those who love God, who are called according to his purpose.' I don't intend this answer to be reductive but expansive: it is a way of elaborating the traditional

Christian idea of *Father, Son and Holy Spirit.*

God: Question 3

Did you practise what you preached?

Answer

No. I tried. But how *do* you deny yourself and attend only to the needs of others? It seems impossible to me and yet I know it is the key to Jesus' moral teaching and how he lived himself. Despairing of me, my wife has often protested, 'I don't know how you can stand up there in that pulpit and say all those pious things and then behave like this.' She is right, of course. But I could scarcely stand there, six feet above contradiction, and sanction moral compromise. Just do your best; if you fail we'll all understand. I had to aim as high as Jesus did in the Sermon on the Mount – perfection – in the hope we might get three quarters of the way there. Wasn't that the method of the prophets too?

My preaching was consistent because I had a theological vision, which I hope I have managed to illustrate in this book. I was a theological liberal committed to making Christian ideas accessible not only to the mainstream of churchgoers but to those on the edge and beyond the fringe of traditional Christianity. I hope you won't hold that against me.

God: Question 4

What is your greatest weakness?

Answer

Not being empathic enough. Or do I do myself an injustice? I feel other people's pain, I understand what they are going through, and when it comes to extreme suffering my imagination runs riot. In my fifties, I suffered from an undiagnosed tumour in my spine. For a year I didn't go to bed because it was too painful to lie down. Now I lie awake at night imagining what it must be like to be incarcerated in solitary confinement for long periods.

But do I communicate that empathy? I wish I had a more natural warmth to do so.

Then there's a deep down anger, inherited from my mother, I suspect, which I now have under control, but thirty years ago I could suddenly lose it with the bank clerk, the concert promoter who broke our church rules, or almost anyone who didn't let me have my own way. I let it parade as righteous indignation, but knew it was a demon.

God: Question 5

Would you live the same life again?

Answer

Yes. And, although there are many things, I would have liked to be different. I would take my life a second time round without alteration. I have been happy. Even my childhood, with its austerity, mad parenting, and missed opportunities, is a time I look back on with great affection. I described the bad bits and perhaps omitted to emphasise the beautiful surrounding of Epping Forest where I was brought up and the visits to the *Festival of Britain*, The Science Museum, Sadler's Wells, The Royal Albert Hall, Westminster Abbey and Canterbury Cathedral. My father's cultural life gave me more than I have recognised and, at an early age, introduced me to the vibrancy of live music in concerts halls and theatres. Then I found my own theatre, in the music of Anglican Christian worship, where daily one could be lifted out of the trivial round and common task into a sense of the transcendent, by using a language of sound without the semantic pitfalls of trying to say the unsayable, reaching beyond the limitations of creeds and essays in philosophy, and making *this* conversation possible.

So, I am happy to have spent my life in search of You, because in that search I have found at least something of that ultimate value, which makes my house, cars, holidays, and material possessions of far less importance than I normally attach to them. Now I understand why Jesus put the renouncement of material possessions at the heart of his teaching. It was about sorting out your priorities. Once that is done you are free to love the world as he did.

God: Question 6

What do you most regret?

Answer

There are three or four things I have done in my life, which you know about, but I am too ashamed to mention now in an interview that might be read by other people; nothing criminal, nothing deviant, but treating other persons very meanly without ever making amends.

You taught me from early days the importance of reconciliation and that penitence was only truly valid if accompanied by making amends; as St Paul put it, not letting the sun go down on one's anger. You remember I got it right once or twice, like the evening I had a massive public row with the church treasurer in Southgate and went home without resolving it. I was just getting into bed when I thought this won't do and at 10.30pm went round to his house where we drank whisky and our relationship was transformed.

Some of the unresolved offences nevertheless lie out there written in the history of the universe ineradicable and I presume unforgiven.

But I have another regret; and that is never having had a job in which I could implement my vision for the Church on a big stage. I have felt uncomfortable carping about the lily-livered leadership of so many of those who have been given a platform in the Church and would have liked the advantage of such a platform myself. Maybe, the powers that be (whoever they are – you should know) thought I would bring a sword of division or 'false teaching' and make things even worse.

God: Question 7

Anything you'd like to ask me?

Answer

Well, yes. Several things in fact. When I was acting as Chaplain of Wellington College, a school for 13–18-year-olds, in early 2020, just before the COVID-19 lockdown, I let the students set the agenda for one of my chapel talks by putting their questions to me, however critical. I would be interested to know whether you agreed with my replies.

1. Why would you pick Christianity over any other religion?

    What religion you are very often depends on cultural background: be born in India, you'd likely be Hindu; in the Arab States or Pakistan, likely Muslim; in Europe or America, likely Christian, in Thailand, a Buddhist. This school has a massive Christian chapel because of its cultural heritage and the religion of its founders. They have handed Christianity down to us.

    Why do I choose Christianity myself? I was brought up that way. But, on a much more positive note, I think Christianity helps to make sense of life – I have an intuitive sense that there is an ultimate reality and Good – which we call God.

    I wrote a best-selling book called *Christian Atheist* which explores why some people who struggle with the metaphysical claims of Christianity are nevertheless attracted to other aspects of Christianity. They admire its moral compass, its promotion of community and community values, and its art and music, which they find a helpful aid to thinking about what's important in life. Choral Evensong, which we have sung tonight, comes high on that list.

2. 100 years ago, homosexuality was criticised by the Church. Now that LGBTQ+ is socially acceptable, it seems God's view on homosexuality has changed. How can that be?

Fortunately, here we have a very open and inclusive attitude to homosexuality. I am not so sure that is true in all churches. National social attitudes, reflected in same-sex marriage legislation, for example, have changed, while the more conservative churches still disapprove of homosexuality on the grounds that it is forbidden in the Bible.

I think your question raises the issue of how Christians make moral decisions. Are they dictated from on high (in an ancient holy book) or do we work them out for ourselves? I would say, a bit of both. That is, it is we who must decide what is morally acceptable and, if we are Christians, hopefully we do that in the light of faith.

If we read the New Testament story of Jesus, what we encounter is a range of overriding moral imperatives, such as love, faithfulness, and the inclusion of the marginalised. The New Testament isn't a rule book with regulations for every moral dilemma we face. I think Jesus' story gives a broad-brush picture of how to love – through parables, teaching and his own personal example. Compassionate Christianity now recognises that being human involves very varied sexual feelings and very different attitudes to gender identity, which must be honoured and respected.

Can God have a change of mind? Most theologians and philosophers claim God is 'immutable', which means, being perfect, God cannot change. God's values are those of love, faithfulness and inclusion: we adapt our ethics in the light of our understanding of God's purpose.

3. The final question was asked by many students and each version of it boils down to why do You allow evil in the

world.

If God is omnipotent, why is there pain and suffering?

If God created the world, why does evil exist?

Is all the chaos and disaster in the world a sign of God's absence?

To take that last question first: yes, many argue that the suffering in the world is a sign of God's absence, and it constitutes a compelling argument against the existence of God, which must be engaged with by Christian apologists.

Each of these questions is getting at what we generally call the 'Problem of Evil'. If God is all powerful and all loving, then why does God allow evil? The question implies creation is messed up. So how do we think God's creation ought to be? What we imagine as a perfect world would be very different from what we know. No disease, no thought of moral right and wrong because everything and everyone would act perfectly. If you played golf, you'd always get round in 18. What would be perfect weather, though? Constant sunshine – too dry; rain, too wet. Would a perfect world have exactly the same weather conditions every year to enable the perfect growing of crops, and so on? That last question poses the dilemma: we need seasons for food. We need ice caps north and south for balance of water on the planet. We need tides to help clean the oceans. We need the moon to keep the earth stable in its orbit. Life is a balancing act. And physical life is dangerous. It involves vast forces and we are vulnerable creatures – we see that writ large with the COVID-19 crisis.

Maybe this life we experience is the best that is possible.

Maybe God must act within the constraints of physics.

We want simple, straightforward answers. Scientists and philosophers want answers too, but often have to live with paradox, mystery, and blurred lines because few things are black and white.

At Wellington, our chapel services were designed to last forty minutes and the talk about seven, so I hasten to this final point. Faced with the problem of evil, many students will be familiar with the 'free will' defence. It goes like this: in order for us to be ourselves, God had to give us freedom to do good or to do evil. Therefore, God had to allow evil as part of creation. With free will, we have the potential to fulfil God's ambition for us to make real in the world the godly values of love, peace, honesty, compassion, generosity of spirit. In a perfect world this moral exercise wouldn't be necessary because all would be perfect.

But there is a weakness in this attractive argument: does God give us free will to murder, rape and torture? That would surely be immoral of God. Perhaps, therefore, the free will argument only works when we are choosing between lesser evils. And then there's the problem of natural 'evils': volcanoes, tsunamis, plagues, and earthquakes, referred to in the insurance business, somewhat unfairly, as 'acts of God'. Although many creatures suffer as a result of these natural events, I think they are a necessary by-product of the dangerous balancing act that makes life possible at all.

Here ends the Pearly Gates interview. It will be interesting to see whether I get in.

Four Last Things

I first learned to speak without notes when Vicar of Southgate and there were more services than I had time to prepare talks for. In Oxford, the sermons were usually published in one form or another and therefore had to be written down. It was a bit like a weekly essay crisis, often messing up my Saturday, but the discipline meant you gradually accumulated a vast body of work.

I have included here four examples: 'Impressionist Theology' and 'Theology and the spoken voice' illustrate my attempts to help the congregation think outside the box; 'Funeral Eulogy for Anne Ridler' is both auto-biographical and innovative; and my 'Farewell Sermon' at the University Church just seemed a good way to finish.

Impressionist Theology

I've been doing some revision on the Reformation for a talk I have to give in a few weeks' time on the Reformation. What strikes me is the idea that the big theological issue of the Reformation was to sort out the rules and mechanics of salvation. By salvation I mean how sinful human beings are restored to a right relationship with God after the Fall, when Adam ate the apple.

Of course, it doesn't actually say *apple* in the Bible. In the Latin of the Vulgate, when Adam and Eve eat from the tree of knowledge in the centre of the Garden of Eden, they suddenly recognise good and evil – *bonum et malum*. *Malum* is also the word for apple and since people were keen to identify the forbidden fruit it was a tempting connection to make. The so-called Adam's apple in the human throat got its name from the thought that the forbidden fruit stuck in Adam's throat as he swallowed.

When they thought about salvation, the pre-Reformation Catholic theologians didn't teach that salvation is achieved by good works, as if people could earn God's favour, but that it is freely given by God's grace, *the response to which might be measured by good works*. In practice, this teaching had been corrupted and compromised most infamously in the commercialisation of religion and the sale of indulgences, which marketed the idea that God could be bribed by payments made to his earthly corporate outlet, the Church, into accepting a person into heaven. There's a kind of parallel in the modern payment for honours: a wealthy man gives a chunk of money to the political party in power and, lo and behold, his name appears in the honours list for a knighthood.

Then Martin Luther comes along. We have to remember he was a Catholic monk and not a Protestant – rather like Jesus was a Jew and not a Christian. His critique was from within, not from outside, and his answer, revealed to him, he said, in a monastic upper room – his 'tower' experience – was that salvation is by faith alone, not in any sense earned, but imputed or assigned by God to those who trust in him.

So we've got big theories in theology, grand narratives, but I am not convinced when it comes to faith that people are persuaded by big theories. Big theories often set out to solve questions that are themselves puzzlingly metaphysical and not necessarily the ones we are asking.

When I was on my post-Easter break in Andalusia, we stayed in a nice but plain modern flat with a sea view, albeit across a roof scape of concrete. There were thirty or so books on the bookshelf, none of which I had the slightest inclination to read. But on the coffee table was a National Gallery introduction to impressionist painting which I took up in desperation. It said this:

'The impressionist vocabulary includes without a doubt the direct, living "impression" of a moment, which is often reproduced in what seems a chance detail of a whole event. These are scenes and figures of modern everyday life as opposed to depictions from classical or mythological stories, such as formed the stock-in-trade of traditional art until the end of the nineteenth century. Workers and prostitutes, passers-by in the street or guests in the café – the impressionists were the first to regard such people as art worthy...'

The idea of an impression of a moment and a chance detail of a whole event seemed like how theology works for me. For example, we pray for peace and justice in Syria, but the close-up detail of a fourteen-year-old boy, hanging by his arms, being beaten, concentrates that prayer and makes it real in a quite transformative way. Theology has to be experiential rather than theoretical. I have often referred to experiences – of suffering or love or betrayal or excitement or relief or forgiveness, either given or received – as the *raw material* of theology. And I want to campaign for more natural theology, more experiential theology in church life. School teachers are trained to start from the child's experience and so it ought to be for preachers. And how deductive and explanatory do we have to be, anyway? Isn't it more a matter of prompting a question or provoking a thought?

In our bathroom there's a beautiful conical shell, the colour of pearl. It's big and brilliantly designed, so that the spiralling mollusc is protected from its predators. And I thought just the other day when contemplating it, how amazing that nature had evolved this wonderful object that, if man made, would command a very high price. That seemed to me a theological experience. It wasn't a case for God from the argument from design. It was simply a kind of religious impression from which I deduced nothing in particular.

On the garage wall in our garden there's a bird box I made from the wood of an old wine case. It has the faint letters AUX imprinted on the side, the left overs of Bordeaux. This spring a pair of coal tits nested there and, for a fortnight, faithfully flew in and out with food for their young. Then just as they were about to fledge, the box fell silent and the parent birds perched on the adjacent fig tree seemingly distraught. Inside the box I found one egg unhatched and four dead chicks – dead, I think, from disease. This experience also left me with a religious impression, but I cannot say more than that. I might, I suppose, quote Jesus' words, 'are not two sparrows sold for a farthing? Yet not one of them will fall to the ground unperceived by your Father ... you are of more value than many sparrows.' Although I didn't think of myself as of more value than those coal tits.

I always get Giles Fraser's *Guardian* pieces through Facebook. Yesterday he told the tale of more break-ins and drug abuse at his South Bank church near the Elephant and Castle. A drug addict, now on a therapeutic dose of methadone, returned to make amends for his previous violent behaviour, and offered to do some gardening. Giles writes: he 'spent a few hours digging, arranging a line of rocks to mark a border around the church bins. This felt like a victory to me. The earth was turned over beautifully. And all was swept up afterwards. It wasn't a token job, reluctantly undertaken. I suppose people will think me foolish – but this is why I do the job. That patch of earth feels more important to me than all the stuff we do on Sunday.' Another theological impression.

And, actually, experiences like this seem to me very close to the gospels: workers and prostitutes, passers-by in the street or guests in the café. There are the labourers in the vineyard and the famers sowing their seed and threshing their corn; the woman taken in adultery, whom the self-righteous religious types want to stone to death, and the 'woman in the city, who was a sinner, who brought an alabaster jar of ointment to a Pharisee's house where Jesus was eating. She stood behind him at his feet, weeping, and began to bathe his feet with her tears and to dry them with her hair'. There was that classic passer-by, the diminutive Jericho tax collector, Zacchaeus, who climbed a fig tree to see Jesus and ended up having him to dinner. And in the café category: the guests at the marriage feast in Cana, or the crowds sitting on the ground at the Feeding of the Five Thousand, or the theological soirées with Mary and Martha.

And when criticised for his love of café society Jesus says: 'John the Baptist has come eating no bread and drinking no wine, and you say, "He has a demon"; the Son of Man has come eating and drinking, and you say, "Look, a glutton and a drunkard, a friend of tax-collectors and sinners!"'

The National Gallery booklet said, 'the impressionists were the first to regard such people as art worthy'. I say that in all these gospel impressionist vignettes Jesus sees the common man, the ordinary person, to be as good as the best of us – in his terms loved by God. And thus, in these impressions I find a better articulation of justification/salvation/grace/free restitution/future hope than in any crusty old formula.

Jesus is an impressionist painter with all the interest and sensitivity and compassion of an artist.

Theology and the Spoken Voice

Some of you know that I have recently been on a Swann Hellenic Cruise – a cruise company once dubbed the 'Church of England at Sea'. One of my fellow speakers was not only a devout Roman Catholic, but something of a comedian. He told us a joke about the Holy Trinity planning their summer holidays. 'Let's go to Jerusalem,' says the Father. 'No, I have some unpleasant memories of Jerusalem,' says the Son, 'I'd rather not go there'. 'Okay, well how about Rome?' says the Father. 'That would be nice,' says the Holy Spirit, 'I've never been there.'

Why do I tell you such an awful gag? Because it's common to think of theology as revealed and therefore written in stone. Something systematic and dogmatic as presented by great theologians like Thomas Aquinas or Karl Barth. But I want to explore the idea that natural theology is close to the spoken voice; it grows from stories and preaching and gossip and singing and poetry in ways that are rarely systematic and more experiential.

It occurs to me that there are an enormous number of ecclesiastical jokes – even anthologies of the wit of the Church? And despite the cries of blasphemy from hardliners in all the religions, we like stories that are subversive of ecclesiastical norms or so-called theological 'truths'. Because while we see the importance of norms and standards, we recognise that what we consider to be norms are actually conditional, and that standards are imperfect and that when we take norms and standards and precepts over seriously, they can grow into great hypocrisy bubbles needing to be pricked.

A very great number of the passengers were very elderly, well to do, and prim. On occasions I was put in mind of Miss Marple and Disgusted of Tonbridge Wells: the sort of people who might be offended by anything vulgar. But (although I can only speak for myself) I think there's something in most of us that delights in a little suggestive, unbuttoning humour.

Our comical lecturer told a story of his first child's birth, with some sentimentality. In the hospital his wife had difficulty breastfeeding and the boy was not getting enough sustenance. At the end of the bed was the usual clipboard of charts and notes. Gervase asked the nurse if he might take one of the sheets of paper as a keepsake. 'Why?' she asked. 'Because it's the first thing that has been written about my little boy's life – the beginning of his biography – and I want to treasure it and give to him on his twenty-first birthday. When the twenty-first birthday came along, with great ceremony Dad stood up to open the envelope containing this first piece of biography about his son. It read simply: poor sucker.

Some of you will remember that last term a friend of mine, Professor Phil Davis, gave a controversial sermon in which, amongst many other nuggets, he offered the thought that 'To know the pain of not having a God is no logical proof of the necessity of that God's existence.' When I sent him his travelling expenses and a book token, he reciprocated immediately by sending me a book of essays, *The Death of Adam*, by Marilynne Robinson, an American writer who won the Pulitzer Prize for her novel *Gilead*.

In an essay about Bonhoeffer she writes: 'Great theology is always a kind of giant and intricate poetry, like epic or saga. It is written for those who know the tale already, the urgent messages and the dying words, and who attend to its retelling with a special alertness, because the story has a claim on them and they on it. Theology is also close to the spoken voice. It evokes sermon, sacrament, and liturgy, and of course scripture itself, with all its echoes of song and legend and prayer.'

I would say we are doing theology not only when we intentionally set out to do it by reading, but when we meet on a street corner and talk about the death of a relation, or when we go to one of Penny Boxall's writing classes and try our hand at writing, or when we joke about the foibles of the Church. We do theology in silence; and we do it in this culturally strange thing of hymn singing together, which is one of the triumphs of the Church, I think. Because there is something primal and bonding in both unison and harmonious singing. The words may be laden with doctrine – often rather crass doctrine – but it is not the words that are most important. As a matter of fact, there are only a few hymns that would stand on their own without their tunes as poems to read out in church. It is the dynamic of communal, societal expression that is a religious thing.

In the same essay, Marilynne Robinson quotes Bonhoeffer's remark that 'God is the beyond in the midst of our lives'. That is, God is not only the transcendent other, God is the arresting, surprising, counter cultural, shock of meaning that occasionally jumps out at us in various unexpected ways providing a bridge to what we call the other.

I began with humour and its subversive quality of preventing us from taking ourselves too seriously. Well, *à propos* of nothing in particular, this week I re-read Alan Bennet's small book *The Uncommon Reader*. It's really an essay about the transformative value of books and reading, and the conceit he employs is to imagine what it would be like if our gracious Queen Elizabeth II were to become an avid reader and to be so absorbed by the books she reads that she wastes no opportunity to share these insights with her ministers and Privy Council and those who govern. They on the other hand, being largely philistine in the matter of literature, are completely nonplussed by this seemingly inappropriate and un-royal obsession. It's the sort of thing in the old days one would have been sent to the Tower for writing. Here's an extract in which Her Majesty and the Prime Minister discuss the forthcoming Christmas Broadcast. The Queen says:

'I thought this year one might do something different.'

'Different, ma'am?'

'Yes. If one were to be sitting on a sofa reading or, even more informally, be discovered by the camera curled up with a book...'

'And what would the book be, ma'am?'

'I was actually thinking of poetry.'

'Poetry, ma'am?' he smiled thinly.

'Thomas Hardy, for instance. I read an awfully good poem of his, the other day, about how the Titanic and the iceberg that was to sink her came together. It's called *The Convergence of the Twain*. Do you know it?'

'I don't, ma'am. But how would it help...?'

'Oh surely,' said the Queen, 'it would show, wouldn't it, that fate is something to which we are all subject.'

And so on. The PM of course thought that the public must not be allowed to think that the world cannot be managed. That way chaos – or defeat at the polls...

The point I deduce from this, and I think Alan Bennett wished to make, is that public life would be enhanced if it were less bland and more open to the surprising insight into what is ultimately important. Reading can do this for you and so can the theology, particularly when it is close to the spoken voice, because theology is concerned with what ultimately matters. Unfortunately, theology has a reputation for the opposite. For example, in parliamentary discourse, when an argument is thought to be esoteric or convoluted it is often described as *theological*.

What the Church might most usefully offer society are flashing insights into the beyond in the midst of our lives, in the way that a poet, or reader, or musician can sometimes do. And thus we might allow ourselves to become more unbuttoned, less process driven, less conformist to prevailing political method. In a word, more PROPHETIC.

Funeral Eulogy for Anne Ridler 1912–2001

20 October 2001

I first came across Anne Ridler in 1957 when as a schoolboy I learnt one of her poems which had been set for a verse speaking competition. It was called 'The Cranes':

'We thought they were gulls at first, while they were distant —
The two cranes flying out of a normal morning,...'

When I became Vicar here 30 years later I was in awe to find this poet, who had made a mark on me as a teenager, was a member of the congregation. She was involved in a determined correspondence at the time with the then Assistant Priest, Christopher Foster, about which Bible translation should be read in church. The Alternative Services Book published all the Sunday lections in full, but had used, seemingly at random, four different translations. When Anne read in church, as she often did, she wished to be free to deviate from what the ASB dictated. Chris considered this a minor breach of church order, but Anne carried on regardless. She had of course served as the only woman on the panel that translated the New English Bible, but the point was she cared about every word, part of her devotion was to enable the word of God to speak as clearly as it could. As Ronald Gordon wrote in his fine obituary, she was 'as profoundly religious a person as I have ever met'.

It was the same care for worship and meaning that made her badger me year after year to sing John Byrom's hymn, 'Christians awake, salute the happy morn' at the Christmas Day Eucharist. 'It's such a fine hymn,' she pointed out, 'and it's the only day of the year we can sing it.' And so we did, with the extended Ridler family leading with great gusto.

The first verse goes on,

'Rise to adore the mystery of love
Which hosts of angels chanted from above.'

I think it was the adoration of the mystery of love that formed the core of Anne's spiritual life – a mystery that couldn't be fully grasped, but required her constant exploration, both in her relationships and her writing. We see this exemplified most obviously in her love for her family, for Vivian, her four children, and seven grandchildren. You told me how she was always at home for you when you were children, how she wrote you wonderful letters when you were away, how she'd put her work second to your needs. How, when you went to parties in North Oxford, she would cycle all the way from East Oxford to take you, go home, then cycle all the way back to collect you. That reminded me of another reference in Ronald Gordon's obituary: 'I last saw her about a year ago, cycling down the Iffley Road, in atrocious weather battling against a head wind. It seemed she thought advancing years no reason for her not getting about the city in the proper manner.'

It was a privilege for me to be with Anne and Vivian and Jane, Kate, Ben, and Colin, leading prayers in Anne's room just an hour before she died. You said the Lord's Prayer together with such assurance and confidence that it could only have lifted Anne as she approached the gate of heaven. In fact, you couldn't have done more to support her and help her both physically and emotionally in these last few months and I know that she felt immensely pleased and grateful for this love shown in return.

There is a temptation to think when you reach 89 with a strong faith and a list of achievements behind you that death ought to be embraced as a fulfilment, like Francis of Assisi welcoming: 'O thou most kind and tender death/waiting to hush our latest breath.' But as one of you pointed out, having had a happy life together doesn't make death any easier – almost harder. And although, as the frailty of Anne's body failed to support the energy of her spirit, she wanted to die. Just three months ago she had lain in the JR protesting at her diagnosis and looking out at the distant hills saying she still wanted to walk on them. It was a subject she wrote about. In 'Threescore and Ten', speaking of the growing awareness of death, she says,

'To admit
He's there is one thing, but the trick is harder
To welcome and ignore him. For it seems
The old should live as though their days were endless,
Yet also, feeling the glance of death upon them
Think that all time is Now...'

Anne never lost her lust for life because she was young in spirit. The child in her had never grown old. She loved playing with children, playing cards with her grandchildren, writing for children, revealing the humour of opera libretti. She encouraged me to publish some Christmas plays I had written for the Sunday School here at St Mary's. I could never understand how the poet in her could tolerate my silly rhymes and fatuous jokes, until I learnt that she sometimes watched *Neighbours* – as a way of bonding with teenage grandchildren, who were going through the grunting stage of non-communication. She told me she used a dictionary of rhymes herself and thought it one of the poet's tools, and we discussed which was the best. She was never intellectually arrogant or pretentious or elitist about people or their interest and habits.

Here at St Mary's Anne was a member of the PCC, host for the Silent Prayer Group, and Secretary of the Garden Committee, a council of formidable ladies who met each November and spoke in Latin about the plants and shrubs of the churchyard. It was always twilight in the vestry when we met and they would ask me what I thought of *Euonymus alatus* or whether we should plant *Hebe albicans* or *Hebe pinguifolia*. I hadn't got a clue what they were on about, but nodded sagely and said yes, which Anne recorded in her shapely semi-italic hand in the minutes.

But it was her play *The Trial of Thomas Cranmer* that somehow symbolised her greatest contribution to St Mary's, the theological one. She wrote this in 1956 for the quatercentenary of Cranmer's death and it was first performed in this building, where the trial had actually happened, and which still contains a resonance of those distant events and the man who wrote one of the greatest flowerings of the English tongue, the Book of Common Prayer. Some of us here acted in a revival production in 1990, which I know pleased Anne. Not only was it a kind of homage to her mentor T S Eliot, but it was a focus for her theology. Besides, it centred on the great theological issue for which the Protestant archbishop was being tried – the meaning of the sacrament: how is Christ present in the bread and wine? She gives her answer in a poem aptly titled 'A taste for Truth', where she says:

'Wine of our joy and water of our tears

Are not so incompatible as we think

If the atoms did not change, but those who drank.'

In other words, it is not we who somehow change the sacrament, but the sacrament changes us.

Perhaps in the vacillations of the tormented Cranmer she recognised an ambiguity of faith which she felt herself, hope and fear, faith and doubt, pleasure and pain, miracle and disappointment. In 'A taste for Truth' she questions the optimism of Julian of Norwich that all shall be well. She asks could saltwater taste like wine? She remarks how cancer offends God's miracle of creation:

'I cannot forget her dreadful sickness,

Nor reconcile within my mind

Her cheerful life, her cruel end.

Yet in her dying eyes I saw

Bright pain and love inseparable,

Part of the truth and ineluctable'.

Perhaps that is why she came to St Mary's, because as a Christian community we live in that tension and own it as a positive way of seeing through the glass darkly, but in the hope nevertheless of seeing face to face. The tension was present just now in the reading from 'A Matter of Life and Death'. These 'sad short-coming lives of ours' contain a 'secret for some resurrection'. And that is a salvation 'not by merit, but by grace'. The matter of life and death, the crucial, indispensable issue, is none other than the gracious love of God in our Lord Jesus Christ. Anne believed in that.

Just a few weeks ago my colleague Harriet Harris gave birth to her first child, Ben. She took him to visit the Ridlers and Anne was delighted and said that it was marvellous to see a new life beginning just as an old one was ending. It is a simple story that speaks of her hope, her graciousness, and her love. We thank God for her life and commend her to his eternal keeping.

Farewell Sermon 24 April 2016

I think I've only taken a text for a sermon four or five times whilst I've been Vicar, but this morning I can't resist. From the thirteenth chapter of St John's Gospel, 'I am with you only a little longer ... Where I am going, you cannot come.' I promise you this is the Gospel prescribed by the lectionary for this week.

On my first Sunday there were sixty people in the congregation and today...

In my first week here John Taylor, a former Bishop of Winchester and well-known theologian at the time, led the Chaplains' Mission to a Sheldonian packed with students and local church people, speaking on four successive nights. I sat in the front row, and each evening the chairman announced that anyone wishing to discuss matters raised by Dr Taylor with the Vicar of the University Church was welcome to come to the Old Library afterwards. No one came. Well hardly anyone. Not on any night – except for a few older parishioners anxious to check out the new vicar. On the last evening Marjorie Reeves came up to me very proudly and said, 'I'd like to introduce you to our student.' St Mary's had a token student – a rather introverted mathematician from BNC.

Compared with Cambridge, Oxford seemed to me a conservative place looking backwards to a glorious past. Radcliffe Square was pitch black at night with no lighting west of Catte Street, and when I put very basic floodlighting into the church garden, Fellows of All Souls complained to me of light pollution. I was most often asked, 'What's it like to occupy Newman's pulpit?' Newman had been Vicar 150 years previously. My answer was: daunting at first and that I wasn't very good at it. But preaching week by week has been one of the most enjoyable parts of my ministry; a real dialogue with you all about the theology of life. And an exploration of what we have proudly and confidently labelled 'Liberal Christianity'.

Now today there's an expectation that I will have saved the best for last. But I'm sorry to have to disappoint. Yet in saying that there's an important theological point to tease out. A lot in Christian theology encourages us to look forward to an end time, to a climactic moment of glory, of completion, when Christ will come again to judge the living and the dead. The Rapture. The hope of heaven. But I think it's a mistake to take too much of a postponement attitude, to invest all your hope in the future so that you miss the present. The New Testament itself doesn't fall into that trap entirely and speaks of the reality of the Kingdom of God now. Now is the time. Realised eschatology. So we need to reflect on what God's purpose in creation is now. One response I find attractive is that the creator God desires a physical order where it's possible for his values to be realised. This is it, or at least one manifestation of it. And the life of Christ, of course, is the prime example of how God's values can be made concrete in the temporal order. But we all know when our sun eventually heats up and becomes a red giant, life on earth will become impossible. So climactic ends are not always the best. My friend Keith Ward has an analogy for this: when we listen to a symphony, we don't find its meaning in the last chord but along the way. In the development of a theme; in the slow movement perhaps, we might find an expression of such emotional intensity that it proves to be the passage we remember most.

My ministry which began at St Stephen's, Rochester Row in Westminster in 1968 has spanned a period of massive social change. If you've watched *Call the Midwife* you'll remember the film clips from the 1950s, my childhood years, and how they look more like Victorian London than London today. Even in the late sixties we would walk around the streets of Westminster in Cassock and biretta holding the sacrament under a veil as we took communion to residents of the Peabody Buildings. In the streets people would stand aside and even occasionally genuflect. Between then and now church attendance has diminished by more than half and we live in a multi-cultural, secular society where the majority describe themselves as having no religion at all. But I believe there's still a widespread yearning for faith. The big questions don't go away: the origins of the universe and of life, whether there are universal ethical principles, the meaning of self (who am I?), the idea that there might be something greater out there, the intuitive sense of the Divine Other.

Religion has been assaulted by reductionism on two flanks: first from outside by the scientism of some atheists who hold that the only things to have meaning are those which can be empirically demonstrated, and secondly from within by fundamentalism, and its tributaries, which restricts religious insight to so-called absolute truths conveyed by texts and rules and statements of orthodoxy. One of the claims I have made over the years is that Christian ideas are better served by expansionism, nuance and open-mindedness. Open to the expanding imagery of drama, poetry, interdisciplinary debate; open to the generative reading of biblical texts. Open to the idea of more questions than answers.

Comparisons might be drawn between the RSC (Royal Shakespeare Company) and the Church. Shakespeare's plays are about universal themes such as: power, greed, love, redemption, free will, evil, appearance and reality. But those gems can be hidden beneath their antique language. The RSC has interpreted the plays so that they sparkle before modern audiences for everyone to see their timeless relevance. The Church faces the same challenge.

(Don't deprive us of the original play and its language, just perform it in arresting new ways. The Merchant of Venice in the London Stock Exchange, Henry V in WWI, Romeo and Juliet in Haarlem, The passion of Christ in modern Syria, Jesus'

Temptation in the Wilderness in suburban Leicester or Liverpool or London, Peter's Confession of Faith at Caesarea Philippi in a comprehensive school sixth form. Do you see what I'm getting at? Enculturate the message. Don't try to change it to fit.)

Despite falling attendances (although not at SMV I might say), I don't see a massive decline of spiritual curiosity, but I do see the decline of trust and confidence in organised religion, the Church, which simply hasn't kept up; and when it's tried to keep up has merely put old ideas into new wine skins – to reverse a biblical image – and the old wine remains flat and doesn't stretch those skins with its fermentation. For example, the so called 'fresh expressions': take the unreconstructed church into the streets on a Saturday night, into the clubs and pubs, into the lunchtime retreats of the workplace and so on. Fresh expressions? I don't think so: old expressions in different locations. It can't work.

What I have been trying to say, I think, is that theology isn't big enough to contain what it claims to. And that the Church has resorted to dogma in the attempt to understand the great mystery of life, and from time to time has insisted it is right like an abusive husband.

Nor do I resort to silence. The idea that the meaning of things is such a mystery and the magnitude of the universe so awesome that words cannot begin to penetrate them. Obviously, words (and numbers) can begin to unravel the ultimate questions because that is exactly what humans have done.

You might say, all this fails to take into account revelation, the idea that God has shown us the truth through the Bible and through the life of Christ, who John said was the 'Way the truth and the Life'. I have avoided interpretations of revelation that come to unequivocal conclusions, but have tried to show that the revelatory stories, like the birth narratives and the passion narrative, the Sermon on the Mount, and great parables of the Prodigal Son and the Good Samaritan, are texts that become revelatory when we engage with them and interact with them. They do not in themselves provide an answer, but help us to mine and hew and polish our own answers. To see that Christianity is not a given, not a commodity or possession, or membership card, but a relationship – with each other and with God's purposes, however we discern them.

And so to the future. I do hope above all things that this University Church will maintain its beautiful music, social outreach, and rigorously questioning theology. Oxford has other churches which are models of the Catholic, Anglo-Catholic, evangelical, charismatic, and non-conformist traditions. This church is the one trying to relate to those who are, as you might say, spiritual but not religious, who are attracted by the beauty of holiness, often puzzled by the creeds, and who don't want to give up on the search for a twenty-first-century Christ. You must keep this vision for the sake of the wider Church. And, if you have any missionary zeal, for the sake of all those struggling to connect with Christianity in non-churchy ways. Of course I recognise that there's going to be change here when a new Vicar arrives – and that will be positive and creative. But don't lose the vision.

If I had known in 1986 that I would be in the same job thirty years later, I would never have accepted it, but now Oxford is my home, where I have roots, and there's no other place I would rather have been and no congregation I would rather have had; no other community, both town and gown, I would rather have belonged to. I have loved playing a part in this University and developing the relationship between University and Church, which has grown so creatively during my time here. So I thank all of you for your friendship and support. There are a few of you who were undergraduates when I first arrived and I have baptised your children and seen them grow up and graduate themselves. (But many are new or passing through – that spices up the community.) It will be a wrench leaving you all.

But of course, I haven't been here alone, and although never a typical clergy wife and always her own person, Annette has contributed massively. She was always nice to people, to make up for my failings in that department. In the early days she organised a flourishing Sunday School; her ground-breaking charity, Family Links, grew out of St Mary's, even though it was always a non-religious organisation. She has been a stern critic of my sermons and occasional organisational faux pas, but a firm support.

At this point I can feel the oratorical momentum of the Letter to the Hebrews chapter eleven coming on: 'what more should I say? For time would fail me to tell of Gideon, Barak, Samson, Jephthah, of David and Samuel and the prophets – who through faith conquered kingdoms, administered justice, obtained promises, and shut the mouths of lions.' Our staff will keep the momentum up. Alan, Claire, Ana, Penny, Charlotte B-P and Adam.

In my second job as a curate of Christ Church, Lancaster Gate, beside Kensington Gardens on the North side, I devised a strapline: Our task is to celebrate the love of God openly. Nothing has changed and that has been my aim here at St Mary's over the past three decades.

Acknowledgements

I am most indebted to all the people who played a part in this story and therefore made it what it is and, in the writing of it, to those who read it and offered their critical and insightful advice, especially John Hunt, Penny Boxall, Annette Mountford, Charlotte Mountford, and Sarah Lloyd.

CHRISTIAN ALTERNATIVE
BOOKS

THE NEW OPEN SPACES

Throughout the two thousand years of Christian tradition there
have been, and still are, groups and individuals that exist in
the margins and upon the edge of faith. But in Christianity's
contrapuntal history it has often been these outcasts and
pioneers that have forged contemporary orthodoxy out
of former radicalism as belief evolves to engage with and
encompass the ever-changing social and scientific realities. Real
faith lies not in the comfortable certainties of the Orthodox,
but somewhere in a half-glimpsed hinterland on the dirt track
to Emmaus, where the Death of God meets the Resurrection,
where the supernatural Christ meets the historical Jesus,
and where the revolution liberates both the oppressed and
the oppressors.

Welcome to Christian Alternative... a space at the edge where
the light shines through.
If you have enjoyed this book, why not tell other readers by
posting a review on your preferred book site.
Recent bestsellers from Christian Alternative are:

Bread Not Stones
The Autobiography of An Eventful Life
Una Kroll
The spiritual autobiography of a truly remarkable woman and a history of the struggle for ordination in the Church of England.
Paperback: 978-1-78279-804-0 ebook: 978-1-78279-805-7

The Quaker Way
A Rediscovery
Rex Ambler
Although fairly well known, Quakerism is not well understood. The purpose of this book is to explain how Quakerism works as a spiritual practice.
Paperback: 978-1-78099-657-8 ebook: 978-1-78099-658-5

Blue Sky God
The Evolution of Science and Christianity
Don MacGregor
Quantum consciousness, morphic fields and blue-sky thinking about God and Jesus the Christ.
Paperback: 978-1-84694-937-1 ebook: 978-1-84694-938-8

Celtic Wheel of the Year
Tess Ward
An original and inspiring selection of prayers combining Christian and Celtic Pagan traditions, and interweaving their calendars into a single pattern of prayer for every morning and night of the year.
Paperback: 978-1-90504-795-6

Christian Atheist
Belonging without Believing
Brian Mountford
Christian Atheists don't believe in God but miss him: especially the transcendent beauty of his music, language, ethics, and community.
Paperback: 978-1-84694-439-0 ebook: 978-1-84694-929-6

Compassion Or Apocalypse?
A Comprehensible Guide to the Thoughts of René Girard
James Warren
How René Girard changes the way we think about God and the Bible, and its relevance for our apocalypse-threatened world.
Paperback: 978-1-78279-073-0 ebook: 978-1-78279-072-3

Diary Of A Gay Priest
The Tightrope Walker
Rev. Dr. Malcolm Johnson
Full of anecdotes and amusing stories, but the Church is still a dangerous place for a gay priest.
Paperback: 978-1-78279-002-0 ebook: 978-1-78099-999-9

Do You Need God?
Exploring Different Paths to Spirituality Even For Atheists
Rory J.Q. Barnes
An unbiased guide to the building blocks of spiritual belief.
Paperback: 978-1-78279-380-9 ebook: 978-1-78279-379-3

Readers of ebooks can buy or view any of these bestsellers by clicking on the live link in the title. Most titles are published in paperback and as an ebook. Paperbacks are available in traditional bookshops. Both print and ebook formats are available online.

Find more titles and sign up to our readers' newsletter at
http://www.johnhuntpublishing.com/christianity
Follow us on Facebook at
https://www.facebook.com/ChristianAlternative